Bearing Witness While Black

Bearing Witness While Black

African Americans, Smartphones, and the New Protest #Journalism

ALLISSA V. RICHARDSON

OXFORD
UNIVERSITY PRESS

OXFORD
UNIVERSITY PRESS

Oxford University Press is a department of the University of Oxford. It furthers
the University's objective of excellence in research, scholarship, and education
by publishing worldwide. Oxford is a registered trade mark of Oxford University
Press in the UK and certain other countries.

Published in the United States of America by Oxford University Press
198 Madison Avenue, New York, NY 10016, United States of America.

Library of Congress Cataloging-in-Publication Data
Names: Richardson, Allissa V., author.
Title: Bearing witness while black African Americans, smartphones, and
the new protest #Journalism\Allissa V. Richardson.
Description: New York, NY Oxford University Press, [2020]
Includes bibliographical references and index.
Identifiers LCCN 2019058319 (print) LCCN 2019058320 (ebook)
ISBN 9780190935528 (hardback) | ISBN 9780190935535 (paperback) |
ISBN 9780190935559 (epub) | ISBN 9780190935566 (On-line)
Subjects LCSH Black lives matter movement. African Americans—Violence
against. African Americans and mass media. Mass media and race
relations—United States. Citizen journalism—United States. Racial
profiling in law enforcement—United States. Police brutality—United
States African Americans—Civil rights.
Classification LCC E185.615 .R5215 2019 (print) LCC E185.615 (ebook)
DDC 323.1196073—dc23
LC record available at httpslccn.loc.gov2019058319
LC ebook record available at httpslccn.loc.gov2019058320

I dedicate this book to the littlest witnesses . . .

To my daughter, Brynn, and my son, Bryce—
Whose eyes reflect hope and love and light,
May you always have the courage to bear witness to what you see.
Your life, your thoughts and your words matter.

To Lerato—
Whose eyes lit up every morning when I began a new journalism lesson,
You were a joy to teach in South Africa in the summer of 2011.
Though you left the world much too soon,
I am grateful that smartphones helped you
Tell your story while you lived.
You mattered.

To Dae'Anna—
Whose eyes saw too much from the back seat of that car in July 2016,
I wished that day you were playing with my daughter, who is your age,
Instead of watching your beloved Philando leave this world.
He mattered. Your mommy matters. And so do you.

Contents

Preface

I thought I was going to have to give birth to my son in the dark. When I checked into Maryland's Anne Arundel Medical Center around 1:00 a.m. on Friday, June 6, 2014, the hospital was in the middle of a scheduled power outage. There were halogen floodlights on tripods in the halls of the maternity ward, but the individual rooms were pitch black. I was given the option to turn around and labor at home, but I insisted on staying at the hospital after a few contractions left me breathless. Ten hours later, the sun had risen and set again. I was woozy with exhaustion when I first saw him. There was this little beige wonder, with a shock of dark brown hair and slanted brown eyes. He did not cry when he emerged. He merely squinted in the light of the room, which had been restored that afternoon before his arrival. The doctor patted him on the back firmly. My son gasped, then wailed. The medical team brought his face to my cheek and I kissed it. My son smiled. Everyone in the room laughed, since newborns rarely do that.

Two months later, I watched a grief-stricken Lesley McSpadden wailing on Canfield Drive as her son's body lay in the street for more than four hours. I had never heard of Ferguson, Missouri, before—and I definitely had not known Michael Brown personally—yet the pain on her contorted face touched me. *She is crying for her baby*, I thought. While the rest of the world may have seen a "thug" intimidating a shopkeeper on leaked surveillance footage, I felt that McSpadden simply must have seen her boy, despite all of his faults and mistakes. Like me, I am sure that McSpadden had a birth story that she could recite readily. Only now, that did not matter. His life story was at the mercy of the mainstream media's shifting frames. I followed the Ferguson footage relentlessly. The narrative morphed from "Hands Up, Don't Shoot," to the eventual admission that Brown never uttered these words. I watched as Brown became the unofficial martyr of the #BlackLivesMatter movement, even as the police officer who shot him described him as resembling "a demon" with superhuman strength. Would someone one day see my son this way? After my own little brown boy came into the world, a keen awareness of how he might be viewed came into sharp focus. As an African American male, I realized that he would be under surveillance forever. While shopping in stores. While driving his car. Even while posting silly pictures to his social media page. This, I realized, was a reckoning that many black mothers in the United States face. This was the reckoning that launched a movement.

After Trayvon, After Michael

When George Zimmerman was acquitted in the Trayvon Martin murder trial in July 2013, widespread disbelief and despair shook black communities across the nation. The case had seemed very clear cut. Trayvon Martin was a child. George Zimmerman was a man. Trayvon Martin was unarmed, carrying only a can of Arizona iced tea and a bag of Skittles. George Zimmerman was armed, carrying a loaded 9 mm pistol. Still, the jury saw Trayvon as the threat. Zimmerman went free. A day after the verdict, Alicia Garza wrote a love letter to black people on Facebook. It read, "I continue to be surprised at how little black lives matter. . . . Black people. I love you. I love us. Our lives matter."[1] Her friend and fellow organizer, Patrisse Khan Cullors, reposted her words on Twitter with the hashtag behind it: #BlackLivesMatter. Although people from all walks of life gathered to protest the Zimmerman verdict that year, the #BlackLivesMatter hashtag (and movement) peaked truly in Ferguson after Michael Brown was killed in 2014. In the years that followed, scholars gathered more than 40 million tweets that were tagged with either #Ferguson, #BlackLivesMatter, or both. In my own early days of observing the Ferguson uprisings, I remember something else kept jumping out at me. Amid all of the sensationalized coverage of tear gas and flames, I noticed something smaller and quieter: a steady sea of protestor smartphones. I pored over photographs from the demonstrations. I paused videos I found on Twitter. I peered at livestream footage. And frame after frame, I saw black people clutching their cellphones, gazing back in defiance. This spirit was familiar to me, since I had spent the last several years as a college professor training people of African descent around the world to report news using only cellphones.

I was working at a historically black college in Maryland in 2010 when I got the idea to launch a mobile-first newsroom. This meant my students would report news using only smartphones and tablets. This was not mere curricular innovation though. This was survival. As I said in a 2010 National Public Radio interview, my students did not feel safe carrying expensive camera equipment around in the beautiful, yet blighted section of Baltimore where our campus was located.[2] It was a common occurrence for students to be robbed at gunpoint or knifepoint for their belongings, in broad daylight. Baltimore was a city that had been home once to stable, blue-collar work. But the steel mills were gone. Jobs on the docks, factories, and rail yards were gone. And, as in many other deindustrialized cities across the United States, crime spiked as people fought to feed themselves. My students, all of whom were African American, would discuss these things at great length in my news writing class. They wanted to be journalists, but they were afraid. Afraid to be seen. Afraid to see.

"What if you had a smaller news camera?" I asked them one day in the fall of 2010. I explained that Apple had debuted a new smartphone that summer, which had a front- and rear-facing camera for the first time. I remember one of my students exclaiming that the iPod Touch MP3 player had the same capabilities as the iPhone, and that it cost far less. I reasoned that we could buy ten iPod Touch devices for the price of one fancy news camera, and I set off to raise the money. A few months later, I was the recipient of a Knight Foundation New Voices grant, which awarded me $25,000. I launched the MOJO Lab. MOJO, I decided, would be short for "mobile journalism." The MOJO Lab was the first and only such project in the country at the time. I watched my students' confidence grow. They were filming stories about a city they loved but that care forgot. They were becoming more street smart about how they moved as journalists.

I was growing too. Mobile journalism was taking me around the world. I was invited to South Africa in June 2011 to teach 20 HIV-positive girls how to record documentaries about their lives with mobile devices. Then, just after the Arab Spring revolts in Egypt in September 2011, I was invited to bring mobile journalism to 40 women in Morocco. My students crisscrossed the country, stopping in Marrakesh, Casablanca, Tétouan, Safi, and Rabat to ask citizens of all ages their opinions on the uprisings in Egypt, Tunisia, and Libya. I was intrigued by how the smartphone enabled the world to bear witness to the assassination of Muammar Gaddafi in Libya,[3] the murder of Neda Agha Soltan in Iran,[4] and the protests in Egypt's Tahrir Square.[5]

When I came back to the United States I went on a nationwide speaking tour, evangelizing about the myriad possibilities that smartphones had for journalism. The National Association of Black Journalists named me its Journalism Educator of the Year in 2012. Apple named me a Distinguished Educator in 2013, for my innovative use of their products. Harvard University's Nieman Foundation invited me to its campus, to be a Visiting

Journalism Fellow in 2014. Then Ferguson happened—just two weeks before my PhD program started in August 2014—and I could not stop noticing all of the cellphones in the air. I realized that the predictions I had shared with elite audiences, about what smartphones *might* mean for news, were happening now, in real-time, in some of the most vulnerable U.S. cities. After Mike Brown's death, the incidence of marginalized communities filming fatal police encounters seemed to rise with the chants of #BlackLivesMatter. There was footage of Eric Garner gasping, "I can't breathe,"—11 times—before he died in a New York City police officer's chokehold. There was the footage of Walter Scott being shot in the back by a South Carolina police officer before he handcuffed Scott and planted a Taser next to his dying body. There was also the footage of Freddie Gray screaming in pain as he was loaded into the back of a Baltimore City police wagon, his leg contorted at an odd angle, as if broken. By the time I sat down to write my doctoral dissertation in 2017, this is what came out. This book. This homage to their lives.

Bearing Witness While Black

In the pages that follow, I tell the story of how the perfect storm of smartphones, social media, and social justice raged to create the most powerful black movement of this century. As a journalist and journalism professor, I tell this story through the lens of news production. I do so because news making has been an uncontested space for so long—until now. In the 19th and 20th centuries, wealthy, white, male newspaper publishers, whose names have become legend, decided what made it to the front of American consciousness. William Randolph Hearst. Joseph Pulitzer. Robert R. McCormick. We know their names. In this book, different names carry power. Eric Garner. Mike Brown. Walter Scott. Freddie Gray. Sandra Bland. Alton Sterling. Philando Castile. We know these names because people of color put their bodies on the line to capture their untimely and unjust deaths, with little more than a cellphone. This is what I call "bearing witness while black."

I am making the claim that bearing witness while black is an innovative style of protest journalism that has been centuries in the making. It deserves a special place in the catalog of media studies, alongside the records of citizen journalists who documented the Occupy Movement in 2011 or the Arab Spring revolution that same year. These records from black witnesses belong alongside the many accounts of Jewish witnessing of the Holocaust too. Just as bearing witness to the Holocaust memorializes the roughly 6 million victims of genocide, I argue that black witnessing memorializes the more than 10 million Africans who were sold into bondage across the Atlantic Ocean for nearly 300 years.[6] Black witnessing memorializes the 5,000 African American men, women, and children who continued to be victims of lynching across the United States between 1865 and 1964—nearly a full century after the law said they were free.[7] Black witnessing memorializes the more than 1 million African American and Latinx men and women who have fallen victim to mass incarceration since the late 1970s, when racism learned to disguise itself as a "War on Drugs."[8] Black witnessing memorializes the men, women, and children who have been shot and killed by the very people who are charged with protecting them. In short, black witnessing provides proof of the many eras of anti-black racism, in all of its perverse mutations.

Black witnessing reclaims black lives and stories from the margins. Black witnessing corrects false narratives. Black witnessing gives us new data points around which we can theorize more intersectional ideas of how journalism works. Black witnessing is about seeing and being seen, about being valued and believed. In this spirit, I am building upon the work of Drs. Deen Freelon, Charlton D. McIlwain, and Meredith D. Clark, which went "beyond the hashtags" in 2016 to produce a landmark study of more than 40 million tweets, 100,000 weblinks, and 40 interviews with activists. The team found that "protesters and their supporters were generally able to circulate their own narratives without relying on mainstream news outlets."[9] What's more, they discovered that the activists "succeeded in educating casual observers and amplified marginalized voices." With this book I add new layers to the team's robust study. I interrogate, for the first time, how the smartphone transformed black witnessing. I situate these activists' work squarely in the discipline of journalism studies.

As a black woman who teaches mobile journalism—and was teaching it to black students during the rise of this movement—there will be many times in this story that I must share personal narratives with you. I hope you will forgive my use of autoethnography. I found it insincere to write in the third person throughout this book though, pretending not to be a part of this seismic journalistic shift when I really *was* there, from the very beginning. I build my concept of black witnessing in this book, therefore, by examining the news that African American activists produced at the height of the Black Lives Matter Movement, between 2013 and 2017.

As I write this, Black Lives Matter is celebrating its fifth birthday.[10] The organization has scaled considerably, from a hashtag to 40 domestic chapters and dozens of international affiliates in Berlin, Dublin, London, Toronto, and South Africa. Despite the momentum that the Black Lives Matter campaign achieved since its inception, to date, no other book has been published about the media that was created by black witnesses from within the movement. This book investigates these activists' vibrant news production processes as well as its key documentarians, who belong to three distinct groups. Some of the interviewees for this book lead nonprofit chapters of Black Lives Matter in their hometowns. Others align with allied organizations in the broader Movement for Black Lives, as it is now called, yet they are not part of the formal Black Lives Matter chapter-based network. The third group of activists works independently on anti–police brutality campaigns and claims no formal affiliation to an organization. Still, they exhibit strong ties to the Movement for Black Lives online and in real life. These three groups of activists are unified in their dedication to push discourse about policing into the global news cycle regularly.

These leaders sustain a newsgathering technique that relies on community—for equal parts content and catharsis. They tweet. They livestream. They hit "record" again and again. Still, their work is subject to great precariousness. SnapChat videos and Instagram stories are designed to disappear. Platforms fold and take activists' digital assets with it. The act of bearing witness while black is too fraught with danger to be discarded in this way, though. These stories deserve care and safekeeping. Bearing witness while black, after all, carries with it a moral and legal weight. It is urgent. It is evidence. It is tragedy. It is record.

Bearing witness while black also comes from an oppositional standpoint. I argue in this book that while legacy media outlets are considered members of the "Fourth Estate,"[11] serving as elite watchdogs on *high*, black witnesses report from *below*. Media scholars have called this "*sous*veillance,"—the opposite of *sur*veillance—since the word "sous" is French for "under" and "sur" means "above."[12] Working class black men like Eric Garner or Alton Sterling died literally *underneath* the bent knees or shoes of police officers whose badge endowed a very specific set of privileges.[13] Likewise, the witnesses who captured the Garner and Sterling deaths by cellphone video did so with extreme risk to their own safety, forming the urban equivalent of WikiLeaks[14] for the most beleaguered U.S. neighborhoods.

To investigate how and why black witnesses perform any of this journalistic labor, I established some guiding research questions. First, I wanted to explore the lived experience of bearing witness while black. What are the trials, triumphs, risks, and rewards associated with doing this kind of work? Second, I sought to understand how much activists relied on their smartphones for storytelling. Were the activists livestreaming videos, taking pictures, blogging, and tweeting all from one device, or was their smartphone only good for some things? Third, I wanted to know how anti–police brutality activists used social media in their news production mix. I went beyond the hashtags to see if there was a replicable process that they used to create and circulate protest journalism. I conducted the research for this book in three phases, to answer each of my guiding questions. The first step involved theorizing my own intersectional concept of media witnessing, which served as a framework for the study. Other theories about media witnessing made no mention of race and, thus, would not help me explore why black people use mobile and social media more than any other ethnic group—especially to document social justice issues. In the second phase of my project, I conducted interviews with 15 prominent black witnesses. I thought it was important for them to articulate what they believe their journalistic contributions are, rather than assume I knew because they have been so visible in the mainstream. After the interviews, for the last phase of the research, I analyzed my interviewees' Twitter timelines to observe how they use mobile devices and social media to bear witness. I selected Twitter because African Americans over-indexed on the platform at the height of the Black Lives Matter movement, using it more than any other social network and more than any other ethnic group. One of the most exciting things I found while scraping Twitter during this time period is that the interviewees engage often in a six-step process for reporting movement-related news, which mirrors what many traditional journalists do in a newsroom.

This book is divided, then, into three parts: smartphones, slogans, and selfies. Part I (Smartphones) focuses on how mobile devices closed the so-called digital divide for African Americans in the new millennium. A confluence of speedy Internet connections, Twitter's simple user interface, and black folks' call-and-response communication styles converged to create new journalistic powerhouses. I highlight in this section, however, that this practice—of using the technological medium of the day to bear witness—is not new to black people. For about 200 years, African Americans have used everything from slave narratives to black newspapers and magazines to television and even early social networks to sound the alarm on racial injustice in the United States. First, they bore witness to slavery. Then lynching. Then Jim Crow. And now, to police brutality, which is the next frontier in black liberation.

Part I, therefore, situates what we are seeing happen with smartphones along a historic continuum of black witnessing. Part II (Slogans) extends the argument that today's activists are building upon a legacy of black advocacy journalism by using new tools. This section acknowledges though, that something has shifted. While it may have been prestigious in the 20th century to label one's self a black journalist, all of the activists in this book repudiated this title. Through interviews, they share why. They explain what they believe to be broken in U.S. journalism and why they thought they could do the job better. These activists offer also a rare peek into how they "do" news. I thank them for trusting me enough to share that process. Part III (Selfies), the final section, analyzes the visual iconography that this new generation of black protest journalists created—for better or worse. On the positive side, many activists have juxtaposed memes, original photos, or remixed images from previous black social movements to round out their protest news coverage. Taken together, these digital artifacts have created a new black visual public sphere that future generations of activists surely will study and emulate. Conversely, the images of fatal police shootings that black witnesses have caught on film belong to this black visual public sphere also. While these videos were recorded with noble intent, the images have traumatized African Americans in deeper ways than we thought possible initially. I discuss what this means for the future of black witnessing. Moreover, I explain how police body cameras threaten black witnessing—especially when officers intimidate black witnesses *not* to film and their cameras again become the only record of what happened.

I close this text with some practical calls to action that we all can perform in our communities, as either black witnesses or allies to black witnesses. We all have an obligation to help end police brutality, but it will happen in our lifetime only if we dare not to look away. Despite how numbed we may feel to images of fatal police shootings, I maintain that visual proof matters. We have to keep seeing, tallying, and holding the powerful accountable. In this spirit, my book ends with an epilogue that is as hopeful as it is sorrowful. The good news is many local police departments have reformed their policies on excessive force in response to black witnessing. Some state-level reform laws have been introduced in the names of many of the victims of police brutality too. So, the movement is working.

The bad news is the martyrs on whom it is based never will come back home. The stories of how these unarmed black men, women, and children died—and perhaps not how they came into the world—may well be the narrative that drives our collective memory of them now. This fact resonates with me for a reason. At the beginning of this book, I told you that I thought I would have to give birth to my son in the dark. In many ways, I did. Before he was born, I was in the dark about what it meant truly to be a mother of a black boy in the United States. With my son's birth came an illumination of these things.

As I pressed toward the completion of this book, I grew ever more convinced that Dr. Martin Luther King Jr. was right when he wrote: "Darkness cannot drive out darkness; only light can do that. Hate cannot drive out hate; only love can do that." So, it is with love for marginalized populations, which too often feel unheard, disregarded, or misrepresented by mainstream media, that I offer you this book. Our stories deserve the light.

Acknowledgments

Heavenly Father, I have felt your favor upon me since I began this book in 2014. I started this work at a peak in my life. You had just blessed me with my second child. I had just completed a prestigious fellowship. And my job had just granted me permission to keep working full-time, while attending school full-time in pursuit of my doctorate. Then, as you know, the valleys revealed themselves. Lord, it was then that you took my hand and refused to let it go. I am here today, finishing this book, because of the people you have sent into my life, who would not let me quit or fail. I thank them here.

I would like to thank the activists who participated in this study, who trusted me enough to share their stories. You helped me go beyond the Black Lives Matter hashtags and protest chants and into your everyday lives. At times, as an African American woman, it was hard to hear you speak of the many ways you have been hurt in the pursuit of justice for members of our community. You told me that you have been harassed online, intimidated by federal and state officials on the streets, and even threatened with death. For these reasons, following you for the last few years has been heavy, spiritual work. Every time fresh police brutality news headlines emerged, I worried about you. I thank you for letting me check in on you. I thank you also for being leaders. You are drafting a blueprint for modern protest.

This project never would have come to fruition without the fantastic team at Oxford University Press. To Toni Magyar, thank you for taking the initial pitch for this book idea over the telephone. Thank you Hallie Stebbins and Angela Chnapko, my tireless editors, for believing in the subject matter. Your guidance and expertise was wonderful during this journey as a new author. Thank you to the many insightful, anonymous reviewers who read drafts too. Your feedback was invaluable.

Thank you to Bob Franklin, founding editor of *Digital Journalism*, for publishing the namesake essay *Bearing Witness While Black*. You wrote me personally to say that you enjoyed the piece. That inspired me to elaborate on my ideas, in book length. To Dr. Patricia Hill Collins of the University of Maryland College Park, I am forever grateful for your Black Social Movements class in Fall 2015. I thank you also for sharing your podium with me, allowing me to deliver a lecture on black witnessing as a PhD student. Your books have inspired me since I was 15 years old. To have you as a mentor now is a treasure. Thank you to Dr. Meredith D. Clark, of the University of Virginia, who helped pioneer the study of "Black Twitter," and became a friend in the process. Your weekly accountability calls kept me writing when the weight of the subject matter gave me pause. Special thanks go to Dr. Deen Freelon of the University of North Carolina Chapel Hill for advancing our understanding of the Black Lives Matter Movement through keen social media analysis. I appreciate you reviewing relevant chapters in the earliest phases of this work.

Thank you to my colleagues at the University of Southern California. From the minute I set foot on campus to deliver my job talk, I knew this was a place that would not shy away from tough conversations about race and the media. To President Carol L. Folt, thank you for inviting me to preview this book at our University-wide faculty symposium in Fall 2019. I have met such compassionate partners in this movement since then—on-campus and off—who continue to challenge my own thinking and activism. To Dean Willow Bay, thank you for inspiring me to adapt my doctoral dissertation into a book. You have been a dynamic presence for me since I arrived in Los Angeles, always tapping me to share my ideas with audiences I never could have imagined meeting. To Dr. Gordon Stables, director of the School of Journalism, thank you for being the best ally that a junior faculty member could have. Whether it was allowing me to design courses around the concepts I explore in this book—or funding professional development to hone my digital ethnography skills—you always put Annenberg's full resources behind me. To Dr. Sarah Banet-Weiser, outgoing director of the School of Communication, thank you for inviting me to hold a dual appointment at Annenberg. Having one foot in the School of Journalism and another in the School of Communication really has been the perfect combination of practical and theoretical exposure that I needed to develop this book. Thanks to immediate past dean, Dr. Ernest J. Wilson, III, for welcoming me to Annenberg with abundant resources. To Dr. Margaret McLaughlin, outgoing Senior Associate Dean for Faculty Affairs and Research, thank you for encouraging me to write a book sooner rather than later in my career. To Geoffrey Cowan, thank you for inviting me to apply for a professorship at Annenberg by telephone that fateful afternoon. Thanks to Dr. Henry Jenkins for reading my book proposal before I sent it off to Oxford University Press. To Dr. Manuel Castells, thank you for inviting me to work with you on university-wide innovation projects that infuse the ethos of black witnessing. Special thanks to Dr. Mike Ananny for helping me sharpen this research agenda and for attending my first international lecture as an Annenberg professor. Thanks to my colleagues who listened to my book ideas over lunch or dinner or invited me to your classes: Amara Aguilar, Dr. Francois Bar, Jaime Carias, Bill Celis, K.C. Cole, Laura Davis, Dr. Robeson Taj Frazier, Rebecca Haggerty, Robert Hernandez, Gabriel Kahn, Dr. Colin Maclay, Dr. Josh Kun, Dr. Lisa Pecot-Hebert, Joe Saltzman, Philip Seib, Willa Seidenberg, Roberto Suro, Sandy Tolan, Dr. Alison Trope, Dr. Cristina Visperas, Dr. Diane Winston and Dr. Aimei Yang. Thanks to my fantastic research assistants, Jeeyun Baik, Emily Iverson and Mairead Loschi. Many thanks to Deb Lawler, Rachel Cardenas, Colette Kosty Stroud, Fabian Ledesma, Annie Mateen, Nancy Ruiz, and the fabulous administrative team at Annenberg, who made it possible for me to write this book without worrying about international travel arrangements or research funding. I would like to thank my students at the University of Southern California also. I have watched you find your footing as journalists in a scary time, when nationalism, racism, and xenophobia are spreading at fever pitch. Your resolve, to be guided by truth and inclusion, is inspiring.

I would like to thank my former colleagues and students who have supported me since I began teaching at the university level, more than a decade ago. To Profs. Talisha Dunn-Square, of Bowie State University, and Chelsea Mays-Williams, of the University of Maryland College Park, thanks always for being but a text message away. To Dr. Monifa Love Asante, thank you for loving Indian food as much as I do—and indulging me always in thought-provoking lunchtime chats. You have been a phenomenal mentor. Special thanks to my original research assistant, the amazing Britney Pollard, who helped me locate and interview the activists in this book. To my students at Bowie State University, thank you for being intrepid reporters when the horrors of police brutality hit too close to home. When Freddie Gray died in Baltimore, Maryland, in April 2015, less than 30 miles from our campus, I saw many of you pick up your smartphones and head right into the city. You did not know it, but your instincts to use that tool in your pocket greatly inspired me to continue working on this book. I felt—and still feel—that I needed to document your brand of journalism. For the culture.

I would like to thank Xavier University of Louisiana for providing me the foundation to be successful in academia. To Dr. Norman C. Francis, our illustrious past president, I thank you for encouraging me to be a writer after I penned my first front-page story for our school newspaper. Thanks also to Dean Charles Whitaker of Northwestern University's Medill School of Journalism. You set me on this path 15 years ago when I was your student, recommending me for my first internship at *JET* magazine. To my family at First Baptist Church of Glenarden in Maryland and now at Abundant Living Family Church in California, I thank you for praying me through this book. To Lawrence and Jackie McCoy especially, thank you for helping me see that His Word is true: "I can do all things through Christ who strengthens me" (Philippians 4:13). To the godmothers of my children, Dr. Shauna White and Ms. Hermetta Wright, you have been blessings throughout this process! Thank you Shauna, for babysitting Brynn and Bryce when I needed to write. Thanks also for traveling with me to Europe to support my nerd talks. Thank you Hermetta, for praying with me in the midnight hours. I am forever grateful to you also for allowing me to borrow your beloved mommy, Mrs. Peggy Wright. She opened up her heart and home to care for the children when I needed her most.

Thank you to my dearest cousins David and Anita Downing, who provided steadfast love—and excellent barbecue—to me when I arrived in Los Angeles. You have been opening up your home to me since I was a college girl, and I am grateful that I could speak with you openly about many of the ideas that landed in this book. Thank you to my in-laws, Ms. Arlean Arnold and Mr. Ernest and Mrs. Nancy Richardson, for being wonderful grandparents. I am able to do this work because I can rest easy when the children are with you. To Allister P. Hosten Jr., just when I thought you could not be a better "brudder," you go and become a phenomenal godfather to Brynn and Bryce. Thank you for only being a FaceTime call away when the three of us need to laugh or cry. Thanks also for being part moving company and therapist to me, and part sword fight trainer and Santa Claus to your niece and nephew.

To my children Brynn and Bryce, thank you for loving me and for teaching me how to have balance. Brynn, when I started the doctoral program that led to this book, you were only two years old, singing bits of "Baa Baa, Black Sheep" to me. Now, you are seven years old and reading entire books to me! You tell me that you want to be an artist and author, who animates children's films and writes books. I hope my process of publishing this book will make me an ample mentor for you one day. Bryce, I thank you for being patient with me. You never complained when I trekked to the library to seek more books for my research. You were only four months old when I started this work, but you would squeeze into my baby carrier like a champ, and ride on my back with a smile. You are five years old now and full of goals to be a marine biologist who makes television shows about sea creatures. It is a wonder to see the black boy joy that you possess. To the father of my children, Bryant Richardson, I thank you for believing in mobile journalism, and in me. Although we have transitioned from husband and wife to co-parents, I will always be appreciative of the time you invested, during our marriage, to help me spread the word about mobile journalism. From driving me to speaking engagements across the country to accompanying me to Africa to teach; from listening to drafts of lectures and essays to helping me think up lesson plans; this story of our people and the things they did with smartphones belongs to you too.

As I draw these acknowledgments to a close I would like to thank my parents for always knowing that this moment would come but never pressuring me to get there. To my father Allister P. Hosten Sr. (for whom I am named), I would like to thank you for taking me to the library every weekend when I was a little girl. You always let me check out as many books as I could carry. I remember learning the Dewey Decimal system from you. I developed my love of writing from you. Thank you for being my first editor. I was so afraid of your red pen back then, but I am thankful for it now, Daddy. Thank you, Mommy, for loving me like our God does. Throughout this entire process, you never let me go. Sometimes, I think back to that race I entered during the citywide field day one year. Remember when I thought it was a sprint, when it really was a distance run? I started to walk off the track during the second lap, as everyone else passed me. You came out of the stands and walked the rest of the race with me. You walk with me still. When I was in the thick of reading and writing, you cooked my favorite things. You did my laundry. You packed lunches for the kids. My admiration of you goes back even further than all of this. As a girl I watched you type your own dissertation, bit-by-bit, every night. You worked and went to school full-time, and still managed to be a glamorous mom and wife. And you finished in three years! You set the bar. The day I saw you walk across the stage, hearing them call you *Dr.* Pamela Ruth Downing-Hosten, I was so proud. It was in that moment I saw what I could become. Thank you, Mommy, for showing me always what brilliance and resilience look like. Amen.

PART I
SMARTPHONES

1

Looking as Rebellion

The Concept of Black Witnessing

Before Eric and Alton and Philando, there was Rodney. Four police officers took turns beating him one night in Los Angeles, in 1991. He put his hands up in a position of surrender several times. He writhed on the ground in agony when their blows landed anyway. Someone screamed during the infamous video. At times, it was unclear whether it was Rodney King or a bystander. As the camera capturing the footage went in and out of focus, the ordeal lasted eight minutes and eight seconds on film.[1] I remember watching the video with my parents as it looped on news broadcasts. I was nine years old. My younger brother was turning seven in two days.

"Jesus," I remember my father whispering. Something about the way he said it gave me pause. It was as if my dad was sending a prayer through our television to a man we did not know. I remember asking my father if he was going to be sick. He looked nauseous. He did not answer me. I cannot tell you what my Grenadian dad was thinking at that moment. At nine years old, I knew nothing of post-colonialism, or about the myriad, warring identities that many Afro-Caribbean people feel when they settle in the United States. We had not yet had the conversation I would launch many years later as a college student, when I asked him why he always referred to the West Indies as "back *home*." It was a conversation that highlighted perhaps how my father never felt settled in the United States, even though he had made a family and a life here.

As we watched the assault, my dad said, "Back *home* they don't do these things to people." I do not remember if I responded to him. I do recall thinking that here—in the United States, in our modest house, in Prince George's County, Maryland—this *was* home. This was safety. There was no "back" for me. It would be many years before Ta-Nehisi Coates would write *Between the World and Me*, which put the Prince George's County police department on the map as one of the most brutal, anti-black forces in the nation. My father must have been living with those realities long before Coates' book

Bearing Witness While Black. Allissa V. Richardson, Oxford University Press (2020). © Oxford University Press.
DOI: 10.1093/oso/9780190935528.001.0001

though. That day, as we watched the billy clubs swing upon Rodney King, my father winced, but he never looked away. I can recall clearly a sudden wave of fear gripping me as I watched the news clips. My mind was beginning to do nine-year-old calculus. If this place, the United States, was home; and if, in the United States, the police beat someone who looked like Rodney King so savagely; and if my father was black like Rodney King, then . . . I did not say these words, of course. No one in the family was speaking as we watched. I remember scooting closer to my father on the couch, until I was under his arm. I was under his arm again, a year later, as I watched the city of Los Angeles burning on television. Three of the four police officers were acquitted, my father explained. The jury could not reach a verdict on the last officer. I remember how my father spat out the words. It was a quiet rage, but it was there. I remember asking my dad why everyone was so angry. People who looked like me were yelling at the news cameras. Some were crying. It was my turn to feel queasy.

"Because they had proof, but no one *cared*," my father said flatly.

How could it be that this proof of which my dad spoke—this video evidence—was enough of a smoking gun for black people but not enough to convict the officers involved? Moreover, why did black pockets of Los Angeles go up in flames after its residents saw the video, while the rest of the city (and nation) clucked its tongue, wondering aloud how "those people" could destroy their own neighborhoods? These are the questions I get most often when I lecture about black witnessing. Nearly 30 years after the Rodney King tape, the average onlooker still has a very difficult time understanding how African Americans can go from viewing video evidence of police brutality to feeling compelled to riot. Perhaps even fewer people can fathom why someone would put themselves in an officer's literal crosshairs to record damning footage. As a nation we have, perhaps, become so accustomed to viewing these spectacles as sudden eruptions of violence and mayhem in a black community, rather than as a climactic moment that has been building over decades of abuse at the hands of its police. As a former full-time journalist, I sighed every time I saw cable television news loop images of fire and brimstone in Ferguson in 2014, after police killed Michael Brown, or in Baltimore in 2015, after Freddie Gray's death. I wanted someone on-air to describe instead how black people experience police brutality, and video proof of it, differently from non-black people. How African Americans, like my father in 1991, see themselves in the bodies of the battered. I wanted the news pundits to say bearing witness while black is a specific kind of media witnessing. It is as networked, collective, and communal as the South African philosophy of Ubuntu, which states, "I am because *we* are." Black witnessing carries moral, legal, and even spiritual weight. I grew tired of yelling all of this at my television. So, I wrote this book. I offer a new way of talking about the "looking" that African Americans do through news media. Bearing witness while black—or black witnessing, as I call it interchangeably—needs its own scholarly categorization. It involves more than simply observing tragic images on TV or online. It is more complicated than picking up a smartphone and pressing "record" at the right time. When most African Americans view fatal police shooting videos, something stirs at a cellular level. They want to *do* something with what they just saw. And they want to link it to similar narratives they may have seen before. In this manner, black witnessing is re-flexive, yet reflective. It despairs, but it is enraged too. Black witnessing is not your average gaze. Before now though, we have lumped it in with mere "media witnessing." Here is why this terminology does not work any longer.

What is Media Witnessing?

Paul Frosh and Amit Pinchevski claimed that the term "media witnessing" seems redundant at first glance since every act of witnessing is mediated in some way.[2] At the most basic level, one person offers an account of events to another person who was not there. In journalism, this process is scalable so that one person can tell a story to mass audiences. Frosh and Pinchevski explained that since news production involves three possible processes, this is where simplistic definitions of media witnessing begin to disintegrate. They wrote "[Media witnessing] refers simultaneously to . . . witnesses *in* the media, witnessing *by* the media, and witnessing *through* the media."[3] In the instance of the Philando Castile killing, journalists could interview eyewitnesses to the shooting and quote them in a story; journalists could serve as primary witnesses themselves; or anyone else could use media pro-duction tools to bear witness without a professional journalist as an interme-diary, like Diamond Reynolds did when she livestreamed the tragedy. Frosh and Pinchevski explained further that two historic events created two dis-tinct categories of witnesses: the authoritative, Holocaust-style witness who saw atrocities firsthand and lived to tell about it, and the distant television viewer witnesses of September 11, 2001, who were not in New York when terrorists flew planes into the World Trade Center but remember seeing the events recounted *through* the media. The September 11 witnesses are just as authoritative as Holocaust witnesses, Frosh and Pinchevski insisted, since they contribute to the collective memory of that day.

Not all scholars agree that distant witnessing is just as effective as firsthand viewing, though. John Durham Peters has argued that being present matters. He wrote: "The copy, like hearsay, is indefinitely repeatable; the event is singular, and its witnesses are forever irreplaceable in their privileged relation to it."[4] Peters proposed that we define witnessing on a continuum, in four different ways: being there, live transmission, historicity, and recording. Being there is the strongest kind of witnessing, since it means that one was a part of an assembled audience, such as a concert, game, or theater. Live transmission is the next strongest form of witnessing, since it describes an audience that was part of a simultaneous broadcast. Historicity refers to witnesses who visit a museum or a shrine, where events happened long ago in the same spot, but not necessarily during the lifetime of the witness. Lastly, a recording, presented as a book, CD or video, is the weakest form of witnessing, Peters said, since the viewer does not have to occupy the same space and time as the original event.

Both definitions of media witnessing—as either a tripartite bundle of accounts *by, of,* or *through* the media or a quadripartite matrix divided along planes of space and time—have provided valuable frameworks for media scholars to explain the works of citizen journalists who have reported the tsunami that rocked South East Asia in 2004;[5] the Virginia Tech massacre of 2007;[6] or the shooting of Iranian activist Neda Agha-Soltan in 2009.[7] These frames reach their epistemological limits when studying the Black Lives Matter Movement, though. The Frosh-Pinchevski model does not help us understand why black people are more likely to engage in either frontline or distant witnessing of police brutality than other ethnic groups. Surely, police kill unarmed white people. Why does this imagery fail to proliferate the media landscape as much as the videos of brutality against people of color do? Likewise, Peters' argument—that recording is the weakest form of witnessing—seems to fall apart when one considers the thousands of international Black Lives Matter protesters who were not present to view Michael Brown's death firsthand, but still feel as if they did see it—so powerfully that they took up picket signs in the slain teen's defense. We need a new definition, then, for the kinds of looking that African Americans do—especially during times of crisis.

The Three Elements of Black Witnessing

After many months of observing African Americans' responses to the highly publicized killings of unarmed black men, women, and children in 2014, I began to see some patterns. African Americans wanted—and, perhaps, even needed—to see a firsthand account of what happened in each fresh case study of untimely death. On Facebook timelines and in YouTube comments sections, I noticed that African Americans were dismissive of official police or media reports. They wanted video evidence that came directly from the community itself. I noticed also that African Americans on my social media timelines used various platforms to direct audiences to original videos or blog posts about uprisings in Ferguson, Baltimore, and beyond. Twitter was most popular. It became a news wire service of sorts. Lastly, I saw subgroups of African Americans finding each other on Twitter. I observed cliques of black journalists who worked for legacy media outlets talking to each other. I saw black activists working across different allied organizations collaborating. I saw black people who did not support the movement arguing with those who did.

From all of my lurking, I noted three recurring observations. Black witnessing: (1) assumes an investigative editorial stance to advocate for African American civil rights; (2) co-opts racialized online spaces to serve as its ad-hoc news distribution service; and (3) relies on interlocking black public spheres, which are endowed with varying levels of political agency, to engage diverse audiences. Modern black witnesses can be on the frontline like Feidin Santana was in 2015. Santana filmed Michael Slager (a white police officer) shoot Walter Scott (an unarmed black man) in the back, in North Charleston, South Carolina. Modern black witnesses can be distant witnesses too, who are galvanized to action after viewing video from the frontlines. Distant witnesses are the thousands of people who blocked the Brooklyn Bridge in New York after the cellphone footage of Eric Garner's fatal encounter with the city's police department went viral in late 2014.[8] Three established communication theories support my suggested characteristics of black witnessing. First, I offer a summary of media witnessing during and after the Jewish Holocaust, to illustrate why we should view black witnessing through a similar, ethnocentric frame. Then, I explain how the rise of so-called Black Twitter gave black witnesses an ideal news distribution outlet. Lastly, I explain how three types of black public spheres circulate the news that black witnesses create. By braiding these three established media studies concepts, I offer a new way of thinking about contemporary black looking. This will provide our theoretical framework through the rest of the book, helping us to situate the activists as conscious agents of protest journalism.

The "Crisis of Witnessing" and its Ethnocentrisms

The notion of "bearing witness" has become so intertwined with evidence of Jewish persecution that the Anti-Defamation League trademarked the phrase in 1996 for a national educational campaign about the Holocaust.[9] Historically, bearing witness to the Holocaust meant becoming a martyr, for only the people who died from the atrocities wrought upon them witnessed the entire narrative arc of the tragedy—from the initial encounter with the oppressor on to death. Within this paradigm it is perhaps easy to understand then, why the Greek word for "witness" is *mártys*. While martyrs are to be revered, their deaths still leave us with incomplete narratives. Shoshana Felman and Dori Laub called this extermination of voices the "crisis of witnessing."[10] Since none but those who died in the Holocaust can serve as the complete witnesses—documenting their capture and their death—we are left with the testimonies of the survivors. In the Jewish tradition of witnessing, survivors speak to commemorate the slain and to verify that atrocities transpired. In doing so, Jewish witnesses create a long, thematic thread of narrative that links similar human rights violations to one another throughout history, rather than regarding each new violation as an isolated incident. The story of atrocities committed against black people could benefit from similar framing. Consider, for example, the October 27, 2018, mass shooting at a Pennsylvania synagogue. The gunman, Robert Bowers, posted anti-Semitic statements on many online sites before killing 11 worshippers during the Saturday morning Shabbat service. According to the Federal Bureau of Investigation (FBI), Bowers, 46, wrote: "They're committing genocide to my people. I just want to kill Jews." Leaders in the Jewish community channeled the crisis of witnessing in their responses to the tragedy. Israeli Diaspora Affairs Minister Naftali Bennett told CNN, for example: "Nearly 80 years since Kristallnacht, when the Jews of Europe perished in the flames of their houses of worship, one thing is clear: Anti-Semitism, Jew-hating, is not a distant memory. It's not a thing of the past, nor a chapter in the history books. It is a very real threat." The same CNN story situated Bennett's comments alongside a frightening statistic: In 2017, anti-Semitic incidents in the United States surged nearly 60 percent, according to the Anti-Defamation League.[11]

By presenting the legacy of anti-Semitism as a clear and present danger to Jews living in the United States today, the community has done an excellent job of never letting the country forget how past horrors can be revived. How hate speech can escalate to hate crimes, and even genocide, if left unchecked. African Americans are no strangers to these realities, yet their legacy of subjugation has not been framed historically as a Holocaust. Even though the bones of millions of unnamed Africans line the bottom of the Atlantic Ocean—creating a hidden trail of slave ship trade routes. Even though southern trees bore "strange fruit"—lynching the freed descendants of those who survived the slave ships, cotton fields, and sugar cane plantations. Even though the lynching and the segregation morphed too—twisting into mass incarceration for those on the inside and police brutality for those left on the outside. This spirit of ongoing domestic terror against black people mutated, you see, as the United States grew older. And so we must frame the violence that has occurred—and continues to occur—against black bodies just as Jewish communities do: as long and storied legacies of persecution. For it is only then that we can observe what the long arc of anti-black racism looks like; how it shape-shifts and becomes more impervious to its own eradication, like a virus that has become resistant to a bevy of powerful antibiotics. This is the work I saw black witnesses do in 2014.

When protestors in Ferguson took to the streets to protest the killing of Michael Brown, for example, they used mobile devices and social media to circulate familiar visual tropes that were associated commonly with Dr. Martin Luther King Jr. They were calling on the long dead to help frame the circumstances surrounding the newly departed. In one popular photo an African-American man held a poster that read, "I am a man."[12] This slogan has deep historic roots in the black community.[13] On February 1, 1968, two black sanitation workers in Memphis were crushed to death by a malfunctioning garbage truck. Despite public appeals from colleagues to address the unsafe working conditions for blacks in the industry, the city's white leadership remained silent. Twelve days later, 1,300 black men from the Memphis Department of Public Works went on strike. They dressed in their Sunday best and wielded posters that read: "I am a man." This declaration of black masculinity attracted the attention of Dr. King and other local leaders of the National Association for the Advancement of Colored People (NAACP), who joined the strike.[14] King traveled to Memphis to support the effort in February 1968 and settled in for what he believed would be a long fight. About two months into the campaign, on April 3, 1968, he told the weary group of men: "Like anybody, I would like to live a long life—longevity has its place. But I'm not concerned about that now . . . I've seen the Promised Land. I may not get there with you. But I want you to know tonight that we, as a people, will get to the Promised Land."[15] The next day, as King was leaving the Lorraine Motel for dinner, he was shot on the balcony. When modern protestors in Ferguson carry the "I am a man" posters, they invoke the crisis of King bearing witness, for he is no more able to recount his own death than Michael Brown. Additionally, an Afrocentric crisis of witnessing frame helps explain why the distant black witness in Ferguson, who may not have seen officer Darren Wilson shoot Michael Brown, feels compelled still to behave much like a Holocaust survivor, bearing witness to speak for the slain.

In another contemporary example, African American Ferguson protestors regularly held up their fists in the traditional symbolic gesture of the Black Power Movement of decades past. Many African Americans remember it as the official salute of the Black Panther Party for Self-Defense.[16] In the same year that King was assassinated, Tommie Smith and John Carlos raised their fists at the 1968 Mexico Olympic Games as they accepted their medals. They later told journalists that they were protesting racism.[17] According to an October 17, 1968, BBC report, Smith said: "We are black and we are proud of being black. Black America will understand what we did tonight." Smith and Carlos were blacklisted for their protest for the rest of their lives. Still, they were right: Black America *did* understand what they did. And so the symbol, of the raised fist, has endured.

Another example of how black witnessing very closely resembles Jewish witnessing, by linking narrative threads of atrocity throughout history, is through the invocation of Emmett Till. Till, a black teenager from Chicago, was murdered in 1955 for allegedly flirting with a white woman in a Mississippi convenience store. Till was visiting family from the North at the time, and is said to have not known the extent of Southern-style racism. Till's killers, Roy Bryant and his half-brother J.W. Milam, both were white. Bryant and Milam beat Till, shot him, and then tied barbed wire and a 75 pound fan around his neck. The men cast his body into Mississippi's Tallahatchie River, likely watching it sink to the bottom. The *New York Times* reported: "A jury of twelve white neighbors of the defendants reached the verdict after one hour and five minutes of deliberations." A juror told the *Times* "If we hadn't stopped to drink pop it wouldn't have took that long."[18] Bryant and

Milam later granted *Look* magazine exclusive interviews about how they killed the boy.[19]

Elizabeth Alexander has written extensively about black witnesses' collective memory of viewing Till's corpse, in an effort to explain why today's black tales of injustice tend to begin with him.[20] She cited lines from the late boxer Muhammad Ali's autobiography, in which he recounted seeing the pictures of a maimed Till for the first time. He recalled: "I felt a deep kinship to him when I learned he was born the same year and day that I was. My father and I talked about it at night and dramatized the crime. I couldn't get Emmett out of my mind until one evening I thought of a way to get back at white people for his death."[21] Similarly, Charlyne Hunter-Gault, a celebrated black journalist, explained: "It happened in August, 1955, and maybe because he was more or less our age, it gripped us in a way that perhaps even the lynching of an older black man might not have. . . . Pictures of his limp, water soaked body in the newspapers and in *Jet*, Black America's weekly news bible, were worse than any image we had ever seen outside of a horror movie."[22]

Fifty years after Till's murder, Devin Allen invoked his spirit still in a political fashion choice. Allen's amateur photographs of Baltimore's Freddie Gray uprisings in 2015 made the cover of *TIME* magazine that April.[23] In a posed picture, the celebrated black witness is wearing a T-shirt that lists slain black men who died at the hands of white supremacist vigilantes or law enforcement officers. The list begins with Till and ends with an ellipsis, suggesting that more names are to follow.[24] Former U.S. Attorney General Eric Holder had a similar message in November 2014, after St. Louis officials announced they would not indict Officer Darren Wilson on any charges for killing Michael Brown. Holder said at a tree planting ceremony in Washington, DC: "The struggle goes on. . . . There is an enduring legacy that Emmett Till has left with us that we still have to confront as a nation."[25] By invoking Till, Holder recognized the black witnessing tradition of beginning the narrative thread of deadly, anti-black racism with the Chicago teenager and reminded us that this problem is not new.

In all of these examples—from the resurrected Civil Rights Movement protest posters, to the raised fists of the Black Power era, to the invocation of Emmett Till—black witnessing makes a concerted effort to weave a historic thread between various eras of black trauma and activism. Just as the Jewish Holocaust ended, yet anti-Semitism endures, so too did slavery and Jim Crow end, yet anti-black racism endures. Just as new tragedies against Jewish bodies trigger the community to reflect on its history of persecution, the recurring disregard for black life at the hands of police compels black witnesses to stand in the gap too; especially for those who are no longer here to speak for themselves. This crisis of witnessing—with its urgency and its memorial—is the same.

The "Weighty Baggage"

Black witnesses often put their bodies and their future safety at risk to film police brutality. This martyr mindset stems from what John Durham Peters calls, "weighty baggage." He wrote "the baggage has three main interrelated sources: law, theology, and atrocity."[26] In law, the witness is a privileged source of information upon which a judgment will be based. When one takes the stand to testify, one swears an oath to God to be truthful or else risk punishment. In Christianity, early witnesses became martyrs when they revealed their faith. Additionally, witnessing in the Christian tradition brought with it sacred responsibility as one of the Ten Commandments requires "Thou shalt not bear false witness against thy neighbor."[27] In terms of atrocity, witnessing is a form of connective tissue among black people that transcends place. Although contemporary scholars of media witnessing often argue that cellphone videography places too much distance between the viewer and the victim, African Americans of any socioeconomic class tend to see themselves in the battered body of another black person in these kinds of footage. The line blurs between viewer and victim.[28] It is what I felt and knew at nine years old while watching the Rodney King video: that my African American dad and brother were just as vulnerable to police brutality as King—even in our relative affluence. And I knew this, years before the Boston police racially profiled Harvard University professor Henry Louis Gates Jr., who is black, at his own home in 2009.[29]

When whites see the videos of Eric Garner, Walter Scott, or Freddie Gray being brutalized, however, they may be able to maintain a safe amount of narrative space. They do not carry the weighty baggage of blackness, so they may not understand why seeing such videos makes some black people want to riot. Elizabeth Alexander found evidence of weighty baggage in her analysis of black peoples' reactions to the 1992 acquittals of the four officers who beat Rodney King. One black distant witness said, "When I saw the Rodney King video I thought of myself laying on the ground and getting beat." Another black distant witness said, "Somebody brought a video to school—the video of Rodney King—and then somebody put it on the television and then every-body just started to break windows and everything—then some people got so mad they broke the television."[30]

This weightiness and anguish extends to other persons of color too. This is how allies of black people have become black witnesses too—even if they are not ethnically classified as such.

Consider that George Holliday, who filmed the Rodney King beating in 1991, is Latino. Ramsey Orta, who filmed his friend Eric Garner being choked to death by police in 2014, is Latino. Abdullah Muflahi, who filmed one of the five existing videos of Alton Sterling's last moments in Baton Rouge in 2016, is Yemeni. In all of these situations, the proximity to the victim's blackness conferred a state of being "socially blackened," a term coined by sociologist Patricia Hill Collins:

> Blackening typically means being pushed down a social scale of some kind. . . . People who are Latino, or Middle-Eastern, or women, or dressed poorly, or who either are out of their whitening context or do not explicitly whiten themselves are routinely ignored by people in positions of power and authority and can even be rendered invisible.[31]

This social blackening causes some non-black witnesses to behave just like black witnesses. They understand very quickly that they, too, are vulnerable to police brutality. Moreover, they understand that they need to bear wit-ness to provide proof. They intercede for the victims, therefore, with weighty baggage. Muflahi said of his filming of the Alton Sterling shooting, for ex-ample: "As soon as I finished the video, I put my phone in my pocket. I knew they [police] would take it from me, if they knew I had it. . . . So I kept this video for myself. Otherwise, what proof do I have?"[32]

Proof. It is what my father told me the jurors in Los Angeles had in the 1992 King case, yet ignored. Still, black people and their allies have continued to record—even if they could not be sure that it would bring justice. Just as survivors of the Jewish Holocaust have been compelled to bear witness to atrocity—even though it would not bring back loved ones and even though doing so would not hold all those responsible for the Holocaust account-able for their crimes—black people are using cellphones to keep a record too. Unlike Holocaust survivors, who fled persecution and found asylum in foreign lands, however, groups of repressed blacks in the 21st-century United States have nowhere else to go. There is no *back home* for them. This *is* home. Black witnessing happens, then, in real-time on U.S. soil. As with all witnessing, a medium must carry the message.

The Leverage of Black Twitter as a News Outlet

I JUST SAW SOMEONE DIE OMFG

With these six words, Twitter user @TheePharaoh, also known as Emanuel Freeman, became a frontline black witness. Just after 12 PM on Saturday, August 9, 2014, he tweeted live:

Im about to hyperventilate
@allovevie the police just shot someone dead in front of my crib yo[33]

His next tweet was a photo of Michael Brown lying in the street. An officer who appeared to be Darren Wilson, who was identified later as Brown's killer, stood over his body. Freeman kept tweeting. He described the wails of Brown's mother. He posted another picture of an unidentified officer carrying a rifle. By Sunday, Freeman thanked his Twitter followers for their concern for his safety. By the following Wednesday, he wrote, "I AM DONE TWEETING ABOUT THE SITUATION."[34] Freeman never granted an official interview to legacy media outlets to recount what he witnessed. He did not have to; he had Black Twitter. In Ferguson, Baltimore, and beyond, African Americans have adopted Twitter as their social networking platform of choice for conveying breaking news. Oftentimes, they use the platform to bypass legacy media outlets altogether, as Freeman did, to break news. In other examples, they share what they know about a developing police brutality case in the face of incorrect mainstream reports. None of this, I imagine, is what Twitter's creators had in mind for the social network.

Twitter launched in March 2006, after all, with the simple question: "What are you doing?" In 140 characters or less, everyday people shared what they observed about the world around them and how they perceived themselves in it. Users alternated often between information sources and information seekers in a dynamic system of both strong and loose ties—that is, a network of people they knew well in real life and people they did not know at all.[35] The platform grew rapidly after its inception. The so-called Twitterverse increased 1,382 percent in one year, from 475,000 unique visitors in February

2008 to 7 million in February 2009, making it one of the fastest growing websites of its time. By June 2010, that number had climbed to 28 million unique visitors.[36] While Twitter use exploded, cellphone ownership proliferated alongside it. When Twitter launched in 2006 neither Apple's iPhone nor Samsung's Galaxy series of smartphones had debuted, but 66 percent of all Americans owned a basic cellphone of some kind. When Twitter announced its surge in users in 2010, 85 percent of Americans owned a cellphone. As of 2018, the market is nearly saturated, with 99 percent cellphone ownership among all Americans.[37]

One of the reasons Twitter grew so fast among communities of color, however, was because it could be used easily on mobile devices, and because mobile devices were the primary way that working class African American and Latinx communities accessed the Internet. In 2013—the year the #BlackLivesMatter hashtag was born—the Pew Research Center reported that 16 percent of Latinx youth and 10 percent of black youth used smartphones to access the Internet every day, while only 6 percent of white youth did so.[38] Smartphones and social media lowered the barrier of entry for news production through Twitter, so that any person of color with a mobile device and a WIFI connection could create and disseminate stories throughout a vast network. For African Americans, that network was dubbed, eventually, Black Twitter. Blogger Choire Sicha coined this term in his 2009 post, "What Were Black People Talking About on Twitter Last Night." Sicha wrote, "At the risk of getting randomly harshed on by the Internet, I cannot keep quiet about my obsession with Late Night Black People Twitter, an obsession I know some of you other white people share, because it is awesome."[39]

Not everyone agreed, however, that black participation was welcome on Twitter. A technology blogger, Nick Douglas, recalled that a white colleague lamented to him: "These people don't have real Twitter friends. So they all respond to trending topics. And that's the game, that's how they use Twitter."[40] Journalist Farhad Manjoo delved deeper when he penned the controversial *Slate* piece in 2010, "How Black People Use Twitter," which featured an illustration of Twitter's logo bird with brown feathers instead of its customary blue plumage, donning a hip-hop-style athletic cap. Manjoo posed this litany of questions about Black Twitter:

> Are black people participating in these types of conversations more often than nonblacks? Are other identifiable groups starting similar kinds of

hashtags, but it's only those initiated by African-Americans that are hitting the trending topics list? If that's true, what is it about the way black people use Twitter that makes their conversations so popular?[41]

In October 2015, I interviewed Dr. Meredith D. Clark, who has helped pioneer Black Twitter studies in academic spaces. At the time of our chat, Clark was one of only a handful of scholars in the United States writing about the platform's lively subgroup. She had completed her doctoral dissertation on the phenomenon in 2014 and entitled it cleverly: "To tweet our own cause." I recognized the title immediately as a play on the slogan of the first-ever black newspaper: "We wish to plead our own cause." What heritage did the Black Twitter of today share with *Freedom's Journal*, which was founded in 1827 though? Clark explained that members of Black Twitter were tired of seeing mainstream journalists get it wrong. Like black witnesses before them, the Black Twitter community did not want an "as told to" version of their lives portrayed in the news, she said. They wanted to participate in the storytelling process.

Clark found that Black Twitter users commonly eased into the platform's sub-network in six steps. First, black users self-selected, or made a conscious decision to participate in Black Twitter conversations. Second, users identified themselves publicly on the platform as black. Most users did this by posting a picture of themselves as avatars, instead of photos of an inanimate object, cartoon, or some other vague image. Third, black users "performed" their race by using certain bona fides, such as language choices and popular culture references, to signal their belonging to the group. Fourth, black users deployed black hashtags or "blacktags," as scholar Sanjay Sharma has called them.[42] This signaled further to the group that the black user added to nascent discourse on a culturally relevant topic. Fifth, the user reaffirmed other members by using culturally resonant language. This is the digital version of call and response, or the online equivalent of a black congregation telling its pastor to "Preach!" Lastly, black users solidified their membership in the Black Twitter subgroup when their narratives affected social change. Creators of trending blacktags often noted in their Twitter biographies that they were the originator of it, to avoid cultural erasure and to establish digital credibility. Overall, Clark said, Black Twitter is a "multi-level community and network building process."[43] It should be noted that Black Twitter is not monolithic though. Not all black users comprise Black Twitter. Similarly, not all Black Twitter in-group members share the same ideologies. However, many prominent black witnesses who have garnered national recognition for their coverage of the Black Lives Matter Movement are part of Black Twitter. As such, they create an ad hoc news outlet that breaks news and supplies updates in real time, rivaling some of the most time-honored legacy media. They achieve this by harnessing the power of interlocking layers of the black public sphere.

The Black Public Sphere

I want to add one more caveat to our current conceptualization of bearing witness while black. Already, I have explained how weighty baggage and the desire to intercede for the dead creates an investigative and advocacy-based editorial stance for many black witnesses. Moreover, I have explained why numerous African American activists chose Twitter to be their news distribution tool during the Black Lives Matter movement—especially among subgroups of black people who relied on their cellphone most to access the Internet. What I have not mentioned yet, however, is who the target audiences for all of this Black Twitter news production might be. Truly, black people are using smartphones to create video evidence for each other—especially in the instances of documenting excessive police force. Yet African Americans are making these videos for external audiences too. They want to set the record straight in many cases. Feidin Santana, for example, did not release his exclusive footage of Walter Scott's last moments until he heard a local news outlet report the official lie from the North Charleston police: that Officer Michael Slager shot Scott because he went for his Taser.[44] Similarly, in the case of the Alton Sterling killing in Baton Rouge, cellphone video showed two white police officers wrestling the handcuffed black man to the ground before shooting him in the back several times. Arthur Reed, the black witness who released the fatal exchange to the press, told the *New York Times* that he decided to do so after hearing official news reports in which the police said Sterling reached for a gun. Reed said: "We don't have to beg the media to come and report on the stories. We can put it out on social media now, and the story gets told."[45] Told to whom, though, exactly? Is there one public sphere, or many?

Jürgen Habermas, a philosopher and sociologist, imagined the public sphere as a physical place where men met to discuss matters of political significance. In salons and coffeehouses across late 17th-century Great Britain and 18th-century France, Habermas proposed that dialogue between ordinary people, away from the prying eyes of the state, had the power to shape democracies. Habermas fancied these dignified exchanges as essential to an engaged, civil society.[46] Numerous scholars have challenged Habermas's theory on the basis that it is Eurocentric,[47,48,49] and excludes women,[50,51] people of color,[52,53] and members of the working class. Nancy Fraser wrote perhaps the most famous refutation to Habermas, asserting "[T]he bourgeois conception of the public sphere, as described by Habermas, is not adequate for the critique of the limits of actually existing democracy in late capitalist societies."[54] Instead, she suggests that scholars consider a "multiplicity of publics."[55] African-American scholars built on this idea by proposing a new ethnocentric theory in 1995, when they penned the anthology, *The Black Public Sphere*. In the introduction to the text, its 16 authors asserted:

> The black public sphere—as a critical social imaginary—does not centrally rely on the world of magazines and coffee shops, salons and highbrow tracts. It draws energy from the vernacular practices of street talk and new musics, radio shows and church voices, entrepreneurship and circulation.[56]

By this definition we can consider today's black public sphere as a place where its members connect in virtual and physical spaces around the world. In this manner, Black Twitter is as much a part of the black public sphere as black "barbershops, bibles and BET [Black Entertainment Television]."[57] As straightforward as both definitions may seem, there are several theoretical conditions to consider when we are analyzing black witnessing from within this frame. First, we should note that not all black public spheres are readily visible. Second, not all former loci of black debate continue to serve as effective means of communication. Lastly, to complicate matters further, the black public sphere does not comprise all black people. There are subgroups even within this subgroup, which subjects some black witnesses (such as black members of the LGBTQ community, for example) to be marginalized further still.

Catherine Squires addressed these problems by considering three types of subaltern black spheres: the enclave, the counterpublic, and the satellite. She argued that we should not think of multiple, coexisting spheres merely as counterpublics that are based on a shared marginal identity, such as "people of color, women, homosexuals, religious minorities, and immigrant groups" that have coalesced as a response to exclusionary politics.[58] Instead she wrote

we should classify a black subgroup by the political climate in which it originated, its members' willingness to engage in dialogues with the dominant
public, and its members' agency to create media resources. For these reasons,
I use Squires' definitions of black subaltern public spheres to frame the black
witnesses' approaches to communication.

The enclave. Let us start with the idea that not all black counterpublics are
readily visible. Melissa Harris-Perry has explained:

> At the turn of the century [W.E.B.] Du Bois described black life as an ex-
> istence that occurred behind a veil. He understood that when white
> Americans forcibly separated themselves from blacks, they lowered a dark
> shroud between the races that allowed a certain covert reality for African
> Americans to operate beyond the reach of whites.[59]

Du Bois builds upon this idea of the veil in *The Souls of Black Folk*. He wrote:

> It is a peculiar sensation, this double-consciousness, this sense of always
> looking at one's self through the eyes of others, of measuring one's soul by
> the tape of a world that looks on in amused contempt and pity. One ever
> feels his two-ness—an American, a Negro; two souls, two thoughts, two
> unreconciled strivings; two warring ideals in one dark body, whose dogged
> strength alone keeps it from being torn asunder.[60]

This psychological battle that black people face, even today, forced much
of the black public sphere, during America's infancy, to exist within an enclave. The enclave is a safe space that is hidden from the view of the oppressor.
Its members often possess "few material, political, legal, or media resources,"
yet desire to "preserve culture, foster resistance [and] create strategies of the
future," Squires wrote.[61] An example of such a black public sphere would be
African Americans who lived through slavery. Since slaves lived under the
watchful eyes of their overseers and plantation owners, they either had to
code their discourse about fleeing to freedom in song or meet privately. Free
blacks in the North formed enclaves too, battling slavery by forming abolitionist groups.[62] Squires has explained that even as blacks gained more political clout in the United States, enclaves remained essential because they
provided "independent spaces to retreat to in times of need or during nego-
tiations with outsiders."[63] This explains why the enclaved black public sphere
structure can be found today still, within the walls of the Historically Black

College or University (HBCU),[64] the "Divine Nine" black fraternities or sororities,[65] or within black professional organizations, such as the National Association of Black Journalists.[66]

The counterpublic. Whereas the enclave model of the black public sphere seeks to shelter its participants from the volatile outside world, the counterpublic deliberately ventures "outside of safe, enclave spaces to argue against dominant conceptions of the group and to describe group interests," Squires has explained.[67] While intense oppression gave birth to the enclave, counterpublics emerged because some measure of subjugation subsided, and the oppressed group gained more resources. This emboldened black public sphere then created protest rhetoric and facilitated increased communication between the marginalized and the powerful. The goals of this form of black public sphere are to foster resistance, create coalitions with other marginalized groups, test arguments and strategies for reform in wider publics, and persuade outsiders to change their viewpoints. Members of a black counterpublic often retreat to enclaves, such as the black church, during times of negotiation or strategizing. During the 2014 uprisings in Ferguson, for example, Black Lives Matter activists protested in front of military tanks, yet regrouped inside St. John's United Church of Christ in North St. Louis.[68]

In addition to the protestors, the counterpublic includes frontline cellphone witnesses when they share their footage. They are carrying reports from enclaves to the mainstream to advance change, oftentimes. We see this clearly in the instance of Feidin Santana, who literally shared his footage of Walter Scott with a friend in a black barbershop before he made the decision to turn it over to Scott's family. The black barbershop, which is affectionately called "the black man's country club," was where Santana worked.[69] It was also where he had formed many of his friendships. As an immigrant from the Dominican Republic, he did not have any family in North Charleston. The barbers were his family. Santana's brief departure from that safe space signaled that the promise of justice outweighed the danger he was exposing himself to by leaving the enclave. The counterpublic model of the black public sphere demands that someone must be brave enough to do this. It is what galvanizes distant witnesses and starts a conversation with the mainstream.

The satellite. Squires' final black public sphere type is the satellite, which makes limited attempts to engage with the dominant public sphere. The satellite is often defiant, separatist, and, in some cases, extremist. Squires offers as an example the Nation of Islam. Since its establishment in 1930, the organization has urged blacks to form an independent, self-sustaining state, where reliance upon the government is unnecessary.[70] The Nation of Islam publishes an independent newspaper, the *Final Call*. On the rare occasion that the Nation of Islam ventures into the counterpublic model to challenge the dominant public, it does so with grand displays of racial solidarity, such as the Million Man March in 1995, or with controversial rhetoric through one central voice, such as Louis Farrakhan.[71]

The paradigm of the satellite is intriguing in that it does not place its members in a position of imagined inferiority. In the counterpublic model, Squires argued, "Even when African Americans use the speech norms and institutions of the dominant white public, white perceptions of racial difference may derail black attempts at negotiation." Black spokespersons may be "considered exceptional and not representative of the skills and character of the masses."[72] For this reason, the counterpublic model bears a paradox in that it simultaneously reinforces and challenges myths of black inferiority. Whereas the black counterpublic comes with its proverbial hat (or bullhorn) in its hand, asking the dominant public sphere to make a compromise, the black satellite does not enable the dominant public sphere to exert this form of symbolic leverage over its head: to negotiate is to recognize that the dominant public sphere is more powerful. On the other hand, the satellite misses the opportunity to expose its message to more potential supporters by not engaging publicly. The prolonged satellite model also can be ineffective because it breeds internal bullying and groupthink. If a black witness within the satellite model participates in Black Twitter, for example, does he have to adhere to all of the beliefs of the satellite while engaging publicly, lest the satellite's credibility be threatened? This is an important question, considering the Nation of Islam once silenced Malcolm X from speaking to the press for 90 days after he claimed that the assassination of President John F. Kennedy was a karmic response to centuries of white-on-black violence.[73]

Triangulating Theories

In the 1990s, theories of media witnessing involved either a tripartite bundle of accounts by, of and through the media, or a quadripartite matrix that was divided along planes of space and time, where "being there" mattered more than viewing a reproduced copy of the event. Our current political climate requires an Afrocentric theory of media witnessing though. I claimed, therefore, that black witnessing has three characteristics: (1) it assumes an investigative editorial stance to advocate for African American civil rights; (2) it co-opts racialized online spaces to serve as its ad-hoc news wire; and (3) it relies on interlocking black public spheres, which are endowed with varying levels of political agency, to engage diverse audiences. When we talk about black witnessing with these three characteristics in mind, in the context of recording police brutality especially, it is important to consider that we do so at the risk of engaging in technological determinism. My journalism students often ask me, for example, if smartphones alone explain why fatal police shootings of unarmed African Americans now make headline news. I explain that bearing witness while black actually has deeper roots. I tell them that before Feidin Santana filmed Walter Scott, before Arthur Reed released the Alton Sterling video, and before Diamond Reynolds livestreamed the killing of Philando Castile, historic black figures like Ida B. Wells and Frederick Douglass looked too. And what they saw was monstrous.

2

The Origins of Bearing Witness
While Black

Throughout history, African Americans and select allies have used the technologies of their day to bear witness while black. Before the Civil War, black slaves used autobiographies to document abuse at the hands of their owners, kidnappers, rapists, or wholesalers. In the post-Reconstruction era, black preachers, Pullman porters, and journalists used African American newspapers to tally lynchings and the injustices of Jim Crow. During the Civil Rights Movement of the 1950s and 1960s, black youth courted televised evening news coverage with lunch counter sit-ins and ambitious marches. And now, those working under the banner of anti–police brutality campaigns use smartphones and social media to document the persistent abuse that many African Americans still face at the hands of law enforcement officers.

In this chapter, I connect narrative snapshots in African American media history to our current moment of black journalistic activism. I do not pretend to give a full account of all the intrepid black activists who have leveraged journalism to impact change. Rather, I call our attention to a few exemplars whose legacy lives on today. I am encouraging us to consider the work of today's anti–police brutality activists along a historic continuum. Doing so helps to explain why, as I write this in 2019, black activists are leading a crowdsourced effort to revive Frederick Douglass' *North Star* newspaper, which launched originally in 1847.[1] It explains why in 2016—the year of the back-to-back police shootings of Alton Sterling and Philando Castile—black reporters founded an investigative journalism organization in the name of Ida B. Wells.[2] It explains why the Pulitzer Prize–winning rapper, Kendrick Lamar, brought famous Gordon Parks photographs from the 1960s and 1970s to life in his stirring 2017 music video, *ELEMENT*.[3] And, it is why Beyoncé's *Lemonade* visual album, released in 2016, looks so much like Zora Neale Hurston's fieldwork films from the 1930s, with its portrayals of black people in rural safe spaces.[4] Truly, the legacy of bearing witness while black predates the Rodney King video and its subsequent uprising in 1992. Before the 54

Bearing Witness While Black. Allissa V. Richardson, Oxford University Press (2020). © Oxford University Press.
DOI: 10.1093/oso/9780190935528.001.0001

riot-related deaths in Los Angeles that year; before the 12,000 arrests; before the 2,383 reported injuries, there was a desire simply to be seen as human.[5] It is a basic, yet enduring request that all black witnesses have made throughout time. So, a colleague asked me after a 2018 lecture I gave in Prague, how far back should we go? To the beginning, I said. If we are to examine fully the act of bearing witness while black, we must start in Africa.

Bearing Witness to Bondage: The Slave Narratives (1734–1939)

Along the western coast of Africa, the "talking drum," the *atumpan*, gathered people, announced state business and performed eulogies. The drummer, who was sometimes called an *okerema*, was as much a historian as he was an entertainer. He had to know the names of all former and current rulers in his nation. He had to be prepared to recite their deeds and follies. He had to be ready to fight also, as drummers often documented wars from the frontlines.[6] This style of communication was not one-sided though. Talking drums inspired a participatory communication style among West Africans, which evolved into the call-and-response patterns that we observe in modern black life.[7] It is not uncommon today, for example, to hear a black Baptist congregation exclaim during a sermon "Amen, Pastor!" Likewise, a black woman giving a spirited speech to other black women is likely to be affirmed with a joyful: "Go *off*, sis!" This understanding, that Africans had a viable communication style before transatlantic slavery, brings up the question how much of it was lost when an *okerema* was taken captive. Talking drummers were the first black witnesses, but they were stripped of their medium when they arrived in Western worlds. Their instruments were outlawed. Adopting the dominant culture's mode of communication was also illegal. For black slaves, reading and writing could hasten death. Perhaps this is why the earliest known slave narrative, penned in 1734, is actually a secondhand story of a man who was renamed "Job Solomon Abraham" by his Maryland masters. Thomas Bluett, an Englishman, met Job in America and decided to document his life. Job's African name was Hyuba Jallo, but Bluett wrote that "Job" acclimated to the Christian belief system very easily.[8] The words "beating," "hit," or "strike" do not appear anywhere in this secondhand tale. A century later, in 1845, Frederick Douglass told quite a different story in the first of three famed autobiographies. Douglass recounted that his master told him to remove all of his clothing one day. He stood still, noncompliant and incredulous. Douglass watched as his master snapped three large branches from a gum tree. Then, he trimmed each one neatly with a pocketknife. He asked Douglass to take off his clothing once more. Douglass remained immobile. In a rage, his master pounced upon him "with the fierceness of a tiger" and lashed him "till he had worn out his switches." Douglass's account of this savage beating at the hands of his owner is one of the most celebrated slave narratives of all time.[9] It bore witness to the many indignities of bondage in the United States, giving readers an inside look at life on a Southern plantation.

Does the early "as told to" version of slavery omit many of its atrocities purposefully, or was American slavery in the 1700s much more humane than the bondage blacks experienced in the 1800s? We may never know. Perusing the hundreds of second-hand slave narratives of the 18th century, however, brings up little more than harrowing tales of past lives in exotic Africa, humorous "fish-out-of-water" anecdotes of how slaves adapted to American life, and accounts of what Africans felt upon their return to their homelands, if they were so fortunate.[10] When the nation's literate blacks, like Frederick Douglass, did manage to craft firsthand testimonies, Northern shock usually followed. Abolitionist newspaper editor Nathaniel P. Rogers, for example, described a public address that Douglass gave in 1844, in which he read portions of his as-yet-unpublished memoir. Rogers wrote:

> Douglass finished narrating the story and gradually let out the outraged humanity that was laboring within him, in an indignant and terrible speech. It was not what you would describe as oratory or eloquence. It was sterner— darker—deeper than these. It was the volcanic outbreak of human nature long pent up in slavery and at last bursting its imprisonment.[11]

It could be argued that all of the firsthand slave autobiographies are similar eruptions of anger and despondence. Underneath the rage, however, early black witnessing was concerned with something else too: the fight not to be erased. In a system that was cataloging black bodies for sale only by gender and estimated age—and often not by name—the slave narrative bore witness to one's existence. It proved: *I did not die in the Middle Passage. I am still here.*

Although the Emancipation Proclamation legally abolished slavery in the United States on January 1, 1863, slave narratives endured well into the 20th century, thanks to the federally sponsored Works Progress Administration

(WPA). President Franklin D. Roosevelt instituted the WPA in 1935 as part of his New Deal initiative to create jobs for unskilled workers. Zora Neale Hurston, who was a novelist and folklorist, joined the effort within the WPA's Federal Writers Project (FWP). She traveled to Florida to capture the voices of hundreds of former slaves who founded the country's first all-black town of Eatonville.[12] Hurston feared that a generation of testimony would be lost if anthropologists did not rush to gather these stories. She conducted interviews, recorded slave "work" songs, recorded silent films, and penned essays and novels that were based on her observations of the towns she visited. FWP leadership loved Hurston's work, and soon hired additional workers to launch a full-scale, national search for slaves beyond Florida. As a result, the FWP gathered 2,300 first-person audio accounts from slaves around the country by spring 1939, complete with 500 black-and-white photographs of willing subjects. The collection came to be known as *Slave Narratives: A Folk History of Slavery in the United States*.[13] Perhaps one of the most enduring legacies of Hurston's black witnessing is that it preserved precious voices. Her work allowed the former slaves to be seen as people, with histories and hopes.

Bearing Witness to Lynching: The Black Newspaper as Evidence (1827–1960)

When we consider that the first "slave narratives" likely were not written by slaves at all, then the *Freedom's Journal*'s first printed words become all the more poignant. "We wish to plead our own cause," its editors wrote in its inaugural issue, adding: "Too long have others spoken for us. Too long has the public been deceived by the misrepresentation of things which concern us dearly." Samuel Cornish and John Russwurm founded *Freedom's Journal* in New York City in March 1827.[14] It was the first black newspaper in the United States. Cornish was a prominent minister in New York, who had established one of the first congregations of black Presbyterians in the region. Russwurm was an outspoken abolitionist. During its brief two-year run, *Freedom's Journal* aspired to reach the nation's 300,000 free blacks who "lived under the threat of constant harassment and violence, even in states where slavery was illegal."[15] Its pages featured editorials on abolishing slavery, establishing voting rights, and ending segregation in U.S. public spaces. Cornish and Russwurm disagreed about the way forward a few months into publishing

Freedom's Journal. While Cornish wanted to continue to use his position as a religious leader and newspaper editor to bear witness to slavery, Russwurm grew tired of making moral appeals. He sought to leave the United States altogether. Cornish and Russwurm parted ways in 1829. Cornish stayed in New York. He founded two more newspapers throughout his life: *Weekly Advocate* and *Colored American.* Russwurm left the United States in 1829 for Africa. He settled in Liberia, where he served as secretary of the American Colonization Society and superintendent of education in the capital city of Monrovia.

Media scholar Catherine Squires has noted that newspaper publishing in the days of slavery was a risky pursuit since "the majority of the free Black population was neither literate nor had the income for regular subscriptions." Still, she explained, "when one paper closed down, another often arose to take its place."[16] Frederick Douglass, for example, turned to newspaper publishing in 1847, when he began printing the *North Star.* The newspaper's title paid homage to the constellation that runaway slaves gazed upon and followed to freedom. Douglass used money he earned from his speaking tours to fund the *North Star*'s printing and distribution. His coverage of antislavery efforts in the United States made him the most famous black man in the nation at the dawn of the Civil War. Douglass lived long enough to see chattel slavery end in his lifetime. The Emancipation Proclamation of 1863, the South's surrender in the American Civil War in 1865, and the 13th Amendment to the U.S. Constitution all proclaimed the end of the formal practice of buying and selling black people in the United States. It did not end segregation though. African Americans soon discovered that white supremacists could, and would, devise new ways to oppress them through sharecropping deals, peonage, and convict-leasing systems.[17] By the time Douglass died in 1895, legislators had drafted a flurry of new federal and state laws to restrict the quality of life for blacks across the country. First, President Andrew Johnson vetoed the Civil Rights Act of 1866, which stated that freed slaves could not be discriminated against by any state or local laws. Johnson explained that newly freed slaves had not yet proven worthy of being classified as citizens.[18] Congress tried again, a little over a decade later, with the Civil Rights Act of 1875, which prohibited segregation in public places, such as restaurants and streetcars. The Supreme Court overturned this law in 1883, ruling it unconstitutional. For the roughly four million blacks living in the United States at the turn of the century, Jim Crow laws instead became a way of life. Lynching was the way to enforce them. Between 1882 and 1968, white supremacists carried out 4,743 documented lynchings in the United States. Countless other killings went unreported. Roughly 3,446 of the victims, or 72.7 percent of the slain, were black.[19] I do not know how Douglass felt about this unfinished business as his life came to an end. It is certain, however, that he knew he had a successor in Ida B. Wells. He wrote in a letter to her on October 25, 1892, three years before he died:

> Let me give you thanks for your faithful paper on the lynch abomination now generally practiced against colored people in the South. There has been no word equal to it in convincing power. I have spoken, but my word is feeble in comparison. You give us what you know and testify from actual knowledge. You have dealt with the facts with cool, painstaking fidelity and left those naked and uncontradicted facts to speak for themselves. Brave woman! You have done your people and mine a service, which can neither be weighed nor measured.[20]

Douglass was referring to Wells' publication, *Southern Horrors: Lynch Law in All its Phases*. In it, she tells the story of three local, black grocers who attempted to open a mom-and-pop-style shop in Memphis, Tennessee, in 1892. White agitators did not like that this enterprise was competing with theirs and threatened the owners to shutter the operation, or else. The black grocers armed themselves. When three white men came into the store late one evening, the grocers assumed the white men had come for a lynching and defended themselves with their firearms. The black grocers were promptly thrown in jail despite their attorney's assertion that the shooting had been an act of self-defense. In the early morning, the grocers were dragged from the jail without shoes or hats, Wells wrote, and they were shot alongside the railroad tracks just as a train was passing, to deaden the sound. A jury found that the shooters could not be determined, despite townspeople's observations that there had been four pools of blood—not just three for the grocers— and that a local white man had died shortly after the shootings, most likely because one of the grocers struggled and shot him. This in-depth style of witnessing became the hallmark of Wells' career as a journalist. The bold manner in which she wrote is legend too. Consider this advice that she gave to black Americans living in the post-Reconstruction era South:

> [A] Winchester rifle should have a place of honor in every black home, and it should be used for that protection which the law refuses to give. When the

white man who is always the aggressor knows he runs as great risk of biting the dust every time his Afro-American victim does, he will have greater respect for Afro-American life.[21]

Such fearless writing led a white mob in Memphis to burn down Wells' newspaper office in May 1892, which forced her into a self-imposed exile from the South for the rest of her life. Wells snuck down from the North only to report on a news tip or to tally a lynching, then slipped back up to print pieces in the *New York Age*—a black newspaper that was led by the former slave-cum-politician and public intellectual Timothy Thomas Fortune.[22] Additionally, she published her work in the *Chicago Defender* (another black newspaper) and the *Conservator*, which she owned jointly with her husband, Ferdinand Barnett. Aside from her journalistic activism, Wells spent her lifetime pushing Congress to pass anti-lynching legislature. She penned newspaper pieces with Douglass until his death. She even co-founded the NAACP in 1909. To many activists today, she is the mother of black advocacy journalism. Her most famous maxim is echoed often in activist circles: "The way to right wrongs is to turn the light of truth upon them."[23]

I would be remiss, however, if I did not mention here alongside Ida B. Wells—in this era of the black newspaper as evidence—the thousands of African American men who served as a secret fleet of black witnesses for nearly 100 years: the Pullman porters. The Pullman porter served wealthy passengers aboard the nation's trains. Outside of agricultural peonage, respectable post-Reconstruction era jobs were off limits to blacks living in the South. The perfect storm of racial discrimination, developing railway connectivity, and scarcity of job opportunities led African American men into the porter profession in droves.[24] Pullman porters did everything, such as tote luggage, prepare passenger meals, and even entertain patronizing railway riders. The advantage to the often-demeaning role that the Pullman porter played was that he was socially invisible. Thus, he gathered all kinds of news from well-to-do passengers and took it straight to black newspapers. The Pullman porter tallied lynchings in remote towns. He threw copies of black newspapers off the side of the train for rural communities to pick up and consume. Some even left the profession altogether to become full-time black witnesses, serving as reporters and editors at the top black newspapers of the day, such as James H. Hogans of the *Baltimore Afro-American* and the *New York Age*; Frank "Fay" Young of the *Chicago Defender*; and Joel Augustus

Rogers of the *Pittsburgh Courier*. Even Gordon Parks, who rose to fame as one of the most intriguing photojournalists of the 20th century, got his start as a Pullman porter.

At the height of black newspapers' popularity, the circulations of top publications hovered at just over 350,000 daily subscribers. These numbers dropped dramatically, to just barely 100,000 in 1960.[25] Historians surmise that black newspapers' editorial voices became more moderate in the 1960s. Instead of shouting about U.S. injustices to an audience of like-minded African American people, editors retreated to refined tones, so as not to frighten away advertisers.[26] Their decline in radicalism also mirrored black flight from U.S. ghettoes. As African Americans sought to assimilate and integrate into white culture further, middle and upper class blacks saw their socioeconomic needs as separate from those of working class blacks. This "status" rift, many argue, never has been repaired—even amid today's Black Lives Matter Movement.[27]

Bearing Witness to Jim Crow: The Black Magazine as Evidence (1942–1970)

Mamie Till waited with her future husband, Gene Mobley, on the Old Central Illinois train station platform on September 2, 1955. She was preparing for her son, Emmett, to come back home. Mamie had sent him to Money, Mississippi, to spend time with family just days before, on August 20. Mother and son had rushed to the 63rd Street Station in Chicago, where she had given him his deceased father's ring to wear during his trip. That piece of jewelry proved priceless as police fished Emmett's body out of the Tallahatchie River on August 31, 1955. His corpse was disfigured almost beyond recognition, but his family in Mississippi remembered the ring. Emmett was still wearing it. Now he was on his way back home for his mother to identify whatever else might be left of him. The train slowed to a stop. Then, the stevedores hauled out a pine casket that held her son.

"Lord, take my soul," Mamie cried out, then fainted.[28]

David Jackson captured all of this on camera for his employer, *Jet* magazine. When Mamie rose again to her feet, she made a decision. Jackson should accompany her to the A. A. Rayner Funeral Home, where she would have a closer look at her son. Jackson followed the family to the mortuary. There he took arguably one of the most haunting photographs in U.S. history. In the foreground lay Emmett on an autopsy table, maimed and bloated by the river's waters. His mother and her beau, Gene, stood just behind the table. Mamie appeared to be looking in the direction of Emmett, though not really seeing him. There was a numb vacancy to her expression. But Gene Mobley's posture and eyes said everything. He used his tall, lean frame to cocoon Mamie, gripping her arm and wrist tightly. His eyes were wide and his nose was flared slightly, as if he was holding back tears just long enough for the picture to be taken. Even today, it feels wrong to be in this moment with Mamie and Gene. For just beyond Emmett, another body lay covered in a white sheet.[29] This was a morgue, after all. Still, this space—that normally would be so sacred that only family members could enter—was America's first peek into the Southern horrors of which Ida B. Wells wrote. And *Jet* magazine had the exclusive images. It became the magazine's claim to fame.

John H. Johnson launched Johnson Publishing Company in 1942 with a $500 loan from his mother.[30] His first magazine, *Negro Digest*, debuted in 1942. It was billed as a blend between *Reader's Digest* and the black church "announcements" fliers that congregations of color circulated weekly during services. The first edition sold 3,000 copies. After six months of circulation, its subscription rose to 50,000 copies per month. Johnson used the profits from *Negro Digest* to fund the launch of two more magazines: the monthly *Ebony*, in 1945, and the weekly *JET*, in 1951. In the inaugural issue of *Ebony*, his staff promised that it would "try to mirror the happier side of Negro life—the positive, everyday achievements from Harlem to Hollywood. But when we talk about race as the No. 1 problem of America, we'll talk turkey."[31] But it was *Jet* that became known for its hard-hitting coverage of the blossoming Civil Rights Movement. David Jackson, *Jet's* staff photographer, attended Emmett's three-day wake and funeral in September 1955, for example, at Mamie's invitation. Nearly 50,000 Chicagoans streamed through the Roberts Temple Church of God in Christ on the Southside to get a glimpse of Till. The mortuary had placed a sheet of glass over the casket, yet the sight and smell of his body caused nearly every one in five witnesses to faint. Jackson snapped more photographs, this time of Till in his final resting place. Johnson published the images in the September 15, 1955, issue of *Jet*. The story burst out of black Chicago and onto the front pages of newspapers and magazines throughout the world. When asked why she would authorize the publication of such shocking photos,

Mamie Till Mobley said: "I wanted the world to see what they did to my baby."[32] The Till photographs cemented *Jet*'s status, for a time, as the most authoritative outlet for black witnessing. Famed black comedian Redd Foxx dubbed the magazine the "Negro Bible." Even the critically acclaimed writer Maya Angelou paid homage to the publication with a line in one of her plays. One of her characters quipped, "If it wasn't in *Jet*, it did not happen."[33]

It is ironic that the medium that brought us the tragic Till photograph became a point of contention for black witnesses in the mid-20th century. The wealth gap between the black "haves" and "have-nots" widened after World War II. Whereas the descendants of some free, Northern blacks were sending their third and fourth generations to college, newly immigrated Southerners who were just entering the middle class had a hard time breaking into their black peers' Northern social circles. The "black bourgeoisie," as E. Franklin Frazier called them in his eponymous 1957 book, fostered class division through the glossies. He explained: "The Negro press is not only one of the most successful business enterprises owned and controlled by Negroes; it is the chief medium of communication which creates and perpetuates the world of make-believe for the black bourgeoisie." Frazier lambasted further: "Although the Negro press declares itself to be the spokesman for the Negro group as a whole, it represents essentially the interests and outlook of the black bourgeoisie."[34] Black magazine publishers and editorial staff spent half of the 20th century arguing about Frazier's critique. Should the glossies be reserved for high art and aspirational product placement for African Americans or for long-form journalistic accounts of black life during Jim Crow? Could the glossies do both?

Media scholars have found that *Ebony* magazine broke eventually from the pattern of its sister publication, *Jet*, to avoid spectacles of black death and suffering. *Ebony* instead highlighted "sanctioned symbols of class respectability, achievement, and American national identity."[35] *Ebony* was not above staging portraits for grand effect either. The iconic photograph of Malcolm X peering out of a window while holding a rifle is a rumored "leak" from an *Ebony* photo shoot.[36] *Ebony* readers saw black America largely through Moneta Sleet Jr.'s lens. This premier black witness photographed the Civil Rights Movement extensively in the 1950s and 1960s. He became the first African American to win the Pulitzer Prize for feature photography, in 1969, for his photograph of a grieving Coretta Scott-King at her husband's funeral. Throughout the 1970s, Sleet battled with the magazine's brass to continue covering civil rights issues, but the magazine, most likely under pressure from advertisers, began to focus more on high fashion and entertainment. Sleet remained at the publication, due to its large national audience, but he continued to caution against adopting conformist editorial stances internally.[37]

While *Ebony* was tempering its tone, *LIFE* magazine, upon which it was patterned, was taking bigger editorial risks. It hired the former Pullman porter Gordon Parks in 1948 after his photoessay on a Chicago gangster earned critical acclaim. Parks said his camera was his "weapon of choice" against white supremacy.[38] At *LIFE*, Parks' images spoke directly to the widening religious and class chasms that black America faced during the Civil Rights Movement. His 1942 *American Gothic*, for example, features a lean, elderly African American woman holding a broom in one hand and standing in front of an American flag. Her resigned expression mocks the idea of the American dream for all. A little more than 20 years later, in 1963, Parks' photoessay of the Nation of Islam bore witness to the black Baptist church's loosening grip on its countrymen. For the first time in history, it seemed, a charismatic leader with all of black America's answers was neither Christian nor college educated—he was a Muslim ex-convict named Malcolm X. Parks' images captured these tensions remarkably.

The latter half of the 20th century saw black magazines become more about cosmetics and fashion. Gordon Parks helped establish the creative vision for the newly launched *Essence* magazine in 1970. The storied publication for African American women began as a heavy-hitting voice for black feminists, but soon devolved into the same consumerist editorial traps publications before it had faced.[39] *Essence* owners sold the publication to *TIME*, Inc. in 2000—a move that was criticized widely in the black community.[40] After the *Essence* sale, *Ebony* and *Jet* began to reveal their financial woes. Johnson Publishing Company sold both titles to a black-owned private equity firm in 2016.[41] The only other black-owned magazine left standing at the height of the Black Lives Matter Movement in 2016 was *Black Enterprise*, which had focused always on personal finance and black business rather than overt politics. In 2018, however, an African entrepreneur bought *Essence* back, in a true, full circle moment of black witnessing.[42] Richelieu Dennis, the current *Essence* owner, hails from Liberia—the same African nation that John Russwurm helped colonize after he left *Freedom's Journal* in 1829.

Bearing Witness to the Civil Rights Movement: Talk Radio as Evidence (1938–1982)

Black witnessing through talk radio ran parallel to the eras of black newspaper and magazine publishing. The United States was entering its Second World War and, once again, relied upon the enlistment of black soldiers. African Americans who served in the First World War remembered returning home to second-class status. They did not intend to experience the same treatment at the end of this war. Black newspaper publishers launched the "Double V" campaign, which expressed the desire for two victories: one against foreign enemies and the other against domestic terrorism against blacks.[43] With racial tensions running high, the government sought to produce programming to boost morale for black troops. Radio proved to be the medium that could reach African American soldiers who were stationed around the world. In 1940, Dr. Ambrose Caliver, who was a member of President Franklin D. Roosevelt's so-called Black Cabinet produced *Freedom's People*, a nine-part radio series that showcased African American history and achievements. It featured activists, such as Asa Philip Randolph; musical acts, such as Cab Calloway and Count Basie; and it united both the literate and illiterate populations of African Americans to create brief racial solidarity during wartime.[44] Caliver's program paved the way for radio shows in black America's urban centers, such as *Listen Chicago*, which ran from 1946 to 1952. *Listen's* host, Jack Cooper, proved to be a pioneer in media convergence as well, since he read news regularly from the pages of the *Chicago Defender* and the *Pittsburgh Courier*—both black newspapers— on air.[45] The total number of radio stations that broadcast black programming jumped from 24 to 600 between 1946 and 1955.[46] The combination of black news and music grew audiences around the country, in both rural and urban areas.

William Barlow, a historian of black broadcasting, explained in 1999: "black radio resonates as an electronic reconfiguration of the talking drum tradition. For most African Americans, it is their primary source of music, news, information, and commentary on a daily basis. At the hub of this cultural enterprise are the black radio broadcasters who assemble and send the messages—much like their ancestral precursors, the master drummers."[47] One such "master drummer" was Ralph Waldo "Petey" Greene, who discovered his love of radio while he was imprisoned in Virginia for the armed robbery of a grocery store.[48] He hosted a talk radio program while he was incarcerated and grew a loyal following. When Greene was released, Dewey Hughes hired him in 1966 to host his own show on WOL 1450 AM. Though the two continually clashed on just how far Greene should push the envelope, Greene's raucous talent bore witness to the institutional racism of the North, often inciting irate white callers to dial in death threats to the station.[49] Then, one night in 1968, Greene's power to appeal to his core audience was tested. As the night fell on April 4 and news spread that Dr. Martin Luther King Jr. had been assassinated, riots broke out across black urban centers. Petey Greene broke the news on-air to his listeners. He begged black Washingtonians to remain peaceful. Greene's broadcast is credited with curtailing there much of the violence that engulfed nearly 100 other cities across the United States.[50] Greene died in 1982. Black political talk radio died that year too, many media historians claim. Though regional Black Power Movement–themed radio stations emerged in the late 1960s— especially in Northern California where the Black Panther Party was born— few of Green's peers captured his reach.[51] He, along with Hughes' eventual ex-wife, Cathy, grew the lone station into the media juggernaut that is today's Urban One, which now owns the majority of all radio stations in the United States that target African Americans.

Bearing Witness to the Civil Rights Movement: Television as Evidence (1955–1968)

From 1955, at the beginning of the Montgomery bus boycotts, until Dr. King's assassination in 1968, black civil rights organizations leveraged the power of television to bear witness to segregation. Television made it increasingly difficult to turn away from the violence being waged against Southern blacks by their own law enforcement officers and legislators. Some civil rights organizations, such as the Student Nonviolent Coordinating Committee (SNCC), employed photographers and staged news events, such as sit-ins, to capture whites' attention in the mainstream press. "If you're going to beat us, beat us in the light of day," SNCC co-founder John Lewis said of this media strategy in a 2011 CBS News interview. He added, "It was the media that carried our message to the rest of the nation."[52]

SNCC formed an ad-hoc photo agency in 1962 and sold pictures to the white press to raise money for the organization. Mary King, its communication secretary at the time, explained in a position paper "It is no accident that SNCC workers have learned that if our story is to be told, we will have to write it and photograph it and disseminate it ourselves."[53] Television networks purchased these photographs as fast as the activists could take them. Leigh Raiford has explained "The [Emmett] Till photographs not only whetted the public's appetite for images of violence perpetrated on the black body, but as powerful political emblems, they indicated the potential of photojournalism, the marriage of photography and the media of its dissemination, to promote social awareness and solidarity."[54]

As televisions became more commonplace in U.S. households, key black witnesses were no longer restricted to the professionalized ranks of Pullman porters, wealthy black publishers, or intrepid journalists. It is here, within the televised format, that everyday people could become witnesses through visual media. The paradigm forever shifted. Instead of reading a *Chicago Defender* newspaper article individually, black people could witness Civil Rights Movement demonstrations unfold together. African Americans who were alive in 1963 may remember seeing Dr. Martin Luther King Jr. give his famous "I Have a Dream" speech at the March on Washington for Jobs and Freedom, for example. Some African Americans may recall the evening of March 7, 1965, when ABC pre-empted its scheduled programming to air news of the so-called Bloody Sunday in Selma. As police assaulted peaceful demonstrators who were marching for black enfranchisement, news cameras rolled.[55] These incidents became "Where were you when . . . " moments around which generations could bond. Television invented that kind of synchronous viewing solidarity that could not be matched by print media. Moreover, television made national heroes of the black people who appeared on the frontlines of the Civil Rights Movement. The moving images of John Lewis leading that line of demonstrators to the Edmund Pettus Bridge; of Dr. King behind bars in a Birmingham, Alabama, jail; and so many other iconic leaders of this era owe their longevity, perhaps, to television. Gene Roberts and Hank Klibanoff have claimed also that television helped eradicate an "astonishing ignorance" that the world possessed about Southern-style racism.[56] Television brought the imagery of multiracial coalitions to the fore as well. Images of white pastors locking arms with Dr. King during marches or white students teaching classes in Mississippi's Freedom Summer of 1964 were visual proof that racial inequality in the United States should be everyone's concern.

Bearing Witness to Police Brutality Then: The Early Web as Evidence (1989–2008)

When scholars explored African-Americans' use of technology in the 1990s and the early 2000s, they used phrases such as "digital divide" or "information poverty" to describe blacks' lack of technical resources or skills that would allow them to participate in the new online economy of ideas.[57] Such terms raised questions of social inclusion at the dawn of the new millennium. One group of scholars even suggested that the digital divide was a chasm that threatened global prosperity. "If we are indeed in an Information Age, then not having access to this information is an economic and social handicap," Benjamin Compaine wrote in 2001.[58] Yet before Facebook, there was BlackPlanet (BP). This bears repeating. Before MySpace, Facebook, Twitter, Instagram, and SnapChat, a social network created by African Americans and for African Americans launched in 1999. Not even the panic of the so-called Y2K, end-of-millennium technology crash threatened the growth of this innovative Internet experiment. Omar Wasow—one half of the BP founding duo—explained: "The idea of socializing on the Internet was a new concept. A lot of our competitors were much more focused on publishing content than creating a way for people to socialize. When we came along people in corporate space did not fully get it, but the users took to it immediately."[59] BP cemented itself quickly as a pioneering social network. Wasow explained that the founding team of MySpace based their platform actually on BP's design. He told *Complex* magazine: "The guys who started MySpace were quoted in Business Week magazine saying that they looked at BlackPlanet as a model for MySpace and thought there was an opportunity to do a general market version of what BlackPlanet was. And that was exactly right."[60] Connecting people online was the next frontier in communication, Wasow said.

That new frontier, however, still included the need for African Americans to have a go-to place for culturally relevant news. Meeting new friends and connecting with old ones was a terrific use of the early Web, but black news audiences were looking for substantive takes on important issues still. For this reason, the decline of black newspapers and magazines in the 1970s and 1980s gave way to a rise in online ethnic publications. Ava Greenwell has noted that the *Grio, Root,* and *Loop 21* all emerged in the mid-1990s, migrating the advocacy journalism from old to new online spaces. She found that "their digital method of distribution may be new, but . . . their editorial content was steeped in historical tradition. Their stories often unmuted voices and topics that are silenced in mainstream media."[61] A flurry of black blogs launched during this era, such as *Black America Web, What About Our Daughters?*, and *Crunk Feminist Collective*. Black bloggers convened their first conference, "Blogging While Brown" in 2005. Black bloggers even scored coveted roundtable appearances on legacy media programs, such as National Public Radio's now-defunct *News and Notes* with Farai Chideya. All of these outlets gave black bloggers a space to inform their audiences about fresh cases of police brutality at the top of the century. Their stories picked up where the Rodney King video left off in 1992. There was Amadou Diallo, for example, whom four New York City police shot 41 times in 1999 during an unconstitutional stop-and-frisk incident. The four officers' eventual defense was that they thought Diallo's wallet was a gun. The police were acquitted of all charges.[62,63] Then, there was Sean Bell, also shot fatally by New York police in 2006, on the eve of his wedding. As Bell was leaving his bachelor party at a club in Queens, three officers fired 50 shots into his vehicle. Bell, they claimed, had a gun and was readying himself to shoot another club goer after an altercation. Bell's two friends, who were in the car when the fusillade occurred, disputed this story. No gun ever was found in the car. A judge acquitted all three police anyway.[64]

Media scholars Paul J. Hirschfield and Daniella Simon found that the killing of Amadou Diallo shifted the way mainstream newspapers reported about police brutality. They examined 105 news articles that reported on incidents of deadly force in 23 major daily newspapers between 1997 and 2000. Before Diallo's death, they claimed, most newspaper articles regularly "cast victims of police killings as physical and social threats and situate police actions within legitimate institutional roles." After Diallo's death, however, newspaper articles were "less likely to demonize both police officers and victims, partially reflecting efforts to frame deadly force and police racism as systemic issues."[65] It is difficult to quantify how much of this shift in the framing of police brutality news stories is due to the work of black activists who were protesting and blogging about the Diallo and Bell cases during this time. Both unarmed black men died before the era of hashtags, trending topics, and other readily traceable Web metrics. Suffice it to say, however, that a new generation of black news audiences was being primed to realize that police brutality was the unfinished business of the anti-lynching and civil rights movements. New York City may have been the town that welcomed Ida B. Wells after she left Memphis in the 1890s. But 100 years later, in the 1990s, it was also the city where police fired 91 bullets upon Amadou Diallo and Sean Bell collectively. The ingredients for this current media moment—of smartphone witnessing—were percolating. The rage against a lack of police accountability was there. The early iterations of a social networking platform for African Americans were there. Still, there was not yet a tool that would allow anyone to create and distribute media quickly, without the need for a privileged gatekeeper. Enter the smartphone.

Bearing Witness to Police Brutality Now: Smartphones and Social Media as Evidence (2009–)

It was the evening of Tuesday, November 4, 2008. Watch parties convened in seemingly every corner of the world to see if the United States would elect its first African American president. Political analysts modeled voter scenarios by pinching and stretching touchscreen maps this way and that. Other broadcasts volleyed between shots of people packed into churches, bars, coffee houses, and Chicago's Grant Park. Finally, one after another, all of the major cable television news networks declared that Barack Obama was president-elect of the United States. Grant Park erupted. The audience raised U.S. flags in the air. Even Jesse Jackson, a stoic icon from the Civil Rights Movement, wept openly there.[66]

Two months later, just 20 days before Pres. Barack Obama's inauguration in January 2009, Oscar Grant lay dying on a subway platform in Oakland, California. The 22-year-old African American man had been returning from a New Year's Eve party on a Bay Area Rapid Transit (BART) train. He and his friends were involved in an altercation aboard the lead car. Transit police awaited them at BART's Fruitvale Station. As Grant and his friends disembarked, the police sat them along the wall of the platform, side-by-side. Numerous passengers took out their cellphones and hit "record," creating the first modern examples of video witnessing since the Rodney King tape. The clearest version of their footage showed Grant making a call on his cellphone. Then, Grant stood up. A BART officer, later identified as Johannes Mehserle, loomed over Grant and shoved him to the ground. With a knee in his back and another on his neck, Grant was pinned down. Mehserle handcuffed Grant with assistance from another officer. Then, Mehserle shot him. Grant was unarmed and face down. He was pronounced dead at Oakland's Highland Hospital on New Year's Day 2009.[67]

Many people outside of Oakland may not have heard of the story of Oscar Grant until a feature-length film, *Fruitvale Station*, hit theaters four years later in 2013. Less than a dozen academic papers investigated the structural inequalities that made Grant's untimely death highly likely in a city like Oakland. Even fewer papers—exactly one—focused on the role citizen journalists played in capturing this moment.[68] So, when the star of the film, Michael B. Jordan, lamented to Oprah Winfrey in a 2013 interview, "Black males, we are America's pit bulls," some may have wondered how a country that had elected its first black president was having this conversation still.[69] After all, journalists were framing Pres. Obama as Dr. King's "Dream Realized." The dream *had* come true—for some parts of the United States—but not for all of it. That Grant's death made no national newspaper headlines until protests broke out in Oakland is a testimony, perhaps, to the collective hopes that many Americans shared at the time.[70] We hoped bigotry was aging out of our society. Many of us hoped Obama's win meant the end of systemic oppression for people of color—especially at the hands of police. As people made cross-country travel plans to descend upon Washington, DC's National Mall for the historic inauguration, Oakland began to look a lot like Rodney King's Los Angeles. Fiery demonstrations broke out and more than 100 people were arrested, according to the *Los Angeles Times*.[71] By January 15, 2009, the newspaper reported that Officer Mehserle would be charged with murder. Suddenly, this regional event seemed like an isolated incident that would wrap itself up quickly and tidily. Then came the killing of 17-year-old Trayvon Martin on February 26, 2012. The shifting of that moment—when the United States could no longer claim that racism is dead—is where I begin my contemporary analysis of black witnessing.

Trayvon Martin is the Emmett Till of this generation. My journalism students shared this with me one day in July 2013, after they discovered his postmortem photograph online. Trayvon's murder trial was coming to an end. The saga had become a media spectacle and many of my students were anxious for it to conclude, so that justice could be served. Many of them watched the court proceedings every day on television. They were watching when MSNBC aired a live shot of the jury's viewing of the crime scene, a student explained to me. The broadcast of Trayvon's dead body was brief, but it lasted long enough for *Gawker*, a now defunct news blog, to screen grab it and repost it.[72] To be certain, this was a monumental gaffe on MSNBC's part. For *Gawker*, however, the editorial decision to extend the moment on a blog felt callous and exploitative, my students said angrily. Martin's eyes are wide open, they argued. His mouth is agape, they said. His family has to look at this again and again, they said. My students—at this small, mid-Atlantic Historically Black College—saw themselves in Trayvon, just as a young Muhammad Ali had seen himself in Emmett Till all those years ago. Trayvon was only a year younger than many of my freshmen.

One student told me that she was not prepared for the visceral reaction she would have to his postmortem photograph. She had viewed it already, she said, the night before our class met. "I got sick," she told us, using a polite euphemism to describe what we were all feeling. I remember fiddling with my laptop to hook it to the overhead projector, to prepare for my lecture. I wanted to do anything but look at Trayvon. I knew I would not be able to keep it together if I looked. Still, someone pulled his picture up on a cellphone. They wanted me to *see*—to bear witness.

I experienced the same discomfort I had felt as a college student, 11 years prior, in 2002. I was an undergraduate student at a time when Google was in its infancy. My classmates and I enjoyed querying the search engine for the most obscure things. Google always seemed to have the answers, we marveled. One day though, a few of my classmates and I were in our university computer lab, doing a report on Emmett Till. We figured Google would help us find the infamous photograph faster than if we poked through the periodicals floor of the library for that now legendary *Jet* magazine issue. My classmates were right. Google was quick. Till popped up onscreen within seconds. I looked away immediately, glimpsing only a blur of grainy black and white. My classmates gasped twice—first at the image and then at my confession that I had not seen it before. "It's too sad," I said. Something about my gaze felt wrong. I now realize that my 20-year-old self was not feeling voyeuristic shame. I was feeling kinship—that weighty baggage. How else could I feel on the verge of tears for a boy I had never known? At 20 years old, I did not know how to process this discomfort. I recall my classmates falling silent eventually, and studying the photograph for such a long time. I remember mumbling something about needing to look for a book in the stacks. I walked off before they tried to convince me to look again. There would be no walking off this day during summer school, in July 2013.

My student was standing in front of me, his eyes plaintive and searching. He held his smartphone up to me. "*Look*, professor," he whispered as his eyes filled with tears.

In that moment, I could not look away anymore. My students needed me to be a steadying force for them—to help them articulate the myriad emotions they were feeling. In that moment I recalled my 20-year-old self, wandering around my college library and wondering if my classmates were done looking at Till. I did not want to look because then, I would have to *see*. I would have to see what they did to Mamie Till Mobley's baby. And I would have to make a decision about what my seeing meant for my life. I would have to decide how to situate the ever-present fear that he could be me or someone I loved, alongside middle-class black respectability politics, which dictated that I exhibit stoic black excellence at all times—even through these fears. That is the thing about black witnessing. Black people are supposed to look at communal atrocity, but they are supposed to keep going too. Always. It is an old (and unhealthy) tradition in most black circles. I told my students this, hoping it would buy me some time. Many of them nodded as I went back to fumbling with the HDMI cords at the podium.

"*Look*, professor," my student whispered again. I stopped moving. Slowly, I raised my head. Tears began to flow even before my eyes met his cellphone screen. Then, I saw Trayvon. I covered my mouth and wept silently, gazing at the photograph's every detail. My student's hand shook as he tried to steady the phone through his own tears. Another student began to cry. And then another. Then another. We were witnessing together. And it hurt.

What hurt more was that after all the work it took to bring Trayvon's case to trial, he was being violated again posthumously in this way, my students said. Indeed, it had taken six weeks for police in Sanford, Florida, to arrest Trayvon's killer, George Zimmerman, age 28, for any crime at all in the spring of 2012. It was not until Ta-Nehisi Coates wrote a scathing piece in the *Atlantic* that other national media outlets picked up the story.[73] Suddenly Trayvon's parents, Sybrina Fulton and Tracy Martin, were catapulted into the daily news cycle for more than a year. At times during the eventual court proceedings, it seemed as if African American culture itself—not Zimmerman— was on trial. Trayvon's hoodie. Star witness Rachel Jeantel's thick, Southern, black vernacular and mahogany skin.

Jelani Cobb of the *New Yorker* implored:

[T]he testimony of Rachel Jeantel, a nineteen-year-old rising high-school senior sometimes described as Martin's girlfriend, served as a kind of Rorschach test. When you look at the prosecution's star witness, a young woman, dark-skinned and overweight, her eyes signaling exasperation, what do you see?[74]

America saw a side show, not a crusade for justice, Alexander Abad-Santos wrote in the *Atlantic*.[75] Even though Jeantel was the last person to talk to Trayvon Martin, and should have been treated with compassion, "that certainly didn't stop a lot of people on the Internet from watching and laughing at a 'dumb and stupid' 19-year-old black girl from the Florida 'hood,'" Abad-Santos wrote. Rachel Samara, a journalist for the hip-hop news outlet, *GlobalGrind*, explained further, "I can imagine George Zimmerman's defense is just hoping some of those five white jurors have some prejudices (as most people do), or hell, are even racist, because if they are, their tactic to make Rachel out to be less intelligent, rather than less credible than she actually is, might actually work."[76]

Zimmerman, in the end, was acquitted of second-degree murder on July 13, 2013—a day after *Gawker* published Trayvon's postmortem picture, and in the same year that *Fruitvale Station* hit theaters. These were the early tipping points of the Black Lives Matter movement. In the wake of the Zimmerman verdict, a string of high-profile fatal police shootings of unarmed black men, women, and children began to lead news cycles. The Zimmerman verdict primed black witnesses to hunt for more stories of violence against black bodies, so that, in some way perhaps, Trayvon's death would not be in vain. Endless headlines reported what African Americans already knew to be true: black men aged 15 to 34 are between nine and 16 times more likely to be killed by police than anyone else.[77] Similarly, black people account for only 13 percent of the U.S. population yet make up 31 percent of all fatal police encounters.[78] In the year that I am writing this book, the *Atlantic* tallied these cumulative deaths to report an astonishing figure: in one year, 57,375 years of life were lost to police violence. People killed by police in 2015 and 2016 had a median age of 35, and they still had an average of about 50 years left to live when they died."[79] This is a striking statistic when one considers that the average life expectancy for a black slave living in the South between 1830 and 1920 would have been only one year more—they died typically at age 36.[80] Undeniably, in the last days of the Obama presidency, it became evident that "The Dream" of racial equality never came true for many marginalized people of color in the United States. This fact merely went underreported by major news outlets.

In this new paradigm we have entered, however, news is no longer solely the domain of the elite. African Americans have seized social media platforms to elevate their discourse to the national level, and beyond. The essential role that smartphones played in this shift cannot be understated. Perhaps no other media production device—save for the printing press—has had more impact on the way we create and share news than the smartphone. The first iPhone debuted in June 2007 and sold 1 million units within 74 days.[81] The Samsung Galaxy series, iPhone's closest competitor, premiered three years later, in 2010. It sold 1 million units within 70 days.[82] Today, 98 percent of African Americans own a mobile phone and 75 percent of these are smartphones.[83] Mobile devices are the closest things to the Winchester rifle that Ida B. Wells suggested in the 1890s. In fact, African scholars have designated the smartphone, "the continent's new talking drum."[84] The fusion of smartphones and social media has allowed black witnesses to organize globally, with people they have never met in real life. This has allowed activists to grieve, memorialize, and strategize. Perhaps most importantly, within the context of police brutality, smartphones and social media have allowed black witnesses to connect the historic dots between each high-profile death. Today's black witnesses are able to make the strong case that the modern annihilation of black bodies links back farther in time than Trayvon Martin, Oscar Grant, or even Rodney King.

Today's black witnesses and their ancestors also have created an unbroken chain of brave seers that has spanned more than 200 years. This chain has been sustained by the labor of people like Frederick Douglass, Zora Neale Hurston, and Ida B. Wells, who documented painstakingly the lives and deaths of black slaves and their freed progeny during the post-Reconstruction Era. This chain has been sustained by the voices of people like Ambrose Caliver and Petey Greene, who documented the rise and fall of the Civil Rights Movement through radio. This chain has been sustained by John H. Johnson, who had the perspicacity to honor Mamie Till Mobley's bold wish in his magazine. This chain has been sustained by Mary King and the other enterprising college students of SNCC, who photographed their Civil Rights Movement protests and sold the images to mainstream television news outlets. And today, in our current moment, this chain is sustained by a fresh crop of black witnesses who risk their lives to document police brutality with little more than a smartphone, Twitter and a speedy Internet connection. Black witnessing today requires the labor of young people like my students, who do not let us look away. This generation of black witnesses realizes it has so much unfinished work to do. This generation realizes that it still has something left to say. Something left to *see*. And, if history is any indication, they are right.

3

The New Protest #Journalism

Black Witnessing as Counternarrative

I strolled with my mobile journalism students one afternoon through the close-knit neighborhood of Kliptown in Johannesburg, South Africa. A few of the girls called the town home, and they wanted me to see it before I returned to the United States. Kliptown is a neighborhood of stark contrasts. There are houses made of nothing more than rusty corrugated metal—no insulation or plumbing fills them but there is love bursting inside. There are dirt roads that look as if no cars have driven along them for months, yet children are kicking up their orange dust in rousing soccer games. I remember sitting down to speak with a young woman and her daughter as my students swarmed about, gathering oral histories from their families and friends with an iPod Touch. After a few minutes, the woman asked me to watch her daughter.

"I need to top up," she explained, gesturing just up the road to a giant, shiny, white truck.

"What does 'top up' mean?" I asked, confused. I had been in South Africa for an entire month yet I had not heard that expression.

The woman laughed. "It means 'charge.' I need to charge my phone," she said kindly.

"May I come?" I asked. She shrugged and smiled, slightly amused that I would find this mundane act so interesting.

Still, I wanted to see inside the truck. I walked down the street holding her daughter's hand. When we reached the vehicle, I saw a maze of electric power strips hanging on its interior wall. Dozens of phones were charging there. The woman gave the telecommunications worker a few coins, then her cellphone. I heard a low buzz of power being transferred, from invisible packets of energy to the very visible faces and fingers of the South Africans who seemed delighted to be connected.

Bearing Witness While Black. Allissa V. Richardson, Oxford University Press (2020). © Oxford University Press.
DOI: 10.1093/oso/9780190935528.001.0001

Here we were, in the middle of one of the poorest towns in the world, yet cellphones were helping its residents tap into a collective force of information and knowledge sharing. Kliptown, after all, is the place where anti-apartheid leaders met to draft the Freedom Charter in 1955, which served as a formal list of black South Africans' demands to end its version of Jim Crow laws. The document opens with: "The people shall govern!" I realized that afternoon in Kliptown that the people *were* governing, in their own quietly rebellious way. They were overcoming the cruel system that withheld electricity to their homes yet offered it to them in small bundles to power their phones. The people were texting. They were engaging in e-commerce. They were laughing at jokes. Mobile phones were their *lifelines*, I thought. I found myself thinking this again on July 6, 2016, as I watched Diamond Reynolds livestream the fatal shooting of Philando Castile from their car. Her four-year-old daughter, Dae'Anna, was in the backseat.

"You shot four bullets into him, sir," Reynolds said, in a preternaturally calm voice, holding her cellphone steadily toward the officer.

"Ma'am, keep your hands where they are," the officer shouted at Reynolds, adding, "I told him not to reach for it! I told him to get his hands up."

"You told him to get his ID, sir, his driver's license," I heard Reynolds say in the video. Then, a prayer: "Oh my God, please don't tell me he's dead. Please don't tell me my boyfriend just went like that."

Castile groaned as if he was trying to speak. Then he stopped.

"Jesus," I said as I watched the video, probably in a tone not unlike the one my dad had used while watching the Rodney King video in 1991. Castile was the second black man to be shot fatally by a police officer in 24 hours. Alton Sterling had been killed in Baton Rouge just the day before. This time though, Reynolds' recording marked a watershed moment for black witnessing. When she decided to activate Facebook Live that day, she became the first person to capture police brutality in near real time. It was her *lifeline*. What might have happened to her, or to her daughter Dae'Anna, had her camera not been rolling, I thought to myself. By the afternoon, a local NBC affiliate television station invited me to participate in a Facebook Live chat about the Castile video. I did not hesitate.[1] *Black women and children are unsafe too*, I wanted to yell. But I wanted to cry too. For Dae'Anna. For Diamond. For Philando.

I talked about power relationships between the people and the police on the NBC broadcast and how Diamond Reynolds disrupted them that day. I said a lot of other things too, but I kept thinking during the program about what I could do personally. I felt so helpless. After leaving the studio, I began searching for other activists. I needed to channel my anger. When I got back home, I went online and started googling. The first search retrieval was a CNN story from the year before, entitled "The Disruptors."[2] I wrote down the names of the 13 activists that were featured in the story. Some of them I knew already, from the reading I was doing in my PhD program, or through my time spent on Twitter. Others I did not yet know. I contacted all 13 disruptors via Twitter initially, either through direct message, if they authorized this feature, or on their public walls. Two of the 13 granted me interviews right away. Two activists never responded at all. The remaining nine activists declined my requests for interviews but referred me to an ally in the movement who was still doing press. I later found out that the activists have developed a sophisticated, alternating method of talking to academic researchers and professional journalists to avoid burnout. Within three months of the Sterling-Castile tragedies, I had booked interviews with 15 leading anti–police brutality activists. And for the next year they let me follow them, to see how they formed the vanguard of black witnessing at the peak of the movement. Some of them let me sit in on Black Lives Matter meetings and workshops they hosted. Others visited my mobile journalism classrooms, either in person or with the help of FaceTime, to talk to me and my students. Still others allowed me to visit them in their neighborhoods. They wanted me to know another side of the saga that was being portrayed on televised news. They wanted me to know what activated them. They wanted me to come and see. I want you to see them now too, without further ado.

The Witnesses

Our 15 black witnesses fall into five broad groups: (1) the Black Lives Matter activists; (2) the "Day 1's"; (3) the Masters of Agitprop; (4) the Bards; and (5) the Rogues. The Black Lives Matter activists were leaders who self-identified as members of the formal organization. The Day 1's were the frontline protestors of Ferguson who believed their actions galvanized the movement. The Masters of Agitprop were the creatives who used art as propaganda for the movement. The Bards provided the soundtrack to the movement, blending hip-hop, poetry, and prose to spread news. Lastly, the Rogues were associated loosely with all of these groups, but refused to be labeled Black Lives Matter activists, for a variety of reasons. I should mention that I did not prompt the activists to share their sexual orientations in the short bios that follow. Some said that they wanted me to highlight this part of their identity, to end the historic erasure of black, queer social activists.

The women of Black Lives Matter. Three activists wanted to be identified as Black Lives Matter leaders affiliated with the official organization. Alicia Garza is one of three co-founders of the international group. Her love letter to black people after George Zimmerman's acquittal in the Trayvon Martin murder trial in July 2013 contained the original #BlackLivesMatter hashtag. When Garza's friend (and co-founder of Black Lives Matter), Patrisse Cullors, shared the letter to Twitter it went viral. Garza is based in Oakland, California. She is an award-winning community organizer who championed workplace equality in the Bay Area prior to establishing Black Lives Matter. She self-identifies as a member of the LGBTQ community and emphasizes the inclusion of queer leaders in the movement. I interviewed Garza in person, at a mid-Atlantic university in October 2015, after she facilitated a closed-door workshop on self-care.

Marissa Johnson was a member of the Black Lives Matter Seattle chapter. She gained notoriety in August 2015 when she interrupted presidential hopeful Sen. Bernie Sanders at his Seattle campaign rally. Her assumption of his podium dominated the news headlines for several weeks. Prior to that protest, Johnson organized "die-ins" at local businesses in Seattle to oppose the shooting deaths of unarmed black men by police. One die-in shut down a major downtown mall on Black Friday 2014. Johnson self-identifies as an evangelical Christian, a former theology student, and a "biracial, queer woman." Johnson spoke, via FaceTime, to my mobile journalism class at a Maryland HBCU in February 2017.

Shellonnee Chinn is a member of the Black Lives Matter Rochester, New York, chapter. She is a former educator at a prominent private secondary school in Buffalo, where she taught for 15 years. She claims she was fired after she complained about discriminatory teaching practices in the classrooms and filed suit in federal court against her former employer in 2015. While the case is ongoing, Chinn has taken to social media to report on educational inequalities in her state. My mobile journalism students and I interviewed Chinn via Google Hangout in February 2017. She gave us incredible insight into how she believes U.S. schools—with their metal detectors and armed security guards—normalize police brutality for young people of color.

The "Day 1's." The leaders in this group believe that the movement did not begin until the Ferguson, Missouri, uprisings in August 2014, in the wake of Michael Brown's death. In the months that followed those protests, they called themselves the "Day 1's," to differentiate themselves from activists who did not have actual boots on the ground in the early campaigns. The Day 1's were the movement's first fact checkers, churning out data and eyewitness news from the frontlines that served often as a corrective to legacy media reports.

Brittany Ferrell is a native of St. Louis, Missouri. She was a founder of the now-defunct organization Millennial Activists United (MAU). When she began protesting in the days after Michael Brown's death, she went on Twitter to find like-minded demonstrators in her age group, since she said the earliest activists actually were friends of Brown's mother, Lesley McSpadden. Ferrell found Alexis Templeton and Ashley Yates on Twitter. The three women founded MAU and pushed to have Officer Darren Wilson prosecuted for Brown's murder. Ferrell self-identifies as a mother, a nurse, and Alexis's wife. She and Templeton were married months after meeting for the first time during the protests. My students and I interviewed Ferrell via FaceTime in February 2017. She was gracious enough to take part in one of the longest interviews, even though she was on her way to a 12-hour work shift as a nurse.

Brittany Packnett Cunningham is also a native of St. Louis, Missouri. She is Vice President of National Community Alliances for Teach for America and co-founder of We the Protestors (WTP), which has several initiatives. Campaign Zero, for example, is a 10-point plan to reduce police violence in the United States. Packnett Cunningham created the policy-oriented organization—with DeRay Mckesson, Johnetta Elzie, and Samuel Sinyangwe—after the four met on the frontlines in Ferguson. Packnett Cunningham is a former appointee to Pres. Barack Obama's 21st Century Policing Task Force. She self-identifies as a Christian, a daughter, a sister, and a community activist.

Samuel Sinyangwe is the last of the Day 1's that I interviewed. The 2012 Stanford University political science graduate was working at PolicyLink, a Bay Area social justice nonprofit, when Ferguson erupted in 2014. He said he contacted DeRay Mckesson on Twitter to ask how he could help once he arrived in the city, after noticing Mckesson's trending tweets. Sinyangwe became chief data scientist of WTP. His first project was "Mapping Police Violence," which curated statistics from disparate police databases around the country to a centralized record. Sinyangwe is a native of Orlando, Florida, who said he was inspired to study political science as a means to fight for social justice when Trayvon Martin was killed in his home state. Sinyangwe self-identifies as a son and an eventual political science professor. I interviewed Sinyangwe via FaceTime in February 2017.

The Masters of Agitprop. All of the activists who use art as social propaganda fell into the group Masters of Agitprop. These leaders have created much of the visual culture that we associate with the Black Lives Matter Movement. Devin Allen is the self-taught photographer who shot the now-iconic images of the Freddie Gray protests in April 2015. Allen's pictures of Baltimore in turmoil landed on the cover of *TIME* magazine, making him one of few amateur photographers ever to achieve this feat.[3] He said that the late Gordon Parks, the legendary black photographer for *LIFE* magazine, is his idol. Allen's images hang in the Smithsonian's National Museum of African American History and Culture in Washington, DC. He is a philanthropist who collects donated cameras to disseminate to Baltimore youth. Allen self-identifies as a black man, a father, and a survivor of Baltimore's gang violence. I interviewed Allen in person, in his favorite neighborhood store, City of Gods, in October 2016. It was a near-two hour session in which his friends and neighbors trickled in and out of the shop to hear him speak.

Dread Scott (née Scott Tyler) is a New York-based visual artist who creates live installations, paintings, photographs, prints, and videos about African American human rights issues. In the year of the Sterling-Castile double tragedy, Scott remade the NAACP's historic black flag that read, "A Man Was Lynched Yesterday." The original NAACP flag flew outside the organization's headquarters in the 1930s as the group pushed for anti-lynching legislation in Congress. Scott's 2016 version of the flag read "A Man Was Lynched by Police Yesterday." The reimagined pennant stoked as much controversy as the original. The landlord of the exhibiting museum threatened eviction if it was not removed immediately. Scott self-identifies as a black man and an artist with "Communist sensibilities." We spoke via FaceTime in November 2016.

Lincoln Mondy is the writer and producer of the film, *Black Lives, Black Lungs*. His documentary on the tobacco industry's targeting of African Americans earned him seven visits to the Obama White House to discuss the links between the Black Lives Matter Movement and public health. Mondy is a 2016 graduate of The George Washington University in Washington, DC. He screened his film at his commencement and served as its keynote student speaker. Mondy now serves as senior manager of strategic projects for

Advocates for Youth, a DC-based nonprofit. Mondy self-identifies as a bira-cial black man. I interviewed him in person early one October 2016 morning as we strolled through his neighborhood in Washington, DC.

The Bards. This group of activists comprises poets and musicians. They have attained their status as the most popular of all black witnesses on Twitter by providing prolific updates and thoughts on the movement. Eve Ewing is an alumna of Harvard University's Graduate School of Education and a cur-rent assistant professor in the University of Chicago School of Social Service Administration. She studies inequality in the U.S. public education system. Ewing is a founding editor of *Seven Scribes*, which aspired to create a digital space for African American audiences to enjoy long-form journalism when it launched in 2015. The publication was born after a $10,000 Kickstarter campaign garnered more than $14,000. Ewing uses Twitter to provide updates on black activism in her native Chicago. As the daughter of a profes-sional journalist, she is careful not to label herself as a reporter, however, even though her essays have been published in the *Nation* and *New Yorker*. She self-identifies instead as an essayist, a poet, a cultural organizer, and a black woman. I interviewed Ewing for nearly two and a half hours on FaceTime one rainy afternoon in February 2017. She was incredibly instrumental with linking me to other activists too.

Clint Smith is a PhD candidate in education at Harvard University. He studied alongside Ewing during her time there. He became a leading voice in the Black Lives Matter movement when his TED talks, "How to Raise a Black Son in America" and "The Danger of Silence," went viral, with more than 6 million collective views and counting. Smith's poetry on growing up black in the Deep South, witnessing police brutality, and fearing vio-lent death have become award-winning pieces of literature. His essays have appeared in the *New Yorker* and *American Poetry Review*. Smith identifies as a teacher, a poet, an inequality scholar, and a black man. He splits his time be-tween Cambridge, Massachusetts, and Washington, DC. Smith granted me a FaceTime interview in February 2017.

David Banner (née Lavell William Crump) is a graduate of Southern University and A&M College, an HBCU in Baton Rouge, Louisiana. Banner began his career as a critically acclaimed rapper. After several chart-topping hits and a lucrative record deal, Banner said he began to feel conflicted about the music he was making. In 2007, he testified in a Congressional hearing on explicit rap, which the Democratic Representative from Illinois, Bobby L. Rush, convened. Banner stopped using denigrating lyrics after his testimony. He rebranded himself as a composer and took on Fortune 500 companies as clients, penning music for global advertising campaigns. When the world turned its eyes on Ferguson in 2014, however, Banner's focus shifted again. He became a sought-after lecturer on police brutality and representations of blackness in the media. His Twitter updates during the Ferguson protests earned him invitations to appear on cable news networks and on local TV and radio shows around the country. He visited Ferguson to facilitate meetings between the Bloods and Crips gangs, which called ceasefires to help the city heal after Michael Brown's death. For all of these reasons, supporters of the Black Lives Matter Movement consider Banner a leader in the overarching campaign to end police brutality although he does not identify with the organization. Banner is a self-described hip-hop intellectual and social entrepreneur. He lives and works in Atlanta, Georgia. Banner spoke to my mobile journalism class via Google Hangout in February 2017. When the university's WIFI dropped our laptop connection, Banner was so dedicated to the interview that he finished it through the magic of LTE—chatting with us by FaceTime as we crowded around my cellphone.

The Rogues. This final cohort of leaders has rejected any attempts from journalists or academics to label them as activists working within the Black Lives Matter Movement. All three Rogues, however, have different reasons for doing so. L. Chris Stewart is founding partner of the Atlanta-based law firm, Stewart, Seay & Felton Trial Attorneys, LLC. He has represented the families of both Walter Scott and Alton Sterling in various lawsuits against the police departments and the individual police officers who shot both men. Stewart said he serves as an ally to anyone who is pursuing civil rights for vulnerable populations. While working with local Black Lives Matter chapters is sometimes part of this strategy, he noted that he collaborates with other organizations too. Stewart is the recipient of the 2014 Esquire Award from the National Bar Association. Additionally, his peers designated him a Super Lawyer for the State of Georgia for four straight years, from 2011 to 2015. Stewart self-identifies as a civil rights attorney, a husband, and a Christian. He spoke to me by FaceTime before a day in court, in February 2017.

Ieshia Evans was the subject of the viral photographs of the Alton Sterling protests in August 2016. She was pictured in a peaceful standoff with Baton Rouge police. They were wearing riot gear. She was wearing a sundress. Evans eventually was arrested and charged with obstructing a highway. After being released from jail, she said she planned to return to New York to live a quiet life. When someone created a fake Twitter account in her name, however, she decided to bear witness on the platform with her own verified account. Evans has conducted international interviews about her civil disobedience since she became a media sensation. She emphasized, though, in our interview that she went down to Baton Rouge from her native New York in the summer of 2016 on her own. She is not affiliated with any Black Lives Matter chapters or allied groups. Evans self-identifies as a "regular degular girl from Brooklyn," a mother, and a black woman. Evans spoke to my mobile journalism class via FaceTime one afternoon in February 2017.

Finally, Mark Luckie has toed the line between legacy media and black witnessing. Luckie is a former *Washington Post* National Innovations editor who went on to work as Twitter's first manager of journalism and news in 2012. At the end of his tenure at Twitter in 2015, Luckie lamented the life of an African American staffer at the company in a *USA Today* editorial piece. He wrote "Witnessing firsthand the lack of faces of color instilled in me the desire to apply my technology skills toward the visibility of Blacks in media."[4] Luckie left Twitter to join the staff of Reddit in February 2016. The social bookmarking service named him its first-ever head of journalism and media. Nine months later, however, he quit, citing the same lack of diversity he had witnessed at Twitter. He launched his own site, *Today in #BlackTwitter*, to amplify voices from the Black Lives Matter Movement. He shuttered that webpage in the fall of 2016 though, citing the desire to escape the "litany of hashtags of slain black men and women," which traumatized him, he said. In October 2017, Luckie signed on at Facebook as its strategic partner manager of influencers. His quick departure from that job the following year led to another round of open letters and mainstream media interviews—this time about the company's alleged censorship policies against black users' commentary on the Black Lives Matter Movement and other social justice campaigns.[5] He told the *Guardian* in a November 27, 2018, article, "In some buildings, there are more 'Black Lives Matter' posters than there are actual black people." Luckie offered lots of insight in his interview about how African Americans over-index on many social media platforms, yet are silenced increasingly when they attempt to use those platforms to protest. Luckie self-identifies as a former journalist and a gay, black man. He is based in Atlanta. He participated in an interview via Skype in February 2017.

A Dozen Reasons to Bear Witness

In each high-profile incident of police brutality that occurred between 2014 and 2018, the frontline black witness typically retreated from view. Many of them—like Ramsey Orta who filmed Eric Garner's death in New York— either expressed regret for coming forward or frustration with the media frenzy that invaded their privacy. Remarkably though, distant black witnesses—like our 15 activists—were eager to continue the work of looking when the initial frontline witness left the public sphere. To investigate how and why these activists performed any of this journalistic labor I established some guiding research questions. First, I wanted to explore the lived experience of bearing witness while black. What are the trials, triumphs, risks, and rewards associated with doing this kind of work? Second, I sought to understand how much activists relied on their smartphones for storytelling. Third, I wanted to know how they used social media in their news production mix.

I identified a dozen themes in my talks with the activists: (1) a desire to revise news narratives; (2) a sense of responsibility to bear witness; (3) a belief that their reports could redress police brutality; (4) an abiding love or fond regards for their community; (5) a retrospective appreciation for predecessor activists; (6) an acknowledgment of personal risks they faced by engaging in activism; (7) an unresolved rage against racism and the ongoing lack of police accountability; (8) a desire to see the movement (and victims of fatal police shootings) redeemed in mainstream media; (9) a sense of seeing themselves reflected in the body of a victim; (10) a feeling of mourning or requiem for the victims; (11) a sense of regret, at times, for joining the movement so visibly; and (12) a sense of how their religion did (or did not) influence their decision to bear witness.

Creating the Counternarrative

All 15 activists said that they felt a responsibility to bear witness to the anti– police brutality movement to revise existing news narratives. The activists aimed to challenge racism, sensationalism, or factual errors in legacy news reports. They felt existing news frames encouraged police brutality and public support for "law and order." Additionally, they believed deeply that changing news narratives about black people could help curb police brutality against them. A few of the activists spoke specifically about a cable television news broadcast that angered them most. They recalled that Wolf Blitzer sat behind his news desk on the set of CNN watching the peaceful protests in West Baltimore give way to violence on a late April afternoon in 2015. The community had just buried Freddie Gray, who sustained fatal spinal injuries while in police custody. In the days leading up to Gray's funeral, Black Lives Matter activists asked the Baltimore Police Department for more information about the cause of his death. Answers were not forthcoming. Frustrations mounted. On the day of Gray's funeral, some citizens began to loot stores and destroy property in the city. Blitzer attempted to relay the mêlée, in real time. He said: "This is a picture of a CVS pharmacy, and casually people are just going in there—they're not even running—they're going in there, stealing whatever the hell they want to steal in there, and then they're leaving, and . . . I don't see any police there. Where are the police?"[6]

Just a few hours later, in nearly identical language, CNN's evening news anchor, Don Lemon, asked why the mayor and governor had not called a state of emergency to summon the National Guard to intervene as black youth descended upon Baltimore's tourist district of the Inner Harbor. Both Blitzer and Lemon were pilloried by their journalism colleagues for suggesting that law enforcement officers quell violence, rather than instigate it.[7,8] The *Rolling Stone* specifically described Blitzer as "a man of breathtaking stupidity, who daily belies his catchphrase of 'watching very closely' with a myopia that dwarfs Mr. Magoo's."[9] By focusing on the destruction of buildings, cars, and other material goods, critics said that the underlying causes of the riot, which included police brutality and longstanding disinvestment in Baltimore's poorest and blackest neighborhoods, were ignored.[10,11]

Many news outlets sensationalized the riots too, journalist Natalie Keyssar claimed in a May 3, 2015, *Medium* blog post, writing that: "For about 23½ hours a day since I've been here, I've seen nothing but peaceful protest . . . [but] turning on network news in my hotel room, I see the same loops of these brief moments of violence over and over, with the name of the city plastered across images of fire and mayhem." Keyssar's testimony served as a springboard to explore why the activists I interviewed believe we need fresh news frames about the anti–police brutality movement. Many of the activists said that traditional journalists did not do a good job covering the protests in which they took part. Brittany Packnett Cunningham, for example, one of the Day 1's, had driven to Kansas City in early August 2014 to deliver a series of talks to high-school-aged girls. The afternoon that Michael Brown died, she said she was online when she saw a picture of Brown's stepfather. She recalled: "He had written on a piece of cardboard, 'Ferguson Police just killed my unarmed son.' And I posted it [online], and reposted it, and then I started to follow along with what was happening."

Packnett Cunningham had not known Brown, but Ferguson and St. Louis are "right next door to each other," she explained. She had grown up traveling back and forth in between the two cities, as did most of their residents. To hear that her hometown was in crisis touched her in a very deep way, Packnett Cunningham shared. She said her social media timelines began to flood with images of "very young people going out there, and being met with German Shepherds and an armed police force, when they were unarmed and peaceful." She was stunned. Packnett Cunningham left Kansas City a day early.

"The whole drive back, I remember feeling like, I told these young women today to be leaders *one* day, but the time is now," she said, adding, "Clearly this world is calling for them to step up now." Packnett Cunningham recalled all of this one rainy afternoon in February 2017, as she sat in a Washington, DC, coffee shop. We were on FaceTime. Even though it had been three years since her frontline demonstrations in Ferguson, she remained appalled by how it was portrayed in the mainstream. Much of the black civil disobedience that looped on television actually were acts of self-defense, she explained with a frown:

> CNN was sitting there saying: "People are breaking into the McDonald's—there's more looting happening." Well, we would go on the [live]streams and what we'd be tweeting is that people are being tear-gassed and they're breaking into the McDonald's because they had milk in the McDonald's and milk is what you have to use on tear-gas. Not water. That is the instantaneous correction that you're allowed to have. We challenged the mainstream media, who were outsiders to our community, to tell the truth.

Packnett Cunningham said that she continued to use Twitter to provide updates on the movement after she saw how vulnerable her community would be to legacy media's chosen narratives. "Media needs to always be held accountable," she said, adding, "The same kind of relationship that we should have with the free press, it's the same kind of relationship we should have with Democracy. We should engage with it and reserve our right to criticize."

Brittany Ferrell, another Day 1 as well as busy mother and full-time nurse, sat in her car to chat with me one afternoon, adjusting her smartphone occasionally to maintain our connection on FaceTime. She chose to conduct her interview in the presence of my journalism students, as she is passionate about youth civic engagement. She spoke of her use of Twitter to debunk legacy media reports in the same tone as Packnett Cunningham. She explained, "The upside is it [Twitter] definitely has helped me get the message out to the people who want to support this movement. It allows me a place to tell the truth without any bias or anybody policing the things that I choose to say. . . . It's like we are so much better connected in this struggle via social media because we know where to turn to when we need the truth."

Nearly every activist expressed some level of caution or outright cynicism when I asked if they trusted news media to tell their stories accurately. For Ieshia Evans, one of the Rogues, that answer was a resounding "no." When she participated in her first demonstration in July 2016—to protest Alton Sterling's killing in Baton Rouge—she said she was surprised to see it portrayed in the news as a riot. She told my journalism class one afternoon: "People were boisterous, they were rowdy as far as being very vocal but there was no violence. There was nobody throwing things." My students crowded around the FaceTime session on my laptop as I continued questioning Evans. Some students shook their heads in disbelief. Evans said the police on the scene became increasingly physical and started "pushing the protestors into the grass." She explained that the cops' behavior led to her now-iconic standoff. She recalled: "I don't even know what came over me but, I just decided to stand in the street, like what's your goal here? What's the reason why you guys are decked out in your war gear, and I'm in a sundress?"

Attorney L. Chris Stewart, who traveled to Baton Rouge from his native Atlanta to represent the Sterling family in the summer of 2016, said: "I was down there the whole time. There weren't mass riots everywhere. The demonstrations were really just certain streets, certain areas, and a lot of them were just kind of standoffs between the police and the protestors. You know, you're just kind of at the will of whatever the media says."

That sentiment—of feeling at the mercy of "the media" bears a bit of explication here. "The media" are made up of real people. And real people in the newsroom often rely on shortcuts to report a complex story quicker and easier—for better or worse. A few things have led U.S. journalism to this point, where words like "crime" or "War on Drugs" have become so loaded that they are synonymous with "blackness," for example. Many post-colonial theorists have described "blackness" as an identity that is thrust upon people of African descent, rather than an identity that they have selected for themselves. Frantz Fanon, for example, recounted a time when a white child saw him and exclaimed, "Look, a Negro! *Maman*, a Negro! . . . *Maman*, the Negro's going to eat me."[12] Fanon described the encounter as an out-of-body experience, in which he did not think of himself as the black "Other," until the child singled out the identification for him. In that moment, he imagined the child must be conjuring up all that blackness *means*. He wrote "The Negro is an animal, the Negro is bad, the Negro is wicked, the Negro is ugly."[13] Similarly, Stuart Hall wrote that people racialize "Otherness" by using a set of binary polarities. He theorized:

> There are the rich distinctions which cluster around the supposed link, on the one hand, between the white "races" and intellectual development— refinement, learning and knowledge, a belief in reason, the presence of developed institutions, formal government and law, and a "civilized restraint" in their emotional, sexual and civil life, all of which are associated with "Culture"; and on the other hand, the link between the black "races" and whatever is instinctual—the open expression of emotion and feeling rather than intellect, a lack of "civilized refinement" in sexual and social life, a reliance on custom and ritual, and the lack of developed civil institutions.[14]

In addition to these black/white binaries, Michael Omi and Howard Winant have argued that race might be a fluid social formation (rather than a fixed biological fact) too, which is "constantly being transformed by political struggle." One of the mediated battlegrounds for this struggle is television, they wrote, as it tends to "address the lowest common denominator in order to render programs 'familiar' to an enormous and diverse audience."[15]

Stuart Hall agreed that the visual medium is the strongest way to perpetuate racist stereotypes. He explained that imperialist iconography exploded in printed works at the end of the 19th century, after the Europeans encountered Africans on maiden voyages with increasing frequency.[16] Over time, derogatory photos and videos of black people became "controlling images," according to Sonja M. Brown Givens and Jennifer L. Monahan. Givens and Monahan have written that the particular portrayal of black women on TV shows and in film—as overweight mammies or as promiscuous Jezebels— translates directly to real life discrimination, especially in the workplace.[17] News media deal in these damaging tropes too though. While we know that popular culture exists to entertain us—and that those who are employed in those spaces may be putting on a persona—many people consider what they see on the news to be true. Journalism enjoys an air of veracity that few other mediated platforms can match. The news never has been neutral or objective though—especially about race.[18,19] Instead, it has been influenced always by the dominant racial myths of its day.

Teun A. van Dijk explained in his book, *News as Discourse*, that three strategies work in tandem to make news appear neutral. First, journalists often emphasize the factual nature of events via eyewitnesses, reliable sources, and statistics. Second, news broadcasts use tried-and-true narrative frames that audiences can follow easily. Third, news stories provide information that stirs strong attitudes or emotions, which makes the piece more memorable.[20] I did not have to explain van Dijkian theory to these 15 activists. They identified unfair or incorrect news frames repeatedly in our interviews on their own. For example, Attorney Stewart said he disliked how the news media framed the African American cop killer in Baton Rouge, who emerged after the Alton Sterling shooting, as a member of Black Lives Matter:

The guy who did that heinous crime and shot those officers in Baton Rouge: that had nothing to do with the cases, [or] with Alton Sterling. That was just a deranged individual. . . . [W]e see examples of crazy people doing stuff all the time—I mean Dylann Roof going, shooting up that whole church!—and the narrative in the media wasn't, "All white guys aged 19 or 20 are evil."

Stewart said news coverage like that made him want to start commenting, as much as the law allowed, on social networks like Facebook and Twitter. One of his most proud moments of witnessing occurred in February 2017, he said. He recalled that the Black Lives Matter chapter in Atlanta organized and led a rally to raise awareness about the police killing of an unarmed black man named Deaundre Phillips. Stewart was proud to see such a broad coalition of support in his hometown. "Seventy percent of that crowd was white," he said. When he turned on the news that afternoon, however, he recalled, "they called it a Black Lives Matter rally, and they only showed the black people, which I thought was just hilarious, because everybody out there was just shocked how many white people were out there supporting it, but you didn't see that."

I asked Stewart why he thought the news media in Atlanta framed the story that way. He shook his head and answered: "I get it, I mean that's fine, that [imagery] kills the narrative that white people don't support Black Lives

Matter and all that stuff, [but] through social media, I was able to show what the crowd really looked like." Stewart said he published his pictures and videos to Twitter to highlight the crowd's diversity.[21] He was happy, he said, when he saw the television station change its evening news broadcast to include more accurate images after he held them to task. "[When] social media covers stuff, it's kind of like a snowball effect," Stewart said, adding, "Once it starts rolling and it starts picking up and picking up and picking up, it's just really effective to let people know what's going on. Other than that, you have to rely on TV news, and that's not the most effective way, because you have no control over that."

Battling the Big Three News Myths

Part of crafting a counternarrative to racist news frames or images involves identifying first the prominent news myths that traditional journalists may peddle without even knowing it. Three of the most popular black stereotypes that circulate in the news are: (a) the myth of inherent black criminality, (b) the myth of black marginality, and (c) the myth of post-racialism. The activists told me they want to shatter all of these.

The myth of black criminality. Paul Gilroy has explained in his essay, "The Myth of Black Criminality," that as the U.S. Civil Rights Movement wound down in 1968, after the assassination of Dr. King, the rest of the Western world began to question whether immigration and integration were worthy experiments after all.[22] Particularly in Great Britain, conservative Member of Parliament Enoch Powell urged the UK government to police people of color more rigorously, lest, he said, "In this country in 15 or 20 years' time the black man will have the whip hand over the white man."[23] Powell's "Rivers of Blood" speech described a dystopia where whites are overcrowded by uncouth, foul-smelling "Negroes" and their "wide-grinning piccaninnies."[24] The media coverage that the "Blood" speech garnered discouraged further anti–police brutality legislation and birthed the myth of black criminality, Gilroy explained in 1982:

Indeed the recent history of "law and order" is scarcely separable from the growth of popular racism and nationalism in the period following Enoch Powell's famous intervention. Powell's wide-grinning piccaninnies have grown up, and with the onset of their adulthood, potent imagery of youthful black criminals stalking derelict inner-city streets where the law-abiding are afraid to walk after sunset has been fundamental to the popularization of increasingly repressive criminal justice and welfare state policies.[25]

Several journalism studies have assessed how this theory functions in televised news. Robert Entman found that between 1992 and 1994— immediately following the Rodney King video—African Americans were featured most commonly in crime news stories at both the local and national levels.[26,27] Specifically in Chicago, when journalists decided to include the names of suspects, whites were identified 72 percent of the time, but blacks were named only 28 percent of the time.[28] Entman concluded that nameless-ness dehumanized black suspects and reinforced the idea that bad individual black behavior represented a larger pattern of communal deviance.

Theodore Chiricos and Sarah Eschholz found that blacks and Latinos are four times more likely to be portrayed as suspects than as victims of crime in local Orlando television news, while whites are portrayed evenly.[29] Travis L. Dixon and Daniel Linz reported similar results in their survey of local Los Angeles television news, in that whites were more likely than African Americans and Latinos to be portrayed as victims.[30] News reports also over-represented African Americans as perpetrators of homicide and underrepre-sented Latinos and whites as perpetrators of this crime.[31]

Paula M. Poindexter, Laura Smith, and Don Heider conducted a more lon-gitudinal study of how race and ethnic groups were portrayed in local TV news, from the late 1980s to 1998. The team researched 26 stations across 12 cities. They claimed that while Asians, Latinos, and Native Americans were seldom the subjects of television news reports, African Americans "were more likely to be newsworthy because they had committed a crime."[32] Sixty-nine percent of the news stories that featured black people as the main subjects were about crime, whereas only 28 percent of the news stories that featured white people as the primary subjects were about crime.

I read some of these statistics to Samuel Sinyangwe throughout our inter-view in February 2017. Sinyangwe is a data scientist and one of the Day 1's. He is both enigmatic and nomadic. He wore all black clothing for our video teleconference and declined to comment on where he was based, yet his de-meanor was warm and inviting. He is committed to dispelling news myths about black criminality, he explained. Sinyangwe recalled that he took a leave of absence from his job at PolicyLink, a Bay Area think-tank to protest in Ferguson in 2014. Once he arrived in Missouri, he said he kept hearing the same two narratives: either that shootings like these were one-off events or that all shootings of unarmed black men began because the slain men had resisted arrest. He said: "I think when Mike Brown was killed in Ferguson and the protests started across the country, there was just this huge question about are these police shootings isolated incidents or a broader systemic issue? That was a data question, and every time that that was being asked, people were like, 'Well, we don't have the data.'" Sinyangwe said he discovered that the federal government did not collect data on fatal police shootings, but websites such as *Fatal Encounters* or *KilledbyPolice.net* did, he said. He decided to merge the data from both sites first. Then, he filled in the many statistical gaps. He explained:

> About 40 percent of the records were not identified by race, and so I went through social media profiles—like every social media [platform], like Facebook, Twitter, Instagram—went through obituaries, criminal records databases, and between those could actually identify more than 90 percent of the people in the database. Then for armed or unarmed—nobody was keeping track of that—so I had to go through all of the reports, both the community perspective, the police perspective, all of that, to identify that column. That was the dataset.

Sinyangwe said that being armed with this data made him realize that he could tell different stories about police brutality. I asked him to talk about a time when he believed his investigative reporting shifted an actual narrative in legacy news coverage of an event. His eyes lit up and a wide smile crossed his face. He explained a triumph in Colorado, where a police department challenged his data, only to find out their numbers were incorrect. A college newspaper then published an investigative piece about the department's underreporting of fatal police encounters. Many local newspapers then picked up the students' story.[33] Sinyangwe said:

> They [the police] got embarrassed in that article, but that's the crazy part about the work: it's the people who are supposed to be the professionals, like the criminologists and the professors and the FBI director and the police chiefs, they actually don't have as much data as I have sitting in my computer. It's easy to run circles around them in that way. I think that is cool and empowering.

Once the demonstrations in Ferguson tapered off in 2014, Sinyangwe said he began to analyze his home state of Florida when he realized that Orlando was "off the charts in terms of every level of police violence, whether it was use of force or stops and searches, arrests or killings," he said. Sinyangwe explained that once he realized this trend, he convened a meeting with the leadership of the Orlando Police Department (PD). The officers claimed that the high rates of excessive force were due to equally high rates of tourism. Sinyangwe crunched more numbers. He told Orlando PD that their rates were higher than New Orleans and Las Vegas, which have equal— if not more—annual visitors than Orlando. "They didn't have a response," Sinyangwe said, adding: "Nobody else could come and say, 'Actually, we have the data comparing you to all these other tourist locations.' After that, they were like, 'Okay, we're going to listen.'"

Sinyangwe said he audited the Orlando PD's use of force policy to show that the agency did not have a rule that restricted officers from using lethal force as a final resort. The police department in Tampa, about 90 miles away from Orlando, did.

Sinyangwe said: "We're like, 'Well, you know, Tampa has this policy in place. You guys don't have this policy in place, and this policy is associated with a 25 percent reduction in police brutality,' because we did that analysis."

The final pieces of data that helped convince Orlando PD to change its excessive force policies were his findings on why people were stopped by police in the first place. "We also showed that of the people getting killed by police, those interactions were starting off with people who were suspected of, quote, 'suspicious activity,' or drug possession—like small, minor things that then get escalated into deadly force. That helped debunk this narrative that police were killing people because they were trying to apprehend violent criminals," Sinyangwe said.

After Sinyangwe recounted what he regards as his major victories, I asked how professional journalists respond to his investigative reporting. After all, he tweets all of the statistics he finds in near real time and even fact-checks *their* work. He laughed wryly. He said that some journalists respect his data. Others seem to be waiting for him to make a mistake. He talked about July 2016, for example, as one of the most fast-paced reporting cycles he has endured in the wake of the back-to-back killings of Philando Castile and Alton Sterling. He recalled that after the news first broke about Sterling's death, he engaged in what he called "rapid response." He said:

As soon as that [Sterling shooting] happened, I'm opening my computer, pulling the spreadsheet, pulling all the facts for Baton Rouge. I tweet them all out immediately about the disparities, how they rank with other the [police] departments, about how that's related to policy issues—all of that—so it can then get incorporated in the media coverage. . . . You never know when something's going to happen, and you have to be able to respond immediately to those situations, and you can't fuck up. They [mainstream media] don't have any data, but they're still able to control narratives, and that's crazy, but if we have any problems with our data, like all of a sudden, we are the people you shouldn't listen to. That's a different double standard. Our shit has to be right all the time.

Attorney Stewart said he eschews early news reports and resists the urge to jump into the reporting fray quickly. He opts instead to conduct independent investigations in his capacity as a civil rights lawyer. He said he was sitting in church one Sunday morning in April 2015, for example, when he received an urgent message through Facebook's text messaging feature on his smartphone. It was Walter Scott's niece.

"She messaged me and said it was an emergency and said that her uncle had just gotten killed the night before, and the family really wanted to talk to an attorney. She had seen all of the work that I had done on other civil rights cases on Facebook, and she had gone to our website," Stewart said. He promised to contact her after the worship service concluded. When Stewart eventually connected with Scott's brothers and mother by phone, he said he felt the police department's official report sounded suspicious. Stewart said:

The video wasn't out. You know, we didn't even know there *was* a video. They asked me to look into it online through the articles and tell me what I thought. I looked at the articles that were out in the media, but they were all saying that Walter Scott had tried to kill the officer . . . [and] you have to kind of go with your gut, and it just didn't sound right—a man that age fighting a cop—none of it made sense. The family said if I could be there by the morning, then they would pick me as their lawyer, so we hopped in the car and drove eight hours up there. Then, once we got up there, we started hearing rumors that there was a video.

In both Sinyangwe's and Stewart's work, there is a stated dedication to debunking the persistent myth of black criminality—that African Americans deserve harsher policing strategies because they are predisposed to commit crimes. This is not easy frame to contradict, since doing so often requires time. Sinyangwe, for example, took several months to develop his complete database of fatal police shootings. Many newsrooms today do not have the luxury of working on a project that long. Shortcuts and stereotypes, therefore, become de rigueur under the strain of a daily deadline and cost constraints. Moreover, black trust in legacy media is waning. That Scott's family wanted to talk to an attorney before a member of the press is, perhaps, very telling.

The myth of black marginality. Many of the activists communicated a desire to be seen more fully in the news. Our hometowns and our people are featured only when there is trouble, was a common refrain. Media scholar Christopher P. Campbell has called this phenomenon the myth of marginality. Campbell's studies of local television news in the aftermath of the 1992 Los Angeles riots reported that the newscasts were full of threatening images of minority crime suspects—many shown in police mug shots, others bound in handcuffs closely guarded by police. "Considering the general dearth of minority coverage on the evening news," he wrote, "these may be the most dominant images of nonwhite Americans."[34] Campbell argued that black human-interest stories would balance such coverage, yet television news stories rarely examine everyday black life. He wrote, "the paucity of coverage of minorities and minority life contributes to a myth of marginalization— people of color exist at the periphery of mainstream society and do not merit the attention granted to whites."[35] Clint C. Wilson and Felix Gutierrez said that this inclusion of people of color only to discuss hot-button issues, such as immigration or social welfare, serves to frame minorities as "problem people," who are "projected as people who either have problems or cause problems for society. The legacy of news exclusion thus leads to the majority audience seeing minorities as a social burden."[36]

Campbell suggested that diversity in the newsroom could help correct the myth of marginalization, since people of color might propose stories that simultaneously elucidate universal truths and highlight varied worldviews. At the time of his study in 1995, only 4 percent of local television news directors were people of color, and whites held 92 percent of the supervisory jobs that usually lead to those positions, such as assistant news director, assignment editor, or executive producer.[37] Twenty years later, in 2015, Joshunda Sanders still bemoaned the lack of newsroom diversity. She wrote: "The number of black journalists in traditional media dropped 40 percent since 1997 in a profession that had in its ranks a little more than 36,000 employees by the

2013 count of the American Society of News Editors . . . . [A] 2012 Radio Television Digital News Association diversity study reported that 86 percent of television news directors and 91.3 percent of radio news directors are Caucasian."[38] Sanders called these statistics startling in the face of U.S. demographics, which project that minority ethnic groups will become the majority by 2043.[39]

Devin Allen, one of our Masters of Agitprop, said that all of this is why he tries to show the beauty that he sees in black Baltimore; not just its turmoil. It is why he chose a local clothing store, City of Gods, as our meeting place for the interview, he said. It is his stomping ground. It is his place of peace. Men at the barbershop next door greeted him by his nickname—*Hey, Moody!*—as we walked inside to get started. The homegrown celebrity waved, greeting everyone with an easy grin. Some of the onlookers followed us into the store, standing quietly in the doorway as the interview began.

"I try to tell people with my art in Baltimore, if you see me taking pictures, I'm not wandering around," he said, adding: "All my pictures are in West Baltimore for the most part—you might catch me over East sometimes, but I rarely go in East Baltimore—so you don't see pictures of East Baltimore. I'm not one of these people going out looking for something. This is my life."

Allen mentioned that his earlier work before the Freddie Gray uprisings captured black women with "natural hair, no makeup, not models, just my friends," he said. He endeavored also to photograph the positive things police officers did in his community to provide balance to black-versus-blue tropes. He admitted this was difficult to do initially. He said: "The thing is, I had so many run-ins with the police, and I still do! I'd get pulled over for the dumbest things, but the thing is, growing up in Baltimore, we learned at a very young age how to avoid them."

Like Sinyangwe, Allen said he feels his reportage has created entry points for dialogue between African Americans and police. He explained: "My photography has allowed me into spaces to literally influence some changes. Anytime, I can have an art show and have the [Baltimore City] police Commissioner on the panel," he shook his head incredulously. His eyes began to well with tears. He let out a low whistle and said: "I did an art show for my youth [photographers], and he [the Commissioner] came. I was like, 'I want him on the panel. He needs to be on the panel. He needs to see my kids' work. Period.'"

"This is the area that police are constantly . . . " his voice trailed off, brimming with emotion. In this delicate moment, the men who were gathered to witness Allen's interview—his friends—all averted their gaze from him. It was as if they knew their eyes were viewing a private moment of rawness that many men do not display publicly. Some of his friends sighed, as if they were fighting back tears themselves.

"People are being . . . " Allen's voice cracked. He still was not ready to finish his sentence. He paused to collect himself.

"Take your time," one of the men whispered from the store's doorway.

There was silence. A heaviness that seemed to be honoring the city's dead.

Allen sighed deeply, and after a while explained, "This is where Freddie Gray is *from*, and if you don't smother and kill our kids—this is what they can do."

The men in the room exhaled as Gray's name hit the air. That is when I realized his friends had been holding their breath, waiting to see if Allen could bear to speak of him. To this community, black life is not marginal. It is not something to be highlighted only in times of crisis. Black life is rich, beautiful, and complex, Allen said.

The myth of post-racialism. The last recurrent news myth that the activists sought to disrupt is that of a "post-racial America." Post-racial America is a mythical place where all of the old markers of segregation have fallen away to forge a promised land of equal opportunity. Helen Neville, M. Nikki Coleman, Jameca Woody Falconer, and Deadre Holmes have explained: "Social scientists argue that a color-blind racial framework is a contemporary set of beliefs that serves to minimize, ignore, and/or distort the existence of race and racism; at its core is the belief that racism is a thing of the past and that race and racism do not play an important role in current social and economic realities."[40] The façade of post-racialism is most evident when journalists either use naively optimistic news frames that gloss over lingering racial tensions or apply verbal or visual double standards in their coverage of ethnic minorities. To the first point, Christopher Campbell, for example, has noted that local news outlets' portrayals of Martin Luther King Jr. Day in the early 1980s largely ignored lingering hostilities toward the federal recognition of this holiday and pushed forward, instead, tales of racial harmonies.[41] More recently, news audiences viewed these same tropes in the headlines that announced Pres. Barack Obama's historic win as the first black Commander-in-Chief of the United States in 2008 and 2012. He was "The Dream Realized" for hundreds of newspapers and newscasters who parroted the pronouncement that racism was officially over.[42]

To the second point, racialized double standards in the news contradict the idea of colorblind post-racialism—and most African Americans know it when they see it. For example, early Hurricane Katrina coverage in August 2005 claimed that blacks were "looting" stores for food, while whites were "finding" provisions for their families.[43] Moreover, news anchors described the forced black migrants as Katrina "refugees" within their own country, while whites were regarded as "evacuees."[44] Such nuances in language are not a matter of mere personal preference. The connotations of choosing one word over another during the Katrina aftermath spoke volumes about a journalist's potential view of the story's subject—as either a criminal or a victim; as roaming marauders to be shut out or displaced victims to be welcomed.[45]

Our 15 activists were aware of these kinds of double standards too—especially when it came to coverage of the Black Lives Matter Movement between 2014 and 2018. More than half of them said that they were angered when the media chose words like "race riot" to describe the peaceful demonstrations that they organized in their respective cities. Media scholar Jennifer Heusel has argued that using inflammatory language to report on black protests is a tool that elite media use to delegitimize black political demands. She explained that: "marking a race-conscious protest as a race riot [is a] normal expression of traditional racial hierarchy in the US. Such hierarchy maintains whiteness as invisible and always innocent, and blackness as highly visible and criminal."[46]

Brittany Ferrell, one of our Day 1's nodded when I mentioned this phenomenon to her. I asked what she thought about the framing of the 2017 Women's March in Washington, DC, which was organized to highlight women's rights and, in part, to denounce Pres. Donald Trump's growing catalog of misogynistic behaviors. In an infamous "hot mic" moment, Pres. Trump bragged to an entertainment reporter that a man of his stature simply can "grab them [women] by the pussy" without anyone ever complaining.[47] Women's March participants defiantly (and ironically) donned pink hats, stylized to resemble vaginas, at many of the nationwide protests. Although two of the Women's March organizers are women of color, the demonstration was regarded popularly as a white feminists' march. Ferrell's voice rose in anger as she dissected the media framing she felt the Women's March received. She said:

I feel like a lot of white women went out and they were like, "Oh, this march is *peaceful*." And really putting the emphasis on *peaceful*. And it's like well, you know, our demonstrations were also peaceful, but when you see a sea of white women with pink vagina hats on their heads, white women are not going to be met with the same type of aggression from police officers as a community of traumatized, torn black people who continue over and over and over again to be traumatized. To be told that we don't matter. To be in communities where we don't have food, we don't have jobs, we don't have nothing! White women had the audacity to emphasize how safe their protests were! And it's like of course they were. They're protecting you! No one's protecting us. So [the news media] frame this narrative about how *this* is peaceful, and *this* is not. And it's like no, *this* is valued in society and *we* are not!

Ferrell recomposed herself. She was very near tears. She concluded quietly that black activists working in this moment should create independent media outlets, such as blogs, podcasts, and web video series, to reframe their organizational missions and leaders. Some of the activists said that the myth of post-racialism requires us to reframe even the deceased victims of police brutality. The news media state what seem to be objective facts about victims, they explained, yet those facts carry racist or classist connotations. For example: Eric Garner sold loose cigarettes illegally; Michael Brown robbed a convenience store; Freddie Gray was a petty thief; and Walter Scott had cocaine and alcohol in his blood when a white officer shot him in the back. In other words, if all of these unarmed black men were not in the process of committing crimes when police approached them, then the officers would not have killed them. How does one explain, then, the fact that *armed* white men—especially mass murderers—tend to survive high-profile encounters with police, while many unarmed black men have not? For example, police escorted Dylann Roof—the white man who shot nine black people during a June 17, 2015, worship service in Charleston, South Carolina—from the crime scene wearing a bulletproof vest, and later took him to a fast food restaurant for a meal.[48] Similarly, James Holmes, a white man who shot 12 people dead and injured 70 more in an Aurora, Colorado, movie theater in 2012, lived to stand trial in 2015.[49] Media scholar Jaclyn V. Schildkraut found that the news framed Holmes favorably, as the "Ph.D. student in a prestigious neuroscience program" who was "kind of quirky, just the way you expect smart people to be," "a bright but quiet and enigmatic student," and "a brilliant person that could've done a lot of good."[50]

Nancy A. Heitzeg has stated that this framing of white violent offenders—as the good guy gone bad—is normative. When whites commit heinous acts of violence, it is presented as divergent, while black violence is presumed inherent—even if the victim is black, she explained:

> There have been more mass shootings by white perpetrators, including Adam Lanza who killed his mother, twenty children and six adult staff members at the Sandy Hook Elementary School in Newtown Connecticut, and then himself. And more criminalization of Blackness, including that of Trayvon Martin, who, even as a victim, was demonized in death, and, in effect, put on trial for his very own murder.
>
> This is an old story too, one told and retold in various versions since the end of Reconstruction. It is a story of a white racial frame that largely denies white criminality and defines it when it must as an "aberration" . . . It is a story too of how this is made possible by the persistent attribution of crime to Blackness, the complicity of media in the framing of crime and criminals, and the reliance on differential sources of social control.[51]

Heitzeg's analysis is poignant in light of the fact that "seeing color"—especially in the newsroom—is supposed to be a relic of the 20th century. But given an increasingly polarized viewing public, where people select news now that matches their political leanings more than they ever did before, media scholars have begun to question anew what ideas people take away from daily broadcasts—especially in terms of race.[52] Some studies have shown that it takes only five seconds of exposure to a mug shot of an African American or Latinx youth offender in a newscast to raise the level of fear in a viewer. This increases their support for "law-and-order" policing styles, like the "stop-and-frisk" encounter that led to Amadou Diallo's 41 fatal shots, in 1999.[53,54] Other studies have found that exposure to news stereotypes triggers the perception of a facial threat from an unknown stranger—especially when that stranger is dark-skinned.[55,56]

Another body of research suggests that anti-black stereotypes are becoming ever more sophisticated, relying less on words and more on moving images to convey loaded meanings. Linus Abraham and Osei Appiah wrote: "[R]acial appeals in American politics now take place through visual imagery, without any explicit or overt reference to race . . . . [N]ews stories make implicit links between Blacks and negative thematic issues and concerns—such as violent crime, drugs, poverty, prisons, drug-addicted babies, AIDS, and welfare—by predominantly juxtaposing or illustrating stories with images of African Americans."[57]

Abraham and Appiah called this post-racial practice of cognitive association, "implicit visual propositioning." This theory states that people file away a single, lasting image in one area of their brain, while attaching numerous verbal or textual meanings to that image in another area. In TV news, this has looked like looping photographs of an unsmiling Trayvon Martin wearing a hooded sweatshirt, instead of airing pictures of the teen grinning with his family. This implicit visual propositioning did not go unnoticed. The hashtags #IfTheyGunnedMeDown and #CrimingWhileWhite emerged from a desire to counter what was being suggested as Martin's inherent criminality.[58,59] Youth of all races began to post to social media images of themselves in stereotypical poses that were juxtaposed to wholesome poses, such as smiling graduation pictures, which begged the question, *Which image would the media choose if I was shot by police?* It was a compelling, yet damning question for mainstream news media to consider.

News frames, after all, help us categorize complex concepts into tidy, digestible dichotomies, for better or for worse. At their best, news frames make certain stories recognizable to us. We know a good sports underdog story, for example, when we see one. What may be harder to see though are news frames at their worst. Persistent news myths perpetuate the tendency to frame African Americans as inherently criminal, dismissively marginal, or simply "playing the race card" in a supposedly colorblind United States that has moved past all of that. These myths work in tandem to produce cumulative cognitive effects in news audiences, some of which are now knee-jerk in nature. This is the prevailing journalistic cause that black witnesses have taken up: to seize power from these negative images and narratives. Just like the woman I met in Kliptown in 2011—who had to walk a quarter of a mile to charge her cellphone in a truck—these activists can see, very clearly, who holds the power. And they want it.

PART II
SLOGANS

4

#StayWoke

A Day in the Life of an Activist

Dread Scott's smartphone was pinging. Twitter notification banners flashed across his screen as he sped to open the mobile application. The self-proclaimed "artivist" thumbed, "@SunsaraTaylor @SoulRevision @uniqueloves following what? What's going on that I should be following?" Within minutes, his audience shared that a young, black activist (#EricSheppard) was trending on Twitter for stomping on a U.S. flag. His friends wanted him to retweet Sheppard's exhibition, since it was reminiscent of an artistic demonstration that he created almost 20 years ago entitled, "What is the Proper Way to Display a US Flag?" Like Sheppard, Scott encouraged those visiting the exhibit to trample Old Glory, to highlight social injustice in the United States. Pres. George H. W. Bush called it "disgraceful" when it debuted, the *Chicago Sun-Times* reported on March 16, 1989. As Scott recounted in an hour-long interview in October 2016, this process of rapid-fire communication among activists is made possible by mobile devices, Twitter, and speedy Internet connectivity. That was clear. What was less clear, however, was what happens in the lives of activists after these messages are sent around the world.

What are the rewards of bearing witness while black? What are the consequences? And, perhaps most importantly, what do they expect will happen once their version of the news reaches the masses? These activists are not unlike their ancestors in that they believe journalism can help them seek redress for the black lives lost to police brutality. Moreover, all of the activists spoke of a responsibility to stay involved in the movement, even though the continual exposure to images of police brutality weighed on them. None of this is without risk though, and they shared what bearing witness has meant for them personally and professionally. Some even admitted, quietly and reluctantly, that they regret ever seeing at all. In this chapter I delve deeper into what it truly means to be on the front lines of this style of maverick news production. Certainly, black witnessing has a long and storied history in the

Bearing Witness While Black. Allissa V. Richardson, Oxford University Press (2020). © Oxford University Press.
DOI: 10.1093/oso/9780190935528.001.0001

United States. But this generation of storytellers has a different "angle," to borrow a term from the newsroom. Gone are the days when black protestors intoned, "We shall overcome!" To hear that song now is to feel the plaintive resolve of a people who believed change was coming. It was full of long-suffering. In 2014, however, a more insistent mantra arose. "Stay woke!" protestors in Ferguson urged their supporters. It was equal parts warning and admonishment. Be cautious, black millennial activists were saying, lest we become lulled into the dream of a post-racial United States that does not yet exist. Be vigilant too, they chided, because the ancestors' wins—everything from Civil Rights legislation to Affirmative Action policies—were under siege.

For Redress of Grievances

All of the activists said that they believed their bearing witness had the power to affect social and political change. They believed their reporting could re-dress excessive force policies in police departments across the United States. In the course of their work though, the activists realized that the very social networks upon which they relied needed overhauling too. They shared with me the myriad problems that arose in their attempts to bear witness. It turns out, many of them said, it is not so easy to exercise one's First Amendment rights, to speak freely and assemble peaceably—online or in real life. The act of looking, they said, can be considered criminal.

Redressing excessive force. To many of the activists, their use of social networks has become an essential part of their workflow. They believe in the equalizing power of Twitter, for example, but are aware of its limitations still.

Attorney Stewart explained that Twitter has allowed him to provide bal-anced views of what reforming police brutality would require systemically. As a lawyer, he said he has seen both sides of law enforcement: the good po-lice officers and the bad ones. Twitter allows him to share these nuanced, ex-pert analyses with a broad audience. He said:

> The majority of police officers are doing a good job. But when the bad ones screw up, they still ride off of the "not having to answer questions," or not being forthright with what really happened, because nobody questions them. That has to stop, because if you did the right thing, then the evidence will show it, and if you abused your powers because you were in a bad mood

or you're just a hothead or whatever it may be, then you don't deserve to wear that badge.

Stewart added that part of his reportage involves educating the public on the importance of the various branches of government. At the time of our interview, then-Sen. Jefferson "Jeff" Sessions III, an Alabama Republican, was in the throes of his Senate confirmation hearing for the position of U.S. Attorney General. It was one of Pres. Trump's more controversial nominations, as many civil rights advocacy groups believed that a Sessions appointment would turn back the clock on civil rights legislation. Sessions, a former prosecutor, promised at the time of his confirmation hearings to support Pres. Trump's call for a return to a "law and order" agenda, which included tougher enforcement of the laws that govern gun trafficking, illegal drug sales and immigration.[1] Two Democratic senators—Cory Booker of New Jersey and Elizabeth Warren of Massachusetts—offered unprecedented testimonies against Sessions. Never before had sitting senators opposed a fellow legislator's nomination in the confirmation process. I asked Attorney Stewart what he thought all of this meant for the movement in February 2017. He said:

> People really don't fully understand the power that the Department of Justice has in civil rights. Under the last [Obama] administration the DOJ had more investigations ever in the history of the department, and it's very important. One way that I've tried to explain it is . . . let's say with Walter Scott, with the state prosecution, if there was no federal investigation, [Officer Michael Slager] would be free.

Stewart added that in many jurisdictions, state prosecutors and local police officers all know each other personally, which makes it even more unlikely that a state will indict a cop who shot someone fatally. In these cases, families of the victims benefit from the federal government stepping in, to provide a presumably impartial investigation, Stewart explained.

These select peeks into the inner workings of the movement are what Sinyangwe said he likes to offer on Twitter as well. He said his involvement with Campaign Zero placed him at the table with nearly all of the Democratic presidential hopefuls of the 2016 election cycle. His Twitter updates positioned him as the "policy shop within the movement," he said. For example, after Black Lives Matter activists interrupted former presidential hopeful

Martin O'Malley at a Netroots Nation political conference in July 2015, Sinyangwe said that the candidate "got embarrassed" and asked for his help. He explained:

> He [O'Malley] already had a disastrous campaign, so at that point, his campaign was desperate and they needed to know what they could do to make up for this, and they hadn't yet released an agenda. They reached out to us. . . . They were like, "Look, we need an agenda on policing that is real," and so we drafted their entire agenda and they adopted it pretty much word-for-word.

Sinyangwe said he met with Sen. Bernie Sanders and Sec. Hillary Clinton soon after the O'Malley assist, to create their platforms too. His Twitter timeline bears witness to his campaigns for redress. Pictures of him seated at the table with the candidates dot his timeline alongside his statistics and policy suggestions.[2,3]

Redressing "algorithms of oppression." While social networks have been a boon for anti–police brutality activists, these platforms are pushing back now against the protestors who hijacked them to broadcast their political demands. Mark Luckie, one of our Rogues, published an open letter to Facebook shortly before he quit in 2018. In it, he claimed: "Facebook has a black people problem."[4] He added that African Americans use the platform more than any other ethnicity, yet their content is censored in ways that undermine this democratized flow of information. Luckie wrote, for example: "African Americans are more likely to use Facebook to communicate with family and friends daily. . . . Sixty-three percent use Facebook to communicate with family, and 60 percent use Facebook to communicate with friends at least once a day, compared to 53 percent and 54 percent of the total population, respectively."[5] Despite African Americans' over-indexing on the platform, however, Luckie argued that Facebook moderators (who are often non-black) often designated black witnesses' chats about community organizing, or public lamentations about another fatal police shooting, as hate speech. He said that black activists and their allies have had their posts removed, their accounts suspended or even closed outright. Punishing black users for leveraging Facebook to bear witness is what led Luckie to leave the company, he explained. He wrote in his open letter:

> Being stationed at Facebook headquarters has required a great deal of sacrifice—being cut off from family, friends, and my now former fiancé,

compromising my health and my sense of security. I've done all this willingly because I strongly believe in this company and its ability to positively impact the world. But to continue to witness and be in the center of the systematic disenfranchisement of underrepresented voices, however unintentional, is more than I'm willing to sacrifice personally. I've lost the will and the desire to advocate on behalf of Facebook.

Luckie's letter confirmed for many activists that their use of these social media platforms is very precarious. Consider this story of two women: Diamond Reynolds and Korryn Gaines. Diamond Reynolds's Facebook Live broadcast of Philando Castile's death was able to "air" on the network, without interruption on July 6, 2016. A day after the livestream, Facebook CEO Mark Zuckerberg posted to his own platform to say that while he was sad Reynolds had to record such tragic footage, he felt resolute in his company's mission to provide everyone in the world the ability to connect with others online—especially during a crisis.

He wrote on July 7, 2016: "The images we've seen this week are graphic and heartbreaking, and they shine a light on the fear that millions of members of our community live with every day. While I hope we never have to see another video like Diamond's, it reminds us why coming together to build a more open and connected world is so important—and how far we still have to go."[6]

I found myself nodding in agreement as I read Zuckerberg's post that day, yet shaking my head in disbelief less than one month later when I heard what happened to Korryn Gaines. On August 1, 2016, Facebook cut Gaines's livestream as she tried to broadcast her fatal standoff with local law enforcement officers on Instagram, which Facebook owns. Gaines, 23, began filming the Baltimore County police when they entered her apartment complex. They were there to serve her with an arrest warrant after she failed to appear in court on charges related to a traffic stop. Gaines refused to come outside of her unit. She armed herself instead, with a shotgun and a smartphone. The police called in a SWAT team and hostage negotiators. After six hours of engagement, officers asked Facebook to deactivate all of Gaines's social media accounts.[7,8] Then they stormed into Gaines's apartment and shot her fatally. Her five-year-old son, Kodi, was next to her when she died. Bullets grazed his face, but he lived. Herein lies the crisis of witnessing of which I spoke in chapter 1: Gaines was unable to bear witness to her own death. The social medium that would have empowered her instead silenced her.

Despite Facebook's initial claims to want to connect people in the wake of the Castile killing, Mark Luckie said that African Americans on its platforms now may find themselves subject to a different kind of policing—of the cybercultural variety. Facebook regularly censors Black Lives Matter dialogue and organizing as hate speech, Luckie said. In some cases, the platform deletes user posts without explanation. In other instances, Facebook suspends or deletes a user's entire account—also without explanation.

Safiya Umoja Noble, author of *Algorithms of Oppression*, has explained that the ecology of the Web regularly reinforces racism in this way. She wrote "On the Internet and in our everyday uses of technology, discrimination is also embedded in computer code and, increasingly, in artificial intelligence technologies that we are reliant on, by choice or not."[9] In terms of black witnessing, both people and abstract digital formulae alike can serve as gatekeepers to documenting police brutality. Noble had not yet published her groundbreaking book when I interviewed Mark Luckie in 2017. Facebook's CEO, Mark Zuckerberg, had not yet testified before the Senate about his company's massive data breaches of user information.[10] And Christopher Wylie of Cambridge Analytica had not yet blown the whistle on the company and its unethical harvesting of profile data from at least 80 million Facebook users, without their permission, to build a massive political marketing database.[11] Still, Luckie hinted at all of this one afternoon in February 2017, before it was headline fodder. I asked him about algorithms on Twitter and Reddit, where he worked during the height of the Black Lives Matter Movement, in 2016 and 2017. Did the algorithms "know" who was a black activist? Were there secret lists within each platform of the black influencers? Luckie declined to elaborate on the algorithms that underpin the architecture of Facebook, Twitter, or Reddit. Instead, he said that all of these social networking companies surveil black users under the catchall guise of preventing hate speech—even when their language does not violate the site's stated terms of use. Luckie said he traveled from one company to the next, in hopes that some of the bigger social networks would have better mechanisms in place for allowing African Americans to socialize and organize freely. Instead, he said he found the problem spans all of the major platforms. He explained:

I left Twitter because I felt it was not catering to a group of people who were using the site more than anyone else. . . . Then I joined Reddit [and] once again a company was not speaking to me as an African American. So I said, you know, it's time to kick rocks. I never considered myself an activist before, but now I see that I am. These online spaces were not really designed with us [African Americans] in mind, but we are using them anyway. And it baffles them.

Luckie said he launched *Today in #BlackTwitter* in 2016 because he wanted like-minded users to find each other easily. Beyond hashtags, Twitter offered no content curation services for discrete audiences while Luckie was there. He said it was a feature he pushed for internally as a Twitter employee, yet it never materialized. As an independent witness, however, he could be that news aggregator, he said. Luckie told Black Entertainment Television (BET) in January 2016: "Black people want to see positive representation of themselves. Too often in mainstream media, culture and business, we are excluded based on who we are and what we look like. So, I created this for the same reason that HBCU's exist, which is to reflect the culture we have and why it's so important."[12] Luckie added that *Today in Black Twitter*, which ceased its digital publication in 2017, was designed to curate black topics of interest even when they were not trending on Twitter. It was Luckie's attempt to report on African American news steadily—especially when mainstream news' interest in sensational-ized events waned.

In a sardonic twist, some activists have created their own methods for over-coming Twitter's trending topics algorithms. They have learned to manipu-late what they want to raise to prominence on the platform. Brittany Packnett Cunningham, for example, said she does not tweet the current president's full name, instead using the abbreviated "Tr*mp" as a stand-in. "It started off as a joke," she explained, adding, "I feel there's a power we give him every time we say his name. It feeds that [ego] to keep saying his name. So I want to be able to refer to him without feeding that—without feeding the trend." She laughed as bemused patrons in the Washington, DC, coffee shop gazed her way. In both Luckie's and Packnett Cunningham's cases, the activists were aware of how social media platforms worked for and against them. They knew that the same social network that allowed distant witnesses to say goodbye to Philando Castile was robbed of the opportunity to be there virtu-ally for Korryn Gaines. That Gaines died without a complete video account—despite her efforts to bear witness—is one of the many reasons why, perhaps, Baltimore County awarded her family an unprecedented $37 million in a civil suit in February 2018. Her life—even up to its final, controversial, tragic moments—had value.[13]

Risking it All

There is a tendency to view the labor of black witnesses through a lens of altruistic nobility. That may be because early scholarship on citizen journalism tended to contain words and phrases like "democratize" and "challenging authority." Researchers have marveled at how citizens in Tunisia and Egypt practiced sousveillance in 2011's so-called Arab Spring revolts to circumvent traditional media outlets, which were run by oppressive political regimes, to publish video directly to Twitter.[14,15,16] Those who put themselves in harm's way to document political unrest in their countries were heralded as "mediated martyrs"[17] who dared to "overthrow the protest paradigm."[18] In terms of police brutality, Hans Toch likened cop-watchers to Greek choruses. He wrote: "The involvement of spectators in police–citizen confrontations invites comparison with the role played by the chorus in classic Greek tragedies. The chorus has been called the moral barometer of the play in classical Greek theatre because chorus members constantly offered opinions on wickedness, punishment, and righteousness."[19] Ben Brucato offered further evidence of smartphone-toting protestors behaving like Greek choruses during the Occupy Wall Street movement in 2011, stating: "Their use of video streaming apps to live-broadcast such events—while chanting "The whole world is watching!"—showed how protesters framed watching as intercession."[20]

While all these sentiments resonated with the activists, many of them said that not enough has been written about the risks that they face while bearing witness. Eve Ewing, for example, referenced a passage in bell hooks' *Black Looks: Race and Representation*, where hooks argued:

> An effective strategy of white supremacist terror and dehumanization during slavery centered around white control of the black gaze. Black slaves, and later manumitted servants, could be brutally punished for looking, for appearing to observe the whites they were serving, as only a subject can observe, or see.[21]

The "brutally punished" portion of the passage is what goes unsaid, the activists shared. Since black witnesses assume an "oppositional gaze," to establish a degree of narrative power, they become vulnerable to retaliation from local police or subject to surveillance from even higher ranks of government.[22] Samuel Sinyangwe described an eerie telephone call that he received just before the 2016 Republican National Convention (RNC) commenced. His easy smile disappeared as he recalled this during the interview:

> The FBI showed up at my door one day before the RNC and I wasn't home, so I get a call from a no-caller-ID number and they're like, "Is this Samuel Sinyangwe?" I'm like, "Yes," and they're like, "Well, this is—" I forget his name. "Something with the FBI—FBI district office—San Francisco and I'm at your door, but you're not home so I'm leaving my business card under your door, but we want to talk to you about your plans for the RNC Convention, and I want to encourage you not to go." I was like, "What? You're trying to tell me not to go?" First of all, I didn't have any plans . . . Then they're like, "Well, we also want to talk to you. Can you come down to our office?" I was like, "I'll get back to you about my schedule." I ain't going in for questioning, so I didn't go in, and they didn't reach out to me again.

Sinyangwe said hackers have doxxed his social media accounts also, and posted his home address on Twitter. I asked him if he and his colleagues have learned to protect themselves from surveillance. Sinyangwe confirmed that they use their smartphones in different ways now that they have become more prominent activists. Without giving away their exact techniques, he spoke of using certain mobile apps that encrypt his communication. Additionally he said that he rarely tweets with Twitter's geolocation feature activated, to avoid real-time tracking of his whereabouts. "I just assume that we're all being surveilled at this point. We try to do what we can do to make it harder to monitor our activities," Sinyangwe said. He added that he tries to remember that his labor as a data scientist distances him, to a degree, from the threats of bodily harm. "My work is not as hard as every single day being in the streets. I'm crunching numbers. I'm doing reports. I'm meeting with legislators, but I'm not getting tear-gassed while I'm doing that. There's a privilege associated with that that keeps me grounded. It could be 10 times harder," he said, shaking his head.

Brittany Ferrell likely would agree. She *was* on the frontlines in Ferguson. She explained: "I felt like I didn't know if I would make it home at night [during the protests]. There was so much happening every night. There were the police that were shooting rubber and wooden bullets at protestors and tear-gas. There were gunshots that were being let off. There were dogs. There was fire. There was so much. And it was like we almost became inured to the fact that we might be harmed physically . . . we still went out night after night after night," she said.

Ferrell's voice trailed off as she stared out of the window of her car. She had been speaking to my mobile journalism class by FaceTime, but she paused poignantly now, for many moments, seeming to get lost in her memories. As we waited for her to resume, a young woman in the front row of the lecture hall dabbed at tears with her jacket sleeve.

"She really risked it all, Professor," that student told me after class, adding, "I am in awe of how these people put their bodies out there—in the way!—for all of us."

A couple of weeks later we listened, as a class, to Marissa Johnson's account of how she used her body to get in the way—and what happened afterward. Johnson said she brought white allies to form a human barricade around her when she interrupted Sen. Bernie Sanders at the podium. She said she does not think she would have made it to her car without them after she finished her speech. They formed a phalanx around Johnson as she left the stage. The audience spit at her and hurled racial epithets. Then, because they could not reach her, she said, they bit one of her white allies on the arm.

"I've gotten thousands of death threats," Johnson explained, adding, "I still do, a year-and-a-half later. Every time something would happen in the [presidential] election again, I'd get new death threats."

Johnson emphasized that her experiences are not unique. She said: "If you're doing effective work, that's what's on the table. If you're afraid of that to the extent that you're not going to do that kind of stuff, then you end up doing work that's less revolutionary. The tactics that we chose—if you're really aware of the legacy of people who take that road—then you understand that everything up to death is on the table."

My students and I sat in silence for a moment, letting her words sink in. I was reminded of my interview a few weeks before with Attorney Stewart. He admitted then: "When I go to court, I have to hire armed security to go with me. That's not fun."

Brittany Ferrell said that being followed is even more unnerving. She recalled the first time that it happened. She was out running errands when an unmarked car drove up to her, and "a white man with a camera leans out of the passenger side window and starts snapping photos [of me]," she said. She explained further: "This is a movement that they know we are winning. This is not just a *moment* for us. This is a very real black movement. There's not a day that goes by that I don't think about who's listening, who's watching. I've become inured to feeling like safety is an illusion."

Ferrell said that the cameraman became a fixture in the days leading up to her March 2017 sentencing date. When I inquired about the charges against her, she said a woman drove through a crowd of Black Lives Matter protestors who had blocked off I-70 in St. Louis to commemorate the one-year anniversary of Michael Brown's death in August 2015. "[She] used her vehicle to try and run protestors over," Ferrell said as tears began to brim in her eyes. She added: "I allegedly struck her driver's side door with my size 6 shoe and now I'm facing a felony. It's definitely political retaliation towards the movement. It's definitely an effort for them to make an example out of me." Ferrell remarked that her felony charge is made all the more bitter when she considered the fact that "The same prosecutor [Robert P. McCulloch] who failed to indict [Officer] Darren Wilson [for killing Michael Brown] is now trying to convict me of a felony for allegedly kicking a vehicle." Someone in my class gasped at her revelation. Many more students shook their heads in disbelief. Ferrell eventually was given a suspended sentence and granted probation as part of a plea deal in March 2017. The Black Lives Matter Movement then turned its attention to voting McCulloch, who was running for an eighth term, out of office. The movement supported Wesley Bell, 43, an African American native of Ferguson and then a city councilman. Bell defeated McCulloch soundly in August 2018 by more than 24,000 votes—56 percent to 43 percent—to become the first black St. Louis County prosecutor.[23]

Still, the activists shared that the risks associated with bearing witness while black are manifold. Some activists said, for example, that they were angry when they realized that Ramsey Orta—the Eric Garner video witness—was the only one arrested in the aftermath of Garner's death. Police charged Orta, 22, with two counts of criminal possession of a weapon in August 2014.[24] A New York grand jury decided not to indict Officer Daniel Pantaleo, who choked Garner to death, for any wrongdoing. In fact, Sally Goldenberg of *Politico* reported that after killing Garner, Pantaleo earned a raise in salary. Goldenberg explained:

Pantaleo earned $119,996 in fiscal year 2016, which includes earnings between July 1, 2015 and June 30, 2016. His base pay was $78,026 and he earned $23,220 in overtime, according to a review of payroll records. He received an additional $12,853 in unspecified pay, which could include retroactive pay or bonuses. Pantaleo's earnings in 2016 represent a 35 percent increase in overtime pay, and a 14 percent overall increase from the previous fiscal year, which began shortly before Garner's death on July 17, 2014. In that 12-month period, ending June 30, 2015, Pantaleo earned $105,061, with $76,488 base pay, $17,109 in overtime and $11,673 in additional earnings, records show.[25]

Although the New York PD (NYPD) stripped Pantaleo of his gun and badge after the Garner killing, he remains on what the force calls "modified duty." The U.S. Department of Justice, under Attorney General Eric Holder, pledged to investigate the Garner case independently. When the administration changed, however, the new Attorney General Jeff Sessions vowed to roll back the agency's probes into excessive force cases nationwide. Though Sessions did not hold his appointed position very long—just shy of eight months to be exact—he issued the anti–police brutality movement a "parting shot," Christy E. Lopez of The Marshall Project said. The nonprofit news organization covers the U.S. criminal justice system. Lopez posted to its site on November 19, 2018:

> On his last day as US attorney general, Jeff Sessions issued a memo making it more difficult for Justice Department officials to obtain court-enforced agreements to stop civil rights abuses by local police departments. . . . Sessions' memo also takes pains to emphasize that states are "sovereign" with "special and protected roles" and that, when investigating them, the Justice Department must afford states the "respect and comity deserving of a separate sovereign." . . . Sessions' memo is consistent with his past statements and his long history of states' rights arguments to disadvantage poor people and people of color. In his view, the Justice Department should be more concerned about protecting states from the burden of abiding by federal law than about protecting individuals from being hurt or killed by the state.[26]

The Sessions memo jeopardized—and, in some cases, dismantled completely—the legally binding consent decrees that the Eric Holder-led Justice Department negotiated with police departments in Ferguson, Baltimore, New Orleans, Cleveland, and Los Angeles.[27] It was a crushing blow to the movement.

Garner's family, meanwhile, continued to wait for a criminal investigation to commence. The civil suit against the NYPD was filed already. In July 2015,

New York City agreed to pay Eric Garner's family $5.9 million in damages. For Eric Garner's daughter, Erica, however, the damage was too great to overcome. On December 30, 2017, the 27-year-old new mother died after suffering a heart attack. She had just given birth to a baby boy, three months before.

Her mother, Esaw Garner, told CNN in a December 31, 2017, broadcast: "She never recovered from when her father died. . . . I warned her every day, you have to slow down, you have to relax and slow down."[28]

Some activists argued that Garner died of a broken heart after trying (and failing) for four years to take her father's case to court in New York City. Others said that she was a living example of what prolonged stress and poor postnatal care look like for black women. A 2017 ProPublica study revealed, for example, that between 2006 and 2010, black women in New York City, where Erica Garner lived, were 12 times more likely to die after childbirth than white women—up from seven times more likely between 2001 and 2005.[29] In either scenario—broken heart or broken healthcare system—the discussion circled back inevitably to the real consequences black witnesses face for watching police officers.

The Regrets

"Sometimes I regret just not minding my business," Ramsey Orta told *TIME* magazine in 2016. In the article, he described the near-constant police harassment he experienced after filming Eric Garner's death. In the interviews I conducted, only one of the activists shared this level of regret for entering the political fray. Marissa Johnson said that she knew what she was getting into when she usurped Sen. Bernie Sanders's platform to deliver her message, but she did not anticipate the long-term effects it would have on her psyche and her career prospects. Johnson lamented:

> I'm really happy about what we were able to contribute to history and trying to advance the people's agenda forward. That being said, had I known what it would cost me personally, I don't know that I would've. I'm not at that point yet where I would say, "Yeah, I would have still done it," knowing what I know now because I lost a lot for a long time as a result of that moment.

When I asked Johnson about specific losses she cared to discuss, she said she has suffered from post-traumatic stress disorder, limited career options, and continual harassment online and in real life. "It colors everything you do and colors your legacy," she explained, adding, "I've always been kind of a do-gooder so I never would have imagined that I would go viral for something that was so controversial."

Taking Responsibility for the Culture

Despite the many risks of black witnessing, the activists expressed the occupational ethos that many professional journalists likely would say that they have. For example, the activists all spoke of being guided by a sense of responsibility to inform people about the facts. Moreover, the activists frequently said that their Black Lives Matter reportage stemmed from a duty to: (a) use their education or professional skills for social justice; and (b) open doors for future activists and storytellers. Both of these are time-honored reasons for bearing witness while black. Gordon Parks once wrote, for example "I use my camera as a weapon against all the things I dislike about America—poverty, racism, discrimination."[30] Devin Allen spoke of his photography in similar terms, 50 years later. He said:

> I believe if you're a writer, the pen is your weapon. That's like if you're a rapper or a singer: Your voice is your weapon. That's why I think it's so important that as black artists, we need to focus on these issues, because your voice reaches the masses. My pictures reach the masses.

Allen noted that he is self-taught. The road to bearing witness to the world has been filled with on-the-job training, he said. He feels obligated, therefore, to share what he has learned with other would-be black witnesses. "I didn't know what the hell a grant was growing up," he said, laughing. The men in the small Baltimore clothing store, where we had all gathered for the interview, chuckled along with Allen.

"Preach!" someone said from the threshold of the shop, in true call-and-response fashion. More laughter followed.

Allen continued: "This stuff, they didn't teach us in school. Now, I'm working on two grants right now." He said he has shown Baltimore youth how to identify and apply for project funding. His workshops are advertised on his Twitter timeline.

Eve Ewing, our Chicago Bard, said she uses Twitter in a similar way. When I spoke to her in February 2017 via FaceTime, she had just arrived at the University of Chicago on a prestigious fellowship that would allow her a year to write, without teaching duties, before advancing to an assistant professorship. She was working on a book, *Electric Arches*. FaceTime connected us one cold, rainy day in February 2017. She told me to take as long as I needed with the interview, as she was in no rush to go outside, she said. "I can go long," she promised with a smile. She was gracious with her time indeed, granting the longest interview of all the activists, at nearly 90 minutes.

We laughed about the gunmetal gray skies that dominate Chicago winters. I admitted that I had chickened out of living there beyond journalism school at Northwestern University—giving it really only two years after graduating before I fled. "It's too cold," I said simply. She nodded. It was a lot of other things too, I did not say. But Dr. Ewing already knew that. She is an inequality scholar and a respected frontline activist in Chicago. She shared that when she helped organize a demonstration in front of the Chicago PD's Homan Square facility in North Lawndale in July 2016, she realized the movement needed many more resources than people tend to consider initially. The Homan Square facility is a so-called "black site" of illegal interrogation, she said, where Chicago police allegedly take African Americans in without legal representation, subject them to torture, and coerce them into making false confessions.[31] Activists from Black Lives Matter, Black Youth Project 100, and the #LetUsBreathe Collective worked as a coalition to produce a sit-in they dubbed the "Freedom Square Occupation."[32] For one month, they chained themselves together in front of the facility, demanding answers on behalf of black families who claimed their relatives remained missing for weeks after their arrests. Ewing said she never stopped tweeting during her involvement. She recalled:

When [we] first set up, we spent a lot of time communicating and people were like, "Eve can you make this flyer in an hour?" "Can you do this or this?" . . . Me and my friend Xavier were like, "Okay everybody has to eat tonight. We both have cars. Let's go to the grocery store and get a bunch of meat that we can grill and a bunch of chips." After that day I put out these tweets and was like, the revolution needs graphic designers. The revolution needs people that can show up to meetings. The revolution needs people that can paint, people that can sew, people that can set up security systems on people's phones so that their phones don't get hacked, people that know how to pitch a tent, people that own sound systems and know how to do audio/visual stuff.

Since Ewing posted her Twitter thread on how people can use their talents to fuel the movement, it has become a mantra of sorts for organizers, who often ask her permission to recite it at meetings, she said.[33] Ewing said she is happy that she can use her communication skills as a professor to teach wide audiences of people about the true labor behind protest.

Dread Scott said he felt a similar urge to educate when he began to bear witness. The Master of Agitprop said he found the 2014 cellphone video of Eric Garner being choked to death incredibly difficult to watch. He leaned toward his laptop's webcam as if we were sitting across from each other in a coffee shop. "If you have children, what do you tell them when you say, 'Well yeah, there was video of Eric Garner being choked to death,' and yet his killers walk free? What do you tell them? It actually points to really clearly you actually have to fight," he said.

There are barriers to fighting though, David Banner said. He explained that he would like to see more wealthy rappers, like himself, involved in the movement, but understands why this is not so. "As much dope music as I've put out, I don't make money on rap. Black folks don't buy rap and it's so sad because one of the reasons why you don't have more of a revolution there in rap is because black folks don't support it," he lamented, adding: "Everybody wants Jay-Z to speak up. Why should he? Y'all ain't buying his albums; Samsung did. Y'all want help from a black [celebrity] and y'all want it for free. If you're a successful rapper, 9 times out of 10, you get paid by some white folks. So why should they fight for you when [white] people are supporting them?" Banner added: "The revolution is not going to come from someone who has benefited from white supremacy." He said he felt a responsibility to be one of the few rappers to challenge these power structures.

Responsibility to open doors. One unexpected theme that arose from the activists' interviews was the degree to which the participants were thinking about future generations of activists and storytellers. While I imagined they envisioned themselves on a continuum of black activism, having assumed the mantle from a prior leader, there was much talk about what the brave new world would look like for their descendants too. Some spoke of their own children in these terms. Others talked about the broader community of black youth around the world.

Devin Allen, for example, said he is bearing witness now because, "I'm trying to open up doors. My daughter loves photography. She can walk through those doors now [because] I walked through these doors." He added, "At the end of the day, these doors open about this big." He held his index finger and thumb a small distance apart and said: "Then they shut behind us. We need to knock these doors down and make sure they are not rebuilt." In a broader sense, Allen said he is bearing witness for all black children in his Baltimore neighborhood too. "I'm teaching them how to love their own situation through photography. I give kids cameras. They go out. I might never see them again, but they have a piece of me with them."

Brittany Ferrell, one of the Day 1's, is a parent too. She said that she still remains active in the movement, despite facing protest-related felony charges in St. Louis because:

I am a mother. I have a soon-to-be 9-year-old daughter . . . I think a lot of times I look at the great sacrifice that it's going to take for black people to get free, and for her and so many kids like her, [and it is] so worth it. You know? We get to train them up in this movement and let them know this is their life's work.

The realization that this work will be long term is daunting to some, but not discouraging. In fact, it strengthens many participants' resolve to bear witness, to mark milestones that will keep future generations assured that progress is being made. Filmmaker Lincoln Mondy said, for example, "There's that aspect of me having to remind myself that this, unfortunately, might not happen in my lifetime. I think having that in mind—I am passing the baton off to my children in the future generation, and instilling the passion to be a trouble maker and to get stuff done but also making sure that they take care of themselves—it's hard."

Mondy sighed as he and I strolled by a group of all-white women doing aerobics on the sidewalk in his northwest Washington, DC, neighborhood of Mount Vernon Square. WTOP radio—a local outlet—claimed that the community was one of the nation's "most gentrified" ZIP codes of 2018.[34] Mondy paused for a minute. I gazed on too, as a native Washingtonian, remembering a time when Mount Vernon Square and the neighboring community of Shaw, were primarily black. It was difficult to fathom that the area, which started as an enclave for freed slaves, had seen so many of its black descendants pushed out at the turn of the 21st century. I told Mondy, who was a recent transplant to DC, that Harlem Renaissance luminaries, such as Langston Hughes and Duke Ellington, had lived nearby. His eyes widened. "Un-be-liev-able," he whispered, uttering every syllable of the word. We continued walking in silence. The aerobics teacher's perky instructions echoed behind us.

5

#WorkWoke

The Movement as a Labor of Love

I had just disembarked an eight-hour flight from New York City to Milan, Italy. After waiting in line at customs for nearly an hour, I was ready to gain entry into Europe. I wanted a stamp in my passport and a cool bed. It was a humid, mid-July day in 2016, and it had been two weeks since the back-to-back shootings of Alton Sterling and Philando Castile in the United States. I was in Milan to lecture about the rise of hate speech online amid the Black Lives Matter Movement, which was in full bloom. But as I attempted to enter Milan that day, hate speech was being lobbed at me in real life. As I inched closer to the front of the customs line, I saw the next available agent wrap up his admission of an elderly white couple into the country.

"Benvenuto," the agent said to the pair in a thick, Italian accent. I remember thinking of how melodic the word "welcome" sounded in his language. He smiled at the couple and waved goodbye. I glanced left and right, to see if any other agents were open. No one else was free yet. His was the only available line, so I approached the window.

"Hello," I said with a smile, placing my passport on the counter. The agent stared at me, never picking up my identification. My smile faltered. Something about the way he looked at me unnerved me. It was an unflinching, contemptuous gaze. I stared back, unwilling to look away first. I wanted to know what was wrong. My brow probably furrowed. The agent never said a word. He simply picked up a nearby newspaper and began to pretend reading it.

My best friend, Dr. Shauna White, had accompanied me abroad. She was standing at the window to my left. She, too, is a black woman. All of the customs agents near her window were laughing uncontrollably. When I looked over at her, tears were brimming in her eyes. In the nearly 20 years since I had known her, I have never seen her face set with such fear.

"Just come over here with me," Shauna said. I glanced back at my customs agent, who was now smirking while he continued his fake newspaper

Bearing Witness While Black. Allissa V. Richardson, Oxford University Press (2020). © Oxford University Press.
DOI: 10.1093/oso/9780190935528.001.0001

reading. A sense of dread began to fall over me as I realized what was happening. The agent did not want to let me into Italy because I was black. The next agent confirmed this for me. I walked over to Shauna's line. She gripped my forearm tightly. I tried again to slide my passport under the window to the new customs agent.

"Africana," the agent hissed, without looking at my passport. I shook my head no. I did not understand why he was calling me African only. I suspected it had something to do with the thick braids I was wearing in my hair.

"Africana," he hissed again, sneering this time like a dog baring his teeth.

"African-*American*," I said. A lump was forming in my throat. The agent appeared peeved. At long last, he looked down at my passport. He frowned at its seal.

"Americana?!," he exclaimed.

"Yes, I am African-American," I said.

The new customs agent yelled something across the aisle to the fake-newspaper-reading customs agent. The agent who denied me simply shrugged. I then watched as he set down his newspaper for a white woman who approached his window.

"What is your business here?," the new agent asked, suddenly speaking flawless English.

"I am delivering a lecture," I said, adding, "I am a university professor."

"A professor!" he scoffed. There was more banter in Italian and more laughter and more sneering. The agent flipped through all of the pages of my passport, asking me what I had done in South Africa and Morocco if I was not indeed African. I told him that I had lectured and taught there too. He frowned. More banter. More scoffing. Then, I felt it. Underneath the sadness of being judged instantly, I was furious. I was enraged that I could do nothing to protect myself in the face of these officials. They were the closest things to law enforcement walking around in that section of the airport, and I was certain that any false move on my part could, and would, be cause for detention—or worse. The lump grew larger in my throat as I thought of Sandra Bland.

The July just before my trip to Italy, Bland had died in police custody in Waller County Jail in Hempstead, Texas. Official reports said she hanged herself, but Black Twitter had other theories. The hashtag #SayHerName trended that summer, to draw attention to the fact that black women often are victims of fatal police force too. Kimberlé Crenshaw, the legal scholar who coined the term intersectionality in 1994, was the mastermind behind the parallel movement. At the time, #SayHerName resonated with me because I never thought Bland's official cause of death was true—especially after viewing the controversial police dashcam video. Now, in the airport in Milan, I had a frightening thought: *What if these customs agents detain me, torture me and later say I killed myself?* I have no way of knowing whether Shauna was thinking this too. I only felt her gripping my arm, as if to say, *Where you go, I will go.* After several more minutes of interrogation, the agent unceremoniously tossed my passport back to me through the window as hard as he could. It hit the floor. This sent the other customs agents into fresh fits of laughter. I heard someone behind me gasp. When I turned I saw it was the white woman whom the former agent decided to serve, after ignoring me.

"Oh my God. I am so sorry," she whispered as she bent down to pick up my passport for me. I saw her passport as she handed me mine. She was American too. Tears welled in her eyes. She pressed my passport into my hand and gave me a reassuring tap.

"I'm sorry," the woman said again, this time glaring at the customs agents.

Still, I said nothing. I was frozen. Afraid. Angry. Humiliated. I walked out of customs and into the baggage claim area on the other side of the door.

"Can you believe that?" I asked Shauna. She shook her head no. As we grabbed our suitcases from the conveyor belt, I realized that both of us were trembling. We did not speak again about the incident until a few days later, when we were in the airport in Rome trying to catch a hop to Berlin, to my next lecture on the circuit.

"Allissa, *look*," Shauna said excitedly, pointing to a man reading a magazine. On the cover a black woman faced off with a white police officer. She wore a sundress. He wore riot gear. Her face was defiant, yet calm. A visor covered his eyes, yet the square set of his exposed jaw signaled exasperation—or, perhaps, something more. The cover titles were in Italian, but I recognized the name "Alton Sterling." That is when I realized that Black Lives Matter was international news. I also felt viscerally, for the first time in my adult life, the rage that many African Americans feel when bad cops strip their humanity through acts big and small.

I had been harassed by police only once before in my life, during college in New Orleans, and I do not know that I had the language then to call it that. I was driving back to my dorm from an off-campus graduation party in my little green Mazda 626. I had been celebrating the coming commencement of one of my closest friends, Ryane. She was one year ahead of me, so I had stayed in New Orleans beyond my semester's final exam period instead of going straight home to Maryland, to see her walk across the stage to earn her degree. Another friend, Lauren, did the same. I remember the three of us laughing as we rode along in my car. I do not remember exactly what we were talking about, but I do recall that it was cut short by the wailing of police sirens behind me. I looked down at the speedometer. I was within the speed limit. I wondered what was wrong. I heard my mother's voice in my head. *If the cops stop you at night, pull over into a well-lit area. Keep your hands on the steering wheel. Explain everything you are going to do, before you even make a move.* I put my hands on the steering wheel. I watched in my side rearview mirror as a white policeman, tall and lean, strode out of his car. He had dark hair, piercing blue eyes, and an aquiline nose. He leaned into the car, resting his elbows on my door.

I will never forget what he said: "Y'all sure look beautiful tonight." His Cajun accent was thick. He pushed his head into my car to get a closer look at Lauren, who was in the passenger seat. Then, he craned his neck to see Ryane in the back, his cheek touching mine as he did so. I do not remember breathing. The officer chuckled a bit as he began to pull his head out of the car. I continued to look straight ahead.

"Y'all smell good too," he said, laughing. "Where y'all coming from?"

"From a graduation party, sir," I said, instantly hating the way I sounded. My throat felt tight. The words came out shrill and nervous.

"Oh!" he exclaimed, adding, "Y'all are college girls. Well, congratulations." He crossed his arms. I turned to look at him, but continued gripping the wheel. His eyes danced. He was having fun.

"Officer, can you tell me why you pulled me over?" I asked.

He mocked me in a sing-song, high-pitched voice, restating my question amid laughter. He shook his head and rocked back and forth on his heels.

"I pulled you over because y'all look nice. I want to know where the party's at," he said.

Lauren, Ryane, and I were speechless. I do not remember any of us saying anything. This was happening in 2001—in the era before smartphones and #SayHerName. All I knew to do then was to get the officer's badge number. My eyes fixated on it, and I began reciting the digits silently in my head.

"Well!" the officer exclaimed in mock exasperation, adding: "Since no one is going to tell me where the party is, I guess I'll have to let you go. But I don't want to." He leaned inside my door again suddenly, which made me jump a bit. His face was right next to mine again. I felt his breath on my cheek again.

"Y'all be safe now, mmm-kay?," he said. He tapped my car door once, letting me know that I was free to go. I rolled up the window quickly, but I did not drive off immediately. I wanted him to leave first. I remember feeling scared that he may say I gave chase. As his cruiser rolled past my car, he gave a pretend military-style salute and grinned.

"Ryane, Lauren, remember this badge number," I said, preparing to recite it to my friends as I pulled off. I remember being surprised when they said they had memorized it too already. We rode back to Ryane's apartment in silence. As soon as we got inside, we used her telephone to call the New Orleans PD. We wanted to report an incident of harassment, we said. We gave the officer's badge number. The voice on the other end was male and very stern.

"We don't have an officer with that badge number here," he said. "Do you have a license plate number or cruiser number?" Ryane had both. She offered them. There was a brief moment of silence. Then: "That car is not registered to NOPD. Good night." The dial tone rang loudly in our ears. All of our mouths hung agape. We had been dismissed.

In Italy, I kept thinking back on the quiet terror that the New Orleans traffic stop held for me and my friends that night in 2001. None of us ever talked about the incident again after that—even as we recalled the raucous fun we had at the graduation party that evening. Nearly 18 years later, as I read Patrisse Khan Cullors' memoir, I identified immediately with what the Black Lives Matter founder wrote as she explained the aftershocks of police brutality. She said that victims "will be silent in the way we often hear of the silence of rape victims. They will be worried, maybe, that no one will believe them."[1] That night, no one *did* believe us, even when we fought silence. Instead, the so-called "blue code of silence" prevailed.

The incident happened so quickly, I did not have time to process all that could have gone wrong during that traffic stop. We could have been raped. We could have been killed. We could have not made it to our own college graduations. Yet, all of us were "good girls." All of us were biology pre-med students who were pledging our lives to care for the wellbeing of perfect strangers. We all hailed from Prince George's County, Maryland, which, at the time, was the wealthiest black district in the entire country.[2] But, none of that mattered when the police officer saw us drive by. He used his badge to hang the specter of harm over our 20-year-old heads.

More specifically, that officer attempted to control the movements of three black, female bodies through fear—just as the Italian customs agent tried to ban my physical entry into his country. In the context of police brutality, Armond R. Towns has explained: "The murder of Black women by police— disproportionately while driving—speaks to a long-held White mastery over mobility maintained by controlling the movements of people of color of all genders, sexualities, and classes."

In a related 2015 study, entitled *Say Her Name: Resisting Police Brutality Against Black Women*, Kimberlé Crenshaw reported that of the women stopped by police in New York, 13.4 percent were white, 53.4 percent black, and 27.5 percent Latina.[3] Reading all of this many years after my own late night traffic stop contextualized just how widespread and varied police brutality can be. Some might say that my experience is not true brutality, since I survived the traffic stop. None of us were fondled. No racial epithets were hurled at us. What was taken from me that night, however, was the sense that all cops work to protect me. Until that point, my 1980s baby acculturation had taught me that police were the good guys. The Drug Abuse Resistance Education (DARE) program, which was a byproduct of the War on Drugs, placed police officers in elementary-school classrooms across the country. I remember Officer Blue, a beautiful black woman who looked like Eddie Murphy's love interest in *Coming to America*, visiting my sixth-grade class every two weeks. Officer Blue dispensed common sense "stay out of trouble," and "say no to drugs" advice. It was advice I had followed. Ryane and Lauren, who were alumna of both Prince George's County public schools and DARE, had followed the advice too. Still, we found ourselves on the receiving end of sexual harassment by a member of the New Orleans PD, which did not want to admit that it had happened.

So, if I—as a black college honors student then and as a relatively privileged black professional traveling in Europe on business now—could be harassed by law enforcement officers in passing, then how much more vulnerable is a working class black woman to such abuse at the hands of cops who have access to her every single day in her own community? The culmination of all of these feelings swirled as I stared at that cover photo of Ieshia Evans, because I understood that the racial tension I felt abroad would not necessarily subside when I got back home. Black people truly are unwelcome in most places they go around the world, I realized that summer. I felt such profound sadness witnessing this firsthand. Yet I realized this is essential, perhaps, to understanding the lived experience of bearing witness while black. This is work that is rooted in anger and in firsthand experiences of police harassment, just as much as it is rooted in love. While there is a deep rage among the activists and, arguably among many black people, that African Americans often are defenseless in the face of police brutality, there is an equally deep love that these activists have for black people, which will not allow them to give up on the idea of holding bad cops accountable for their actions. In this chapter, the activists share the six things that inspired them to bear witness beyond a precipitating event: rage, regards, reflection, retrospect, redemption, and religion. For the activists, the work starts with fury but culminates in other outputs—just as it did for me that day in the Milan airport, where I made up my mind to finish this book.[4]

Reconciling Rage

Devin Allen knows rage. He said that his rapid rise to fame brought with it a flood of jealous carpetbagger-types who were looking to capitalize on his work. He alleged that a white freelance photographer exploited the children in his community by conducting an offensive photo shoot, for example. Allen explained:

> He decided that he wanted to pose kids with toy guns with their middle finger up and then try to sell it to a publication. The first thing you know as journalist, if you pose someone, you have to state that this is a posed image. He tried to sell it but couldn't sell it because he didn't have the kids' names. Then he had the nerve to go back to the youth center and ask for their names and their parents' permission to try to sell this image.

Allen said he turned to Twitter to apologize publicly to the families of those affected. He said that it was not the only incident in which he had to do so, however. He spoke of another episode, where a professional journalist loaned Allen a camera to teach photography to Baltimore youth for a few days. Allen said he forgot to take the SD memory card out of the camera, and the journalist tried to pass the children's images off as his own. Allen said he was devastated that he had left his youth vulnerable to appropriation. "I felt bad because I was a gateway for this guy in the community, and people trusted him," Allen said. He shook his head ruefully.

Ieshia Evans said that bearing witness on Twitter since protesting Baton Rouge was born, partly, out of rage toward the U.S. justice system. She said that she is still in disbelief that peaceful protest is really "not a First Amendment right for everybody," as she was arrested during her stand. "I had to ask what I was being charged with. The officer . . . told me he didn't know. I didn't even know what I was being charged with until my bond was posted—until they had an amount for me to bail out of jail with. Until then I didn't know what I was being detained for in *prison*! Not jail. Not no central bookings. It's real in Louisiana." Evans said the process went against everything she thought she knew about the judicial process. Students in my journalism class, who had been silent till that point in the interview, gasped.

Similarly, Shellonnee Chinn said that she has tweeted to show people just how long it takes a case to go through the judicial process. Chinn spoke to my same collective of journalism students one week after the Ieshia Evans interview. She said she wanted young people to hear how to fight *through* the system. "It takes years," she explained to them, shaking her head with a frown. Still, she argued, fighting in court is one of the hallmarks of the Civil Rights Movement, she said, and it should still be part of the modern protest arsenal.

With Warm Regards

Love guides most of the persistent storytelling in which the 15 activists engage, despite their pain. Many of them spoke of feeling led to report their version of the news out of "regards" for black people, to heal historic wounds, and make communities healthy again. Moreover, the activists said that they have provided updates on the Black Lives Matter Movement to show love for queer-affirming spaces, for self, and, to a lesser degree, for one's enemies. Alicia Garza, for example, reminded me in our October 2015 interview that the Black Lives Matter Movement began as a love letter to African Americans. Garza had just wrapped a self-care workshop at a large, mid-Atlantic university that morning and had downtime before lunch. I approached her as she left the dais. I asked if I could have the name of her publicist, so I could arrange an interview for a later date. Instead, Garza turned off the ringer on her smartphone. "Let's do it now," she said with a smile. I had assumed Garza would need a break after facilitating the emotional workshop. Though I am not at liberty to divulge all that was discussed in that private space, suffice it to say that the student leaders who attended were largely people of color on the predominantly white campus, who spoke of the real threats they faced by confronting racism there. Garza was a calm, active listener through the students' tears, offering many bits of actionable advice. She received a standing ovation at the end.

Some of the workshop participants milled in the hallway where we had gone to escape the excited, post-workshop rowdiness. Garza used words such as "collective" and "unified" when she spoke of her ultimate goals for the Black Lives Matter organization. She talked about "making visible folks who feel invisible." She said: "I've been that person before, that felt isolated, that felt weird and like an anomaly because I'm one of the only black folks in a space. And so it feels really good to come together and love on each other and encourage each other to hold our heads high."

Garza added, "We really wanted to focus on making sure that black folks were getting organized and that we were grounded in the principles of love for ourselves, love for each other, love for humanity, and also that we were grounded in the principles of building power for our collective liberation."

Several of the students who had followed us into the hall politely snapped their fingers in agreement as she spoke, as if they were at a poetry slam. It was a respectful, quieter version of call-and-response, all for the benefit of my video camera. I laughed quietly and kept rolling. About a year later, Eve Ewing spoke of her love for her news audience and storytelling partners on Twitter in similar tones as Garza. "I definitely feel a sense of community and fellowship with other black people on Twitter, especially black women on Twitter. I also think that the black media maker space on Twitter is really special and a lot of us know each other in real life or have relationships with each other."

Love for queer-affirming spaces. Some activists asked that I disclose and/ or emphasize their sexual orientation, to end the historic erasure of queer activists' contributions to black social movements. These activists spoke often about the love they have for those who are marginalized three times over, as black, female, queer leaders. Brittany Ferrell explained that MAU formed to nurture women who self-identified this way. "I began to notice that people began looking for this charismatic male leader. They romanticized the early Civil Rights Movement. They were looking for their Malcolm [X] or their Martin [Luther King Jr.]," she said.

My class nodded in agreement. We were interviewing Ferrell during my mobile journalism lecture, via FaceTime. One of the young men in my class asked if she ever felt belittled in any way, as a woman activist. She scoffed. "We [MAU] had a lot of young people, a lot of queer people, and a lot of women who were doing so much work that was not being recognized. Their work was not being taken seriously, but it was the work that we felt like a lot of men got the credit for."

She continued: "We wanted to create a space for young people regardless of your identity and regardless of your gender, your sexuality, if you are ready to do this work for black lives, this is your space. We wanted to open that up so people could feel safe coming into this with their whole selves, not to feel like they have to fit in anybody's box."

When I asked if Ferrell has experienced resistance from other activists due to self-identifying as a queer leader, Ferrell nodded. At best, she said, black male leaders within the movement have called her troublesome for highlighting their sexism—especially in terms of hoarding media opportunities or only doing certain kinds of work. At worst, Ferrell said she has experienced vehement opposition from other black activists who believe her sexuality threatens the movement's credibility outright. She said:

> There are different people in this struggle where their blackness is intersecting with their sexuality [and] intersecting with their gender. So it's been a struggle for myself and other women in this Movement because a lot of times you can be labeled as divisive when calling out sexism, but it's our duty to do that. It's our duty to do that because all that's going to happen if we don't is people are going to recreate structures that are going to continue to marginalize people: women, queer people, trans folks.

Some of the students in my journalism class snapped their fingers affirmatively, just as black youth at the other school had for Alicia Garza. Ferrell smiled at them through FaceTime. Ferrell met her wife, Alexis Templeton, while protesting in Ferguson, she explained. I asked how they maintain love in a movement, when history has shown that so many activists have been unable to do so. She sighed deeply and said:

> It has its own set of traumas honestly. We were forged in the fire . . . but I can definitely say that because of this experience, it's a love that has never really felt like any other love that I've ever experienced. Knowing that somebody is so committed to something in the same way that you are and that they are on this journey to make sure that they're whole and they're healthy in the same way that you are—it's something very powerful about the type of love that Alexis and I have grown into during this Movement.

Love for "self." Ferrell spoke of her daughter often in our interview too. Not only is Ferrell teaching her to love black people, she said she is training her daughter to practice self-love too. "She needs to grow up in this and to learn what it means to live as your whole self, your true self, and to love radically, and to fight for freedom, and to really walk in this purpose of your commitment and love to black people," Ferrell said. She added: "I think that she has kept my feet to the fire. She has kept me constantly evaluating how do I do this work in the most transformative and honest and radical but tender way?"

Devin Allen is rearing a black girl too, in his native Baltimore. He grinned when he spoke of her. He said he never really paid much attention to legacy media's standards of beauty until she was born. Now, he uses his photographic witnessing to capture various versions of black beauty, so he can share it with her.

"I'm raising a daughter," he said, adding: "We're constantly being tormented about our skin tones—this light skin versus dark skin thing—these are things that media is constantly portraying. We've been taught not to love ourselves. That's the thing. It's always something wrong. Our hair's too thick. Our nose is too big. It's like this reverse thing where they want to make us uncomfortable in our skin so that they can jump in it."

Allen points to his Afro. He said, "It's like, for instance, my hair. I was told, 'Oh my God, I love your hair. It's so intimidating.' Is that a compliment? Are you intimidated by my hair? I want people to see my photography, [and] make people comfortable with my skin."

Love for perceived enemies. To a lesser degree, some activists talked about having love for their perceived enemies, which include Internet trolls or warring political parties. Mark Luckie said that when he transitioned from life as a tech executive to become an outspoken voice on race, he experienced a lot of online harassment. "People said things like, 'I follow you for journalism. Why are you talking about black people all of the time?' or 'Diversity is stupid. You're stupid,'" he recalled. Luckie said he was ready for the pushback, however, adding, "I say there is no gray area. If you are not going to commit to this fully, then you should not get involved. I joke all of the time and say that there is probably an FBI file on me somewhere because of the things I tweet and the fact that I have been to the [Obama] White House several times for various events. I am okay with that, in knowing that I am trying to connect with my community."

Similarly, Brittany Packnett Cunningham said she had to cultivate her own community while sidestepping trolls online. This has been difficult, however, when trolls sometimes have come from within the movement, she said. Many of her Twitter followers criticized her when she publicly endorsed Sec. Hillary Clinton in the 2016 presidential election cycle, for example. There had been scuttlebutt among many movement leaders about which Democratic candidate deserved the black vote most. Alicia Garza, for example, conducted an interview with scholar-journalist Melissa Harris-Perry for *Elle*, in which she said she would not support Clinton. When Packnett Cunningham tweeted her choice on October 21, 2016, therefore, mixed reactions followed. She spoke in terms of love for her enemies that trolled her that day:

> I see everybody—including the [Trump] folks in the White House that I don't think should be there—as God's children. So for me, the foundation is that I'm doing this out of a sense of duty towards love and justice. That none of us are perfect but all of us are sinners saved by Grace because God loved us that much and so therefore we need to love ourselves and one another that much to fight for justice.

Packnett Cunningham added that her emphasis on love as fuel for the movement has sustained her when she has felt attacked on all sides.

Reflections: "It Could Have Been Me"

Only one activist said that he began reporting movement-related news because he saw himself reflected in the body of a high-profile victim. Samuel Sinyangwe, one of the Day 1's, explained:

> I used to literally stop at 7-Eleven every day and get a sweet tea—Arizona Sweet Tea and some Starburst or some Skittles and walk home—and so seeing Trayvon get killed and the system refuse to hold Zimmerman accountable, I think, was very personal to me in the sense that that was about 15 minutes away from where I lived. It was like I could've been Trayvon. Trayvon could've been my little brother. In that way I think it made this issue very personal and that's what put me on this trajectory to really be thinking more deeply about police violence and the way that the system enables that to happen.

Sinyangwe was an outlier, however, in that most of the other activists were more likely to see themselves reflected in their hometowns. In many interviews, the beleaguered city itself became a character in the story—a character that loomed larger, oftentimes, than the victim of police violence. While the killing of an unarmed black man, woman, or child certainly served as a tipping point in many participants' minds, they said, they were more likely to speak up empathetically on behalf of the African Americans who are still alive and still facing oppressive conditions in their local communities. Brittany Packnett Cunningham, for example, described her overwhelming sense of heartbreak for her birthplace as demonstrations in Ferguson became increasingly violent:

> I went to high school in Ferguson. Ferguson is home for me and I've always been very active in my community. When I saw what was going on at home that activism just grew. I could not *not* do something. I could not *not* take action in my own community—especially when they were facing the type of terror that they were from the police.

Devin Allen said he will never leave Baltimore to bear witness elsewhere, for this reason. He said he is invited to photograph protests in other cities and he has always declined. "I can't spread myself too thin," he said, adding: "That's why everything I do is Baltimore-based. I created something, but if I leave it's going to be that gap. I feel like Baltimore needs me." Allen's friends in the clothing shop nodded, while some held up Black Power-esque fists. Allen mentioned also that if he does take speaking engagements abroad or even out-of-state, he does so in order to be able to take a portion of his honorarium to buy more cameras for Baltimore youth.

Paying Homage to the Ancestors

The activists have a way of rattling off names of Civil Rights Movement icons as if they were family members. Some said that they channeled deliberately the aesthetics of past black activists to acknowledge their roots. Alicia Garza said that she and the co-founders of the Black Lives Matter Movement, for example, studied historic black activism and noticed a trend that they wanted to reverse.

"As a black woman who is queer," she said, "I think one of the things that just feels important for us to understand is that black women and women of color have been kind of the very foundation of what it's meant to get free, and then we're pushed aside or kind of erased."

Garza smiled, adding, "I guess my response to that is this is a moment where we can shift that, and I think what we're seeing is that we're watching old ways of being go away and new ways of being come in."

I asked Garza how successful she feels she has been in this endeavor to highlight black women's social work—especially since legacy media often anointed DeRay Mckesson, an openly gay black man, the leader of Black Lives Matter. His Twitter following dwarfs hers. (Mckesson never responded to my requests for an interview, despite many attempts.) Garza shook her head emphatically, but her answer is very measured:

> One of the things that we can continue to do is craft our organizations, our culture, our demonstrations, our Movement in way that not only makes visible the leadership and the work of women of color, and queer women, and trans women, and poor women, but that we also name what those contributions are. That we be very specific about what it is that we contribute. It's important for us to fight for our space without fighting each other.

The students who were milling in the hallway snapped their fingers in agreement again. Garza smiled at them. Another retrospective motif that one of the activists conjured was that of the Civil Rights Movement-era "sit-in" demonstration. Marissa Johnson said when she looked out at the sea of furious faces during the Sen. Bernie Sanders rally, she felt:

> The utter and vile hatred that white folks have for you . . . It felt very emotional and it felt very spiritual to me in terms of having literally over a thousand angry, white people screaming at you, and you could tell in their voices, they hate you. They really hate you so much, and you're so inconveniencing them and their first thought when they are inconvenienced is violence. It was so similar to sit-ins in terms of what is somebody sitting at your [lunch] counter but inconvenience. In the grand scheme of things, as you really don't like black people, you don't want them there. White supremacy has such a violent, vicious, obviously irrational, response.

Johnson said that she understood why those who wanted to participate in sit-ins during the Civil Rights era had to endure practice protests first, in which their classmates and professors hurled epithets at them, to build their mental fortitude. There is no such training today, she noted. Still, all of the activists I interviewed imagined themselves as receiving the metaphoric baton from an icon in the 1960s Civil Rights Movement or the Black Power Movement of the 1970s. Brittany Packnett Cunningham explained:

> [I]t's the Black Power and Black Arts Movement that influenced me most. Late '60s and '70s folks like Kwame Ture and Gil Scott-Heron and Maya Angelou and Audre Lorde—people who took the foundations of the mid-century Civil Rights Movement and built something intentionally radical on top of it. They had an understanding of direct action and intellectual pragmatism . . . . [T]hey also elevated a level of scholarship that allows us to talk about things the way that we do right now. So without an Audre Lorde you wouldn't have a Kimberlé Crenshaw. Without a Kimberlé Crenshaw we wouldn't be talking about intersectionality. Without a bell hooks, we wouldn't be talking about why the Women's March needs to be intersectional and include a womanist agenda.

In addition to elevating the time-honored rhetoric of black scholars to levels of national discourse, Marissa Johnson said she was conscious even of highlighting a historic black activist's face in her protest. When she made the decision to interrupt Sen. Bernie Sanders, for example, she said she chose to don a T-shirt that read, "Fight like Fannie Lou [Hamer]," to commemorate Hamer's historically overlooked role in the Civil Rights Movement. She thought the shirt was particularly ironic too, insomuch as Pres. Lyndon B. Johnson interrupted Hamer's 1964 televised testimony to the Credentials Committee of the Democratic National Convention. Just as Hamer began to recount the beatings she sustained in police custody after she led black voter drives in her native Mississippi, Pres. Johnson preempted her televised speech with an unscheduled press conference.[5] Marissa Johnson said this time she was "the Johnson doing the interrupting" at the Sanders rally, in Hamer's memory.

Samuel Sinyangwe was the only activist who said that he channels an early 20th-century black activist. His idol, he said with a huge smile, is Ida B. Wells. He said he admires the fact that she was tabulating state-sponsored violence against black bodies long before the Internet made the aggregation of this data simple. He upholds her official report, *The Red Record*, as sacrosanct.[6] He said, "She was doing something very similar in an earlier time where it was much harder to get access to the information and much harder to just exist in that space."

Redeeming the Movement

While few activists spoke directly about wanting to change the image of a particular victim of police violence, they spoke more commonly, instead, about using their reports to undo the casting of the Black Lives Matter Movement and its protestors as violent. In nearly every interview, the activists expressed either anger or disappointment that legacy media consistently failed to mention the source of their frustrations with their local police departments, opting instead for the images of fire, brimstone, and cops clad in riot gear. Moreover, many of the participants said they believe the Black Lives Matter organization has not been disambiguated enough from the broader Movement for Black Lives in mainstream media. This creates a plethora of problems when it comes to reporting the major actors in a prominent campaign, Eve Ewing explained:

> It's a pet peeve of mine in the media when people call everything "Black Lives Matter." One of the most egregious examples being referring to things that DeRay Mckesson does as being under Black Lives Matter when in fact they are extremely separate . . . it's really lazy reporting to be honest. Especially here in Chicago, Black Lives Matter Chicago is one organization and they work in partnership with other orgs, but they say all of the time, please don't credit us for things that Assata's Daughters did, or that We Charge Genocide did.

Brittany Packnett Cunningham said that she tweets to inform the public about the coalitions that her organization, Campaign Zero, has formed with kindred groups in the movement. She explained:

> We know that people have been mislabeling the Movement after one single organization, but we are a collective Movement. So, I often remind people that past black movements were the same way. We called it the Civil Rights Movement. Correctly so, but there were lots of organizations who had lots of different tactics, aims, leaders, and constituents. They were oriented towards the same goal: a goal of racial equity and freedom. Goals of economic empowerment. Goals of the American dream. Right? Where it's liberty and the pursuit of happiness. So in the same way that SNCC, SCLC and NAACP and Core and the Panthers all had different tactics—and maybe in some ways even had some different aims—they were all a part of a

broader Movement. And that is exactly how Campaign Zero stands up with organizations like Black Lives Matter, the Black Youth Project, et cetera.[7]

Some activists spoke specifically about efforts to report on the movement to keep its momentum alive. Marissa Johnson said that there may be a temptation to frame the movement as dead, since some leaders are not as visible as they were at its inception in 2013. She explained:

People are like, "Oh, whatever happened to the Movement?" And what they mean is why aren't you protesting the same ways? Why aren't you confronting in the same ways? They are not understanding or acknowledging that people who have really decided to stick in this work, like myself, have moved on to other strategies that are more sustainable—especially in the era of [Pres.] Trump. A lot of work will be underground.

The final news frame that requires additional redemption, according to many of the activists, is the recurring failure to link police brutality to other systemic problems in some beleaguered black communities. Two participants, for example, said that national talks about police brutality should dovetail with discussions about U.S. public schools and black public health disparities. Eve Ewing explained: "I think that education and education policy issues are very frequently underrepresented in conversations about the Movement for Black Lives and that's something that I push back on a lot." Ewing published *Ghosts in the Schoolyard: Racism and School Closings on Chicago's South Side* in 2018, which highlighted the mass closure of public schools on Chicago's Southside. The city shuttered 53 schools in 2013, displacing at least 12,000 children—94% of whom were low-income and 88% were African-American. For Ewing, it is impossible to separate any storytelling about fatal police force from narratives of purposeful black "miseducation" in her hometown. Both cruelties disregard black futures, she said.

Similarly, Lincoln Mondy, who produced the documentary *Black Lives, Black Lungs*, said that he tweets to frame black public health issues and police brutality as interrelated:

There's an interesting story that one of the interviewees in my documentary told and that was that they were handing a letter to President Obama to get him to ban Menthol . . . but they had to cancel the press conference because there was another killing of a black man. They were supposed to go to Baltimore, but when that happened they had to cancel it and they felt almost silly just because they're like, "Oh, we can't talk about menthol when we're being killed in the streets" but it's also like, why can't we? This is the same. You see what happened on Twitter and your TV yesterday? That's what the tobacco industry's being doing for 50 years!

Mondy said that when he has discussed police brutality on Twitter as a public health issue, journalists have thanked him privately in his direct messages (DMs). Mondy allowed me to scroll through several of the supportive messages on his smartphone as we sat in a Washington, DC, coffee shop. He explained that many reporters have acknowledged that it was not a narrative link they might have made readily. He smiled over his coffee mug and then said that he believed most journalists who work for legacy media do want to "get it right." He said reporters fall short on covering the movement correctly when they do not regard activists as subject-matter experts.

Mark Luckie, the former journalist-cum-social media executive, agreed. He said: "I think the publications that are covering the Movement well, like the *Los Angeles Times* and *Buzzfeed*, have reached out to people who are an actual part of that community to report on what's going on. The organizations that are fishing for clicks are the ones that have tried to use people who really did not know much about those communities and lost the trust of the readers. I have been in a lot of newsrooms. I have seen what works and what does not."

The Role of Religion

Two of the 15 activists said they believe that they are doing "the Lord's work." One participant, Brittany Packnett Cunningham, is the child of two Christian ministers. Marissa Johnson is a former divinity student. Packnett Cunningham referenced religion to describe her childhood and the morals her parents instilled within her. She said: "My father was a pastor and a professor of black church history and black liberation theology. So my upbringing was very steeped in Afrocentric beliefs around community, around support, around understanding my history and the shoulders on which I stand." Packnett Cunningham laughed and added that in her house, "I learned all three verses to 'Lift Every Voice and Sing' [the Black American National Anthem] when I was a kid and had to know them from memory. This was not a game in my household."

Johnson was a bit more conspiratorial. She explained, "One of my influences is Dietrich Bonhoeffer [the German Lutheran pastor and Nazi resistor] because I'm a Christian. Dietrich Bonhoeffer was part of a collective who planned an assassination attempt on Hitler. [This was] a collective of pastors!" She continued: "If you're understanding what's happening in the United States and you understand fascism, then [you understand that] you don't resist in ways that are public. There are underground tactics that have to happen now. There were no protests to free the Jews [during the Holocaust]. That's not what happened. People had to create underground collectives in order to figure out how to break the law."

Other activists only made passing references to a higher power, as in believing that they had a "God-given talent" that they should share with their community. Ieshia Evans, for example, said from her home in Brooklyn, "I'm blessed that God decided to use me as a vessel to spread some type of awareness." Likewise, Devin Allen said the only reason he rose to such heights without formal training was because of God. "I didn't follow I guess the right, the traditional path of a photographer. I picked up a camera three years ago. I taught myself. I used social media. Then I landed on the cover of *TIME* . . . I think that bothers them [professional journalists], like, 'I had to [work for] 20 years. I had to go to school, but this young black kid is doing all these amazing things.' That's my path. That's my God-given gift." He pointed a single finger to the heavens.

Only one activist rejected the role of religion while discussing the movement: David Banner. At the time of his interview with my mobile journalism class in 2017, he had a new album out, called *The God box*. It was his first in seven years. On the track "August," he rhymes:

> You want God?
> I think I seen God in a skirt (in a skirt)
> (Yeah) She had deep black skin,
> But she was looking for herself on the out and not the in.

One of the young women in my class asked Banner what the lyrics meant. Was he riffing on feminism? Was he saying that black people were not being self-reliant enough in the campaign to end fatal police encounters? Banner smiled and nodded eagerly, seemingly pleased that the youth comprehended his message. He replied that organized Christianity can be a hindrance to black people. He explained: "I always ask people all the time, 'What are your demands?' I don't believe in hope. I don't want nobody's hope. White folks don't believe in hope. They're building that Heaven right now. We want Jesus to come back and save us. We want [Pres.] Obama to come back and save us. I don't believe in any of those. They're not coming. I personally believe that Jesus was the symbol that *you* could be a walking God."

One of the young men in my class exclaimed, "Facts! He's keeping it so 100 right now."

The class erupted with laughter. Banner chuckled easily with them, nodding on my smartphone screen via FaceTime. In that moment, I wondered how many of my students ever had imagined themselves that powerful.

6

#BeforeYouWatch

Activist Reports From the Field

In one of Devin Allen's iconic photographs of the Freddie Gray uprisings in Baltimore, two African American men interview a uniformed police officer. The image portrayed the men recording the exchange with an iPhone, which was rigged to a tripod and microphone. It was an image I saved to my computer's clipboard as I began my research. That picture generated so many questions. How do anti–police brutality activists use mobile devices to engage in sustained acts of black witnessing? How do these activists use Twitter as a news outlet to create and circulate protest journalism? To answer these questions, I used a Twitter collection tool called Twecoll to retrieve mobile device metadata associated with each activist's tweets. Twecoll scraped Twitter's application programming interface (API) for the type of device that generated a tweet, the mobile applications that the activists used, and whether the tweet appeared to be scheduled or live. These metrics provided a clearer picture of the activists' reliance on smartphones as an essential element of protest #journalism.

I chose January 2017 to collect my snapshot since many of the activists said in their interviews with me that they were anxious about what a Trump presidency would mean for their work. On the official White House petitions page, for example, someone who wished only to be identified by the initials "J.O." asked on January 22, 2017, that the U.S. government: "Formally recognize black lives matter as a terrorist organization." The petition read, in part: "It is time for the pentagon to be consistent in its actions—and just as they rightfully declared ISIS a terror group, they must declare Black Lives Matter a terror group—on the grounds of principle, integrity, morality, and safety."[1]

Samuel Sinyangwe, one of the Day 1's, told me about the petition in our interview. He was nervous about what being designated a terrorist would mean for his ability to continue bearing witness. "If that happened, I would not be able to fly," he told me, shaking his head. That Sinyangwe thought first of

Bearing Witness While Black. Allissa V. Richardson, Oxford University Press (2020). © Oxford University Press.
DOI: 10.1093/oso/9780190935528.001.0001

his mobility as a precarious privilege made me think of my own time in that Milan airport. I knew that kind of federal label would make it impossible for him to move around the world, to collaborate with police departments in person. This fight not to be silenced, I discovered, fueled much of the journalism I saw the activists create with their mobile devices.

The smartphone has been a gift and a curse for anti–police brutality activists. On the one hand, it has provided unmatched access to like-minded black witnesses. Moreover, smartphones have afforded speedy news distribution and the potential for international reach. At the same time, smartphones—and the metadata they generate each time that activists use them—have made it increasingly easy for federal and local law enforcement authorities to track black witnesses. This practice harks back to the days of the FBI's Counterintelligence Program (COINTELPRO), when federal agents spied on citizens illegally in order to dismantle their burgeoning social movements. This chapter, then, complicates our discussion of bearing witness while black. If the very tool that empowers the activists also has the potential to extinguish them, then the act of using video as evidence may be undone already—even before it had a chance to make real change. This danger, of the chain of black witnesses ending in this generation, is very real.

To analyze the scope of this problem I offer the smartphone's many advantages first. The 15 activists' timelines highlighted some promising news production patterns. They tend to cycle news through Twitter and other related social media in six recurring steps. I counter these findings though, with a discussion of other metadata that have made it easy for intelligence agencies to catalog the activists' activity. Taken together, I offer a cautionary look at what we must not take for granted: our First Amendment rights. If the smartphone helps law enforcement officials trample on African American citizens' rights to assemble peaceably or to speak freely, then bearing witness while black becomes more than a singular fight to end police brutality—it becomes an expanded battle to protect everyone's civil liberties, no matter their race.

The Gift of the Smartphone

Gordon Parks, the legendary photojournalist and black witness, once told Eldridge Cleaver, a militant leader in the Black Panther Party: "You have a 45mm automatic pistol on your lap, and I have a 35mm camera on my lap, and my weapon is just as powerful as yours."[2] For our 15 activists, Parks' claim holds true still. Nearly 83 percent of their tweets originated from Apple iPhone's native mobile application for Twitter. These data confirmed what Sinyangwe shared with me. He told me that the iPhone is the activist's preferred method of communication, as they believed it offered them a level of imperviousness to hacking and other security breaches during Black Lives Matter's infancy. For this reason, perhaps, none of the activists' tweets were marked "Twitter for Android" explicitly. It is possible, however, that some of the tweets marked, "Twitter Web Client," "Mobile Web (M5)," or "Mobile Web (M2)" came from a mobile device that runs on the Android platform. Still, only 9 percent of the tweets pulled in January 2017 came from all three of these options—combined.

In terms of other mobile devices, tablets still are not as ubiquitous as smartphones. Only 2 percent of the activists' tweets originated from an Apple iPad. Still, this rate of adoption is nearly triple the rate at which the activists used desktop computers or laptops to create and share news the month that Pres. Trump assumed office. Less than 1 percent of the activists' tweets in January 2017 came from the Twitter for Mac application.

The last trend I observed was the low adoption of third-party tweet "schedulers," such as Hootsuite, which indicated that the activists tended to report more breaking news than they did "evergreen" stories. As the activists' content is timely, scheduling a tweet in advance seems to be impractical for them. I found only one tweet that originated from Hootsuite. What activists did tend to do most with mobile apps was cross-pollinate their content across various social media platforms. Instagram, the world's leading photo-sharing platform, for example, was the third most popular mobile application that activists used to publish news to Twitter. The witnesses in this cohort were nearly 18 times more likely to push a picture from Instagram to Twitter than they were likely to use the iPhone's native camera app to upload to Twitter directly. This indicated that activists optimized their reach like professional journalists. Just as a local reporter's story might run in their hometown newspaper first, then get picked up by the Associated Press for publication in national news outlets, the activists syndicated their work too. For video they used Periscope—a live-streaming mobile app—to syndicate real-time footage to Twitter. The activists leveraged the app IFTTT too, which creates algorithms for publishing content across platforms. For instance, activists used IFTTT commonly to create a rule that posted all Instagram pictures to Twitter automatically.

All three of these major mobile trends—the over-indexing on Apple iPhone, the low rate of tablet and desktop use to post tweets, and the tendency to syndicate content across social media platforms—suggest that the smartphone has indeed become a critical tool for activist storytelling. This, unfortunately, has left black witnesses ever more vulnerable to state-sponsored surveillance. Every tweet an activist posts to Twitter can potentially reveal where they are, who else is nearby, and even what device they are using. Not even encrypted messages are safe from today's military-grade spying technologies. The activists tried to tell me this in the interviews. Being followed and photographed is not a figment of their imagination. It is domestic warfare—and it is unclear who will win.

The Curse of the Smartphone

About two years after I began writing this book, mainstream media began to report that the FBI and local police departments were using a sophisticated catalog of cellphone reconnaissance devices to spy on activists and other everyday U.S. citizens—most often without the required search warrant. The most common brand of these kinds of devices, known as the Stingray, became the umbrella term that journalists used to describe this smartphone hacking technology. Stingrays work by imitating cellphone towers. A user's smartphone signal and device data are routed to a law enforcement agency instead of a service provider (such as AT&T, Sprint, T-Mobile, or Verizon), without the user's knowledge or permission. Although Stingrays have been around since the 1990s, the technology was not used against law-abiding civilians often, said Jeremy Scahill, a journalist for the *Intercept*, during a March 25, 2016, broadcast of *Democracy Now*. Scahill told *Democracy*'s Juan González:

> The surveillance platforms that were created by and for the NSA [National Security Agency], the CIA [Central Intelligence Agency], other intelligence agencies, [and] the U.S. military—to target the communications of terrorists or adversaries or, you know, drug syndicates, smugglers and others—started to become a common part of police in this country, both on a local and state level, and also the FBI, on a federal level, for using these devices to target people in routine criminal investigations.

Scahill added that although the American Civil Liberties Union (ACLU) has filed many lawsuits and Freedom of Information Act (FOIA) requests to discourage local law enforcement agencies' use of the technology, the number of police forces that deploy Stingrays is astonishing. "There's almost no major law enforcement entity in the U.S. that isn't using some form of a Stingray," he said on *Democracy Now*. What is more, the devices have become more sophisticated as manufacturers gathered more user data and used that to perfect the technology. Now, no brand of smartphone is invulnerable to hacking.

Black Lives Matter activists discovered this firsthand in the movement's early years. In Chicago, as demonstrators assembled to protest the Eric Garner killing in 2014, they broke the news of a black SUV that drove alongside the group. Each passing of the truck caused glitches to occur on the activists' smartphones. A protester tweeted on December 4, 2014: "Wtf is this? It keeps flowing [*sic*] the protest. And it messes up my phone when it drives by #ericgarner."[3] Nearly 1,000 people retweeted the message. Chicago's local CBS affiliate, WBBM, picked up the story two days later, on December 6, 2014.[4] The television news station reported that the activists conducted counterveillance to pinpoint a public radio exchange between police who were at the protest and their department's headquarters.[5] An audio clip, leaked by the hacktivist group Anonymous, revealed that police targeted Chicago organizer Kristiana Rae Colón, the daughter of Chicago alderman Rey Colón. She was the main organizer of a Black Friday protest in the city.[6]

An officer said in the recording: "Yeah one of the girls, an organizer here, she's been on her phone a lot. You guys picking up any information, uh, where they're going, possibly?"

The other officer replied: "Yeah we'll keep an eye on it, we'll let you know if we hear anything."

Colón later told ACLU Massachusetts: "What's happening . . . is a template for how civil liberties can be stripped from citizens in any moment of social unrest. Police forces are more concerned with protecting retail and commerce . . . than they are with protecting the rights of people."[7]

To be clear, spying on civilians via cellphones did not begin with the Black Lives Matter Movement. CBS Chicago reported, for example, that the city's police invested in Stingray technology as early as 2008.[8] Journalists for the outlet interviewed Freddy Martinez, a Chicago-based privacy activist, who filed a FOIA request with the Chicago Police Department (CPD) for evidence that the force purchased the devices. CPD sent Martinez two invoices—one from 2008 and another from 2009—that revealed nearly $150,000 in Stingray purchases.[9]

Three years after a black witness exposed CPD's Stingray use on Twitter, an attorney living in the city filed a federal lawsuit that challenged the force's use of the secret tracking technology. Jerry Boyle told the *Chicago Tribune* that police intercepted data from his device at a Black Lives Matter protest on Martin Luther King Jr. Day in 2015.[10] Boyle is a volunteer for the National Lawyers Guild and attended protests regularly in that capacity to offer pro bono support for activists who were arrested. According to the *Tribune*, Boyle wrote in a press release: "The people of Chicago should be able to exercise their First Amendment rights to freedom of speech, association and assembly without being spied upon by police."[11] Boyle's official lawsuit opens with similar language:

> Modern cell phones are not just another technological convenience. With all they contain and all they may reveal, they hold for many Americans "the privacies of life." The fact that technology now allows an individual to carry such information in his hand does not make the information any less worthy of the protection for which the Founders fought.[12]

The Boyle case is awaiting a date for a jury trial. Chicago is but one of many major metropolitan cities that continues to track activists through their cellphones though. The *Intercept* reported in July 2015 that the Department of Homeland Security (DHS) has monitored the Black Lives Matter Movement nationwide since the Ferguson uprisings.[13] A FOIA request of the department's Office of Operations Coordination revealed that the agency tracked activists' smartphone location data, as well as information that they posted to social media platforms, such as Twitter, Facebook, and the now-defunct Vine. Even peaceful gatherings, such as candlelight vigils and black music festivals, were part of the reconnaissance efforts. Such surveillance calls into question whether DHS, which was created in response to the September 11 terrorist attacks of 2001, has overstepped its initial objectives to become, instead, one of the most indomitable civilian spying agencies that the world ever has seen. A DHS spokesman, S. Y. Lee, told the *Intercept* in an email:

> The Department of Homeland Security fully supports the right of individuals to exercise their First Amendment rights and does not provide

resources to monitor any specific planned or spontaneous protest, rally or public gathering. The DHS National Operations Center statutory authority (Section 515 of the Homeland Security Act (6 U.S.C. § 321d(b))) is limited to providing situational awareness and establishing a common operating picture for the federal government, and for state, local, tribal governments as appropriate, in the event of a natural disaster, act of terrorism, or other man-made disaster, and ensures that critical terrorism and disaster-related information reaches government decision-makers.

DHS documents revealed that the agency provided Google map images of protestor meeting places and live updates of demonstrations in key cities—just as it had done during the Occupy Wall Street movement of 2011. Federal monitoring of lawful gatherings by DHS is an effective deterrent for anti–police brutality protestors, no matter how benign the government claims its watching may be. Consider, for example, that Brittany Ferrell reported that her organization, MAU, dissolved after Ferguson police targeted her at every gathering she convened. The state's eventual lawsuit against her—in which it alleged she kicked a motorist's car when it plowed through a group of protesters—effectively slowed MAU's momentum as its key leader was indicted.

Fellow MAU founder, Ashley Yates, declined to do an interview for this book, yet spoke out about how federal and local authorities were following her too, in a 2016 Netflix docuseries. In *Truth and Power*, Yates recalled that a NYPD officer called her by her Twitter handle, BrownBlaze, as she protested on the frontlines. Just these few instances show that black witnessing remains as potent as ever. The highest levels of government seem to have summoned the ghosts of COINTELPRO, which dismantled many burgeoning social movements in the 20th century. That notorious FBI initiative ran from 1956 until 1971 and, although it was originally designed to root out Communism in the United States, grew to surveil white hate groups, what it deemed "black extremist groups," Puerto Rican groups, indigenous groups, and other leftist movements.[14] Illegal spying and organizational infiltration were common FBI tactics during COINTELPRO's 15-year lifespan. Maurice Mitchell of Blackbird, a group that supports anti–police brutality activists' First Amendment rights, told the *Intercept*, "The fact that our government is doing this—I can only assume to disrupt us—is pretty alarming . . . Directly after 9/11, people said, 'if you're not doing anything wrong you have nothing to worry about.' Well, now we're fighting back against police brutality and extrajudicial killings, yet they are using this supposedly anti-terrorist infra-structure against us."[15]

Mitchell's assessment of the leap the United States made—from post 9/11-vigilance to the Orwellian panopticon that we have now—was made more poignant to me when I realized the relationship between DHS and some of the PDs that came under fire between 2014 and 2018. In Baltimore, for example, not all of the police portrayed in Devin Allen's iconic *TIME* photographs are Baltimore City police. A *VICE* news report indicated that DHS deployed 400 officers from its Federal Protective Service to bolster the city's force.[16] Could it be, then, that all of the post-9/11 terrorist attack threats have waned so in-credibly in the nearly 20 years since the devastating events of that day, that now all our government has to spy on is its own citizens? Moreover, what if we got so efficient at rooting out foreign danger that there really was no other need for DHS? And what if protesting that fact ironically puts us even more on the radar for federal and local surveillance? This story—of how activists and intelligence agencies try to stay one step ahead of one another—is but one of the narratives that black witnesses pushed into the national discourse. As I continued to sift through Twitter, I found many more.

Trends from the Timelines and Frontlines

Even though using Twitter makes activists hyper-visible and, therefore, prone to surveillance, it remained an essential tool for many of the anti–police brutality movement's activists between 2014 and 2018. Between January 1, 2017, and February 15, 2017, I counted for each activist: (1) the total number of tweets sent during the first six weeks of 2017; (2) the number of original tweets versus retweets; (3) the number of @replies sent to address specific users; (4) the number of "favorited" tweets; and (5) each user's indi-vidual average daily rate of tweeting, to observe bursts and lulls of news pro-duction. These data points offered specific insight into an activist's prolificacy and their engagement with the public.

Quantifying commitment. The most prolific Twitter user is one of our Day 1's, Brittany Packnett Cunningham (@MsPackyetti). She generated an average of 70 status updates every day. When she was particularly inspired, Packnett Cunningham tweeted more than double her daily average. On the day of Pres. Trump's inauguration, January 20, 2017, for example, she pro-vided 161 updates. The day after that, as activists from various factions within

the broader Black Lives Matter Movement dialogued about what his election might mean for their varied missions, she tweeted 201 times. Packnett
Cunningham's Day 1 ally, Samuel Sinyangwe (@samswey), is the second
most prolific activist. He posted an average of 67 updates every day. Like
Packnett Cunningham, his all-time high coincided with Trump's assumption
of office. He tweeted 255 times on Inauguration Day, but tapered off the day
after, with only 88 tweets.

This round-robin pattern of participation is worth exploring. I noticed that
very often when Packnett Cunningham's participation was high, Sinyangwe's
was a bit lower on the same day. Then, on the following day, the inverse was
true. For example, on February 8, 2017, legacy media reported that Pres.
Trump made false claims about the U.S. murder rate being at an all-time
high.* The Day 1's engaged in Sinyangwe's so-called rapid response. Packnett
Cunningham tweeted 143 updates about why Trump's statistics were faulty on
February 8; Sinyangwe tweeted 92 updates. The next day, however, Sinyangwe
picked up the baton, posting 104 total tweets that day, while Packnett
Cunningham posted only 44. I should note here that during these two days,
the division of labor in terms of who reported what is fascinating. Sinyangwe
stuck to his role as investigative data scientist, churning out statistics to coun-
teract Trump's narrative of lawlessness in African American urban centers.
But Packnett Cunningham was busy too. She played the role of Capitol Hill
correspondent, reporting through the smokescreen of Trump's news cycle
distraction to the more pressing issues of that week: the contentious Senate
confirmations of Betsy DeVos as secretary of education and Jeff Sessions as attorney general. As Sen. Elizabeth Warren earned her now-infamous rebuke for
reading a letter from the late Coretta Scott King on the floor, which opposed
Sen. Sessions, Packnett Cunningham published a flurry of tweets that kept an
eye on the legislative branch of government. Sinyangwe, meanwhile, attacked
the executive branch's data. Both of the Day 1's said in the interviews that they
took turns reporting so that no one burned out. Sinyangwe explained: "We
were communicating on text chats and we're always interfacing back and forth
about things . . . We're all in different places, so we're doing things virtually."

Eve Ewing, Devin Allen, and Marissa Johnson round out our Top 5 Twitter
users between January 1 and February 15, 2017. Ewing (@eveewing) boasted
a daily average of 62 tweets. Allen (@byDVNLLN) averaged 50 tweets per
day. Lastly, Johnson (@rissaoftheway) clocked about 32 tweets daily. By

---

* *See* the CBS News timeline, *Today in Trump*: http://cbsn.ws/2k2KCpo.

contrast, Alicia Garza (@aliciagarza) posted nothing at all. When I pored over her Twitter timeline (which I summarize later), I saw that she experienced a disproportionate amount of trolling online. This may have turned her away from the platform until her eventual return about one year later.

Some of the activists I interviewed were still finding their voices on Twitter. Shellonnee Chinn (@schinn) and Ieshia Evans (@ieshiaevans) started 2017 slowly, with only a dozen news updates between the two of them. In my interviews with both activists, they explained that they started to share more of their updates on different platforms. Chinn said she created a Facebook page so that people could follow her federal trial, calling it her Casebook.[17] The platform allowed her to upload pertinent documents and audio files in an interface that is more static, she said. Facebook users do not have to scroll through months of Twitter updates now to find a media item, she explained further. Similarly, Evans said that her decline in average daily tweets—from one update per day in 2016, down to one per week in early 2017—is due to a migration to Instagram.* "I'm in my learning phases," she said, adding that she only recently joined in July 2016 after her participation in the Alton Sterling protests in Baton Rouge. She did so because someone made a fake account in her name, she said. She worked with Twitter to create a verified account.

Original content versus pass-along content. I tallied the number of original tweets versus pass-along tweets (also called retweets) that each activist created and shared. User-generated content was that which the activist appeared to have produced firsthand. Pass-along content was information that was transmitted secondhand, either from a legacy media outlet or an ally in the movement. Less commonly, the activists passed along news from detractors of the movement, but only in terms of providing the background necessary to counter it. This was a very important and nuanced designation to make because it revealed the nature of a particular activist's witnessing. Samuel Sinyangwe, for example, is one of the Top 5 most prolific Twitter users in the group. It may be tempting, at first glance, to dismiss his productive Twitter timeline as merely rehashing legacy media news stories, since 81 percent of his updates are retweets. Sinyangwe uses the retweet function, however, to provide context for his firsthand reportage. Before he launches an assault on a faulty statistic or a news myth, he tweets a litany of links to news stories that have reported a story incorrectly, then follows up with his

---

* *See*: https://www.instagram.com/luvempress911

analysis. It is his version of academic citation, adapted for Twitter's discursive sphere. Sinyangwe retweets to side publicly with his Day 1 colleague, Brittany Packnett Cunningham too. He retweets most commonly her posts that suggest specific policy changes.

Marissa Johnson, another Top 5 Twitter user in our group, was a top "retweeter" too; 80 percent of her posts fell into this category. Johnson used the retweet function in the way it was imagined initially, however, to share news secondhand, although not from legacy news outlets. Johnson instead amplifies the voices of local protestors who are tweeting live from a demonstration. In this manner, Johnson shows solidarity for those who are still engaged in frontline campaigns, even though she said that she has shifted her focus to more clandestine forms of organizing. Garza's Twitter timeline reflects a similar pattern before her year-long break from the platform, in that she formerly retweeted live reports of Black Lives Matter chapter protests around the country too, thereby centralizing organizational news. Aside from Sinyangwe and Johnson, the remaining Top 5 Twitter users part ways in terms of shared retweet habits. While Brittany Packnett Cunningham and Devin Allen both retweet about half of the time—54 percent and 49 percent, respectively—Eve Ewing does so only 23 percent of the time. Ewing devotes the majority of her Twitter use to the next metric: audience engagement.

Estimating engagement with @replies. When a Twitter user wants to speak directly to another user, the platform allows them to use the "@" symbol before a Twitter handle. Both users then receive instant notifications when the conversation is updated. A high number of @replies is "an indicator of visibility because it acts as a measure of the extent to which other users have taken note of and gone to the trouble of replying to or mentioning the user," scholars Axel Bruns and Stefan Stieglitz have explained.[18] Mark Luckie, one of our Rogues, was a top audience engager. Nearly 42 percent of his tweets were devoted to speaking to another user directly. Eve Ewing and Clint Smith, the Bards, are the second and third most likely to engage in extended conversation with other users, respectively. Roughly 30 percent of their tweets are conversations with other users. This is noteworthy because both Ewing and Smith were not big retweeters. For Ewing, only 23 percent of her tweets tend to be retweets. For Smith, it is only 22 percent. These statistics suggest that our Bards are the most likely to report original news and opinions. Moreover, they are more likely to engage with the counterpublic, asking and answering questions from people who are inside and outside of the movement. Another remarkable finding was the degree to which David Banner replies to his followers. Although he is a celebrity, he responds to users who tweet him directly about 20 percent of the time, making him a Top 5 conversationalist in this group. Like his fellow Bards, Ewing and Smith, he reports from the frontlines and offers original commentary on the movement too.

The activist who is least likely to engage in conversation on Twitter is Attorney Chris Stewart. His professional code of conduct precludes it, he explained. Stewart said:

> I speak a lot on telling young lawyers how to use social media. You have to be aware of what you're doing and saying. You can't say a thing you wouldn't say in court. Whatever you say on social media, you'd better be able to back it up. . . . When you're talking about a case, don't just get up there making outlandish statements or anything like that to get more followers. I probably could have 50 million followers on stuff if I said flamboyant, outlandish stuff . . . but you know I kind of stick to the facts of the investigation as I can prove it.

Estimating engagement with favorites. The final metric of engagement that I gathered was the "favorite" feature of Twitter. When users like a tweet that they have read, they can click a heart icon that appears underneath the tweet to indicate their approval of it. Like the @reply function, this metric is a measure of visibility, since users have to make an effort to read the tweet and decide whether they like it enough to let the author know that they do. Again, the Bards and the Day 1's lead the cohort in engagement—this time in terms of "favorited" tweets. Clint Smith's tweets were "favorited" nearly 1 million times in the month of January 2017 alone. Packnett Cunningham's tweets garnered 236,449 favorites; Ewing's earned 229,593; Sinyangwe's drew 203,868; and Banner's gleaned 44,252.

The Activists' Editorial Workflow

Perhaps the most fascinating thing to observe in the activists' Twitter timelines was their ability to cycle through six steps of news production, just like professional journalists. The first half of their communication included: (1) observation, (2) discussion, and (3) authentication of potential news stories, leveraging the "@" function of Twitter's architecture to hide in plain sight. Then, activists engaged their audiences through (4) production, (5) publication, and (6) agitation, deploying their hashtags and stories throughout various counterpublics.

Establishing a Digital Enclave

Even though Twitter is public facing, I was surprised to find that it could be used to form a digital enclave. In the early stages of reporting the activists used very few built-in Twitter features, such as @ mentions and hashtags. This contributed to a level of strategic invisibility. I observed, for example, that the @ messaging convention effectively cloaked exchanges between activists, making it very difficult to relocate an original thread by using Twitter's search function. While it is true that Twitter's native search engine does allow one to look up tweets by user with the @ symbol, the search results then display an ambiguous variety of things: the referenced activist's profile page; any @ mention used in the context of a direct conversation between an activist and someone else; or (perhaps most nebulously) an @ mention that refers to the activist, but does not indicate a conversation with her. For example, the hypothetical message, "I loved hearing @aliciagarza speak at my campus today," would appear in a general, big data Twitter search, but not in my granular timeline analysis of Garza's own exchanges with her followers. Thus, I found that using Twitter's @ function to search natively for discrete exchanges between users retrieved noisy data. It is difficult to pinpoint the beginning and end of a conversation using an @ search, so I argue that such exchanges are semiprivate and enclaved—until a Twitter user drills down to evaluate a singular timeline, preferably in chronological order.

But since neither the desktop nor mobile version of Twitter allows one to invert the display of tweets this way—and since Twitter's interface features an endless scroll of results that does not export to Excel easily—to do so would mean following my multistep method, of scraping the individual timeline data from Twitter's platform, then exporting it to a spreadsheet for further analysis. The communicative veil that results from all these cumbersome steps is profound. Activists can discuss breaking news among themselves before distributing a story widely. Their preliminary work includes three phases in the enclave: (1) observation (categorized as pass-along tweets), (2) discussion (categorized as conversational tweets), and (3) authentication of news pegs (categorized as conversational tweets).

Observation. Sometimes breaking news came from pass-along tweets that I coded as headlines or referrals. In the instance of Dread Scott, for example, his Twitter timeline revealed that followers often tweeted him a flurry of links to television station and newspaper headlines. Scott said he read the stories completely before providing his own updates on the platform. At other times, the news production process began with referrals from other activists or supporters. This happened most commonly when legacy media outlets had not yet reported on an issue. A user contacted Alicia Garza directly on her timeline, for instance, to ask for her assistance to highlight a fresh case of police brutality in New York. Garza tweeted to the user, "@tdowlats can you send me an email with more details?"[19] Garza's response, which instructed the user to continue conversing in an even more enclaved space, emphasizes how much of this observation phase tends to occur in semiprivate digital locales. Once a news peg and potential source or subject matter expert was legitimized, however, activists moved into a period of lively discussion.

Discussion. Activists used conversational call-to-action or coalition-building tweets to begin gathering facts about movement-related news stories. In some cases, breaking news of a social injustice called for an in-person meeting of the activists, rather than a social media campaign. Garza, for example, retweeted hours after her request for the aforementioned private email: "RT @BLMNYC: Action tonight at Union Square at 5pm. Organized by our comrades @NYC_ShutItDown." I should note that most tweets in the discussion phase of the enclave mirrored an editorial budget meeting in a traditional newsroom. The activists called on each other to see who had propinquity to the breaking news event or who had the means to travel there. Those who were deemed closest were "assigned" the story and tasked with following up with the group. In other cases, the activists determined that a "pool" of reporters (to borrow common newsroom parlance) would better serve a story.

When two or more allied organizations working under the Black Lives Matter Movement umbrella coordinated their reportage, I deemed this coalition building. Devin Allen's Twitter timeline, for example, revealed that he worked closely with Baltimore BLOC, a nonprofit group in his hometown. On January 26, 2017, he tweeted a crowdsourced request: "RT @BmoreBloc: If you know any immigrant or refugee in need of support here in #Baltimore, please connect with us. #RefugeesWelcome." The thread was filled with responses from those in need of help. Allen then referred those users to deeper enclaved spaces, often giving them email addresses to connect further. Together, Allen and Baltimore BLOC curated eventually dozens of testimonies from immigrants and U.S. citizens who were barred from entering the United States during the 2017 travel ban. Without this discussion phase, it may have been much harder for Allen to locate those affected by the travel ban by himself.

Authentication. The final enclaved step that I observed was authentication. The activists moved often to a fact-checking phase before publishing any stories or engaging further with suspicious Twitter accounts, through conversational tweets coded as retweets or inquiry. Ieshia Evans, for example, said that someone made a fake Twitter account with her likeness. Evans worked with Twitter to verify her account. After she was legitimized online, she drafted a press release to authenticate her online identity further. The bots disappeared, she said.

The activists did not know it, but bots would become even more of a problem as the Black Lives Matter Movement approached its fourth birthday. In January 2018, *Mother Jones* magazine wrote a scathing investigative piece on Russia's infiltration of the movement. The publication found that a Russian disinformation firm created more than two-dozen highly active Black Lives Matter bot accounts on Twitter that fooled even its CEO, Jack Dorsey. The bot known as @Crystal1Johnson was among the most prolific of the fake accounts. She tweeted one day in March 2017: "Nobody is born a racist." Dorsey retweeted the message during a trending #WomensHistoryMonth conversation.[20] When Twitter realized that Johnson's account was a fake, the company deleted it. Twitter took the extraordinary move of releasing to the public the 10 million tweets that were posted from purported Black Lives Matter bots since 2009 too.

Carving out the Counterpublic

When activists were ready to engage, posts of original news stories shared three qualities. First, the post contained numerous hashtags, which facilitated future retrieval. Second, the updates provided a quick summary or editorial stance. Third, the tweets posted messages simultaneously to other social media platforms, such as Facebook or Instagram, through app syndication. I observed three outward-facing phases of this editorial process: (1) production, (2) publication, and (3) agitation. The production phase included tweets that featured the activists "teasing" subsequent news coverage, much like local evening news broadcasts do before air-time. Next, they published the story. Then, the agitation phase inspired heated debate, which sometimes led to imbroglios with the Alternative Right (alt-right), incumbent Democrats, or assumed beneficiaries of white privilege.

Production. Activists most often provided location-based updates to let other users know where news events were taking place. These kinds of tweets often resembled broadcast journalist news tags or print journalism datelines, where the activists began their Twitter threads with "I'm streaming from . . . " or "I'm logging off now from . . . ." Once an activist informed the news audience of her arrival, she usually began on-the-scene coverage with a thesis statement of sorts, which described the battle of the day.

The activists served as national correspondents too, often re-broadcasting hyper-local movement news. These tweets included typically some call-to-action statement. For instance, Garza retweeted a Black Lives Matter chapter update: "CHICAGO JAIL SUPPORT NEEDED AT DIVISION & LARABEE! Badly beaten #AltonSterling #PhilandoCastile demonstrators need your support." A few hours later, she added: "Give & share #BatonRouge bail fund & legal support fund for those arrested last night after #AltonSterling march." The next day, Garza circulated a pledge to encourage her audience to protest in their own cities. "Yes yes and yes. Solutions over sidelines #TakeThePledge https://t.co/hXov4ubMSs."

The process of "signing on," then stating a brief solution for the day was a common pattern. It helped prime potential supporters about a campaign's goals. In other words, these news audiences were shown, essentially, what would be considered a successful day on the frontlines. These kinds of tweets stopped short of providing a live video or minute-by-minute textual updates about a protest. Instead, these kinds of tweets perhaps made audiences want to "stay tuned," to see what would happen next.

Publication. Once activists picked a location and a political position—in terms of the solution they would like to see—they published multimedia news reports. Livestream video footage, photo essays, and text-only stories were the most popular formats.[21] Garza provided a feed of Tamir Rice's mother making a speech in Ohio, for example. Police shot the 12-year-old black boy in a Cleveland, Ohio, park in 2014, as he played with a toy gun. Alicia Garza tweeted: "There is a live-stream for Samaria (Tamir's Mom) Rice's keynote for @M4TF & @KentState May 4 @ 12pm (EDT). Tune In."

Garza then offered live tweets of the speech's most rousing portions. Pictures and videos rounded out the report.

Similarly in April 2016, Chicago activists from three allied groups—Black Lives Matter Chicago, Assata's Daughters, and Black Youth Project 100—chained themselves together to form a human barricade across Lake Shore Drive, one of the city's main thoroughfares, on National Football League Draft Day. Garza collaborated to produce a live dispatch with a local chapter. She tweeted: "@BLMChi @AssataDaughters @BYP_100 shutdown the LakeShore drive https://t.co/IDR7bmcDtj." The hyperlink referred viewers to a live stream of the campaign, which did not end until the women were arrested late into the night. The thread continued with further instructions for news audiences to send the pictures to legacy media outlets to ensure the women's safe release.

The activists engaged in what professional reporters call "enterprise" or "human interest" journalism too. This kind of coverage marked movement-related milestones. Chris Stewart, for example, used Twitter to produce a thread of news stories that commemorated the anniversary of Walter Scott's birthday. He was serving as an attorney for the family at the time. He wrote: "Happy birthday to Walter Scott. Gone but not forgotten. You woke up the world to injustice and civil rights violations." The tweet is punctuated with Stewart's photo essay of a local commemoration of Scott's life.

Agitation. Once a story was pushed into counterpublic spaces, hostile engagements on Twitter seemed to be par-for-the-course for many of our black witnesses. I created the new coding category, "imbroglio" to capture these exchanges. Whether it was an individual troll who attacked every post that an activist made, or an activist's statement of disdain for a political ideology or political party, these debates on Twitter bore very little news value. Techno-culturally speaking, the imbroglios are avoidable, in part, because Twitter does offer a "block user" feature, which prevents trolls from contacting an activist again. In practice, however, the activists said that their opponents create new bots every day to begin fresh rounds of harassment.

They battled most commonly with members of the so-called alt-right movement, the Democratic Party, and seemingly oblivious beneficiaries of white privilege. The alt-right is "a set of far-right ideologies, groups and individuals whose core belief is that 'white identity' is under attack by multi-cultural forces using 'political correctness' and 'social justice' to undermine white people and 'their' civilization," according to the Southern Poverty Law Center. Many of the imbroglios that I observed appeared to debate alt-right political stances. Alicia Garza, for example, engaged in these types of online quarrels most commonly, which may have led her to leave Twitter for nearly a year. When then-presidential candidate Donald Trump took the stage at the RNC on July 21, 2016, for example, she tweeted: "I don't know what I'm watching right now but I imagine this is the kind of speech Hitler would make #FreedomNow."

A user replied the next day, "You don't know much about Hitler do you? He's not calling for gas chambers for blacks, sweetheart."

Another user defended the Black Lives Matter activist, tweeting: "neither did Hitler honey. There's a reason concentration camps where [sic] kept secret."

Nearly a dozen additional commenters joined the fray at this point, and the conversation devolved into name calling, with no further mention of the other RNC news items that the participant had posted.

Garza offered the penultimate tweet of the thread: "I'm not your sweetheart. And you might wanna brush up on your history homie."[22] The activist continued to tweet well into the early morning about what a Trump presidency might mean for Black Lives Matter. She said at 3:00 a.m.: "To all my folks: LGBT, Muslim, Black, undocumented, crip, Latinx, and more—I love you. Time to ride. Fascism must not win #FreedomNow."

Heated exchanges, such as these, highlight the rough transition from conceiving journalism in supportive enclaved discursive spaces to debating those same stories in an increasingly polarized counterpublic.

The New Protest #Journalism

Nearly every iconic picture of the uprisings in Ferguson, Baltimore, New York, and Baton Rouge contained seas of cellphones. What were people doing with these devices? And were some devices better than others, when it came to creating news? Also, I wanted to know what role Twitter played in the production and spread of movement-related news. I searched for any observable, replicable process of storytelling on the platform, and I found it.

To the first point, I discovered the smartphones have been a gift and a curse to today's anti–police brutality activists. The good news is that the devices double as newsrooms in the activist's pockets. I kept hearing—over and over again—how some of these activists met on Twitter first, then in real life second. The thread of connecting to the social network through their smartphones enabled them to organize remotely and massively, in ways that previous black social movements have not been able to do. That more than 80 percent of the activist tweets I observed came from an iPhone is quite telling, in terms of the power that smartphones gives today's activists. In fact, Devin Allen uses *only* an iPhone now to bear witness to his community's healing in Baltimore. He gave the high-end DSLR camera that brought him his acclaim to a local child.

Despite the ease of using mobile devices over fancy equipment, however, it is important to note that activists are giving intelligence agencies ever more access to their most private moments, whether they know it or not. To be fair, surveilling leaders of black social movements is not new. Intelligence agencies wiretapped both Malcolm X and Dr. King's telephone lines and tailed them with photographers regularly. The innovation here, however, if we can call it such, is that smartphones provide more access to personal data than 1960s-era landline telephone taps ever could. These newsrooms in the activists' pockets are also homing devices: beacons that signal their whereabouts, as well as known connections between other leaders on the ground. For these reasons, I am worried for the movement, in this regard. As PDs ramp up financially exploitative practices like asset forfeiture, as they did in Chicago, or ticketing petty offenses, as they did in Ferguson, so too will they become more flush with the cash they need to purchase military grade equipment. Ieshia Evans's question rings in my ears as I write this. She asked my class why that cop met her in "war gear" when she was wearing a sundress. Her word choice was perfect. This *is* a new war. It is bigger than the War on Drugs, in many ways. This is a war against free speech. Just as soon as smartphones put the power to look into the hands of working class people, powerful forces have worked hard to take back that power. I do not think the manufacturers of smartphones ever imagined that they would be leveraged in this way, to document the actions of the previously unaccountable. This time of reckoning is upon us now, however, as black witnesses have awakened a sleeping giant, so to speak. It is evident that recording fatal police encounters—that *seeing*—is a significant threat to the U.S. racial status quo. The scrambling of smartphone signals during protests or the sweeping of cellphone data with Stingray devices is only the beginning of this invasion of privacy and this infringement of First Amendment rights, if we leave it unchecked. It is encouraging to see activists using Twitter to push conversations about illegal surveillance, and other instances of digital excessive force, into the counterpublic.

In this vein, Twitter has become a true, ad-hoc news outlet for all of the 15 activists I interviewed. They comprise a newsroom that engages in a six-step process to do journalism. At an enclaved level, the witnesses situate their missives a priori within the Black Twitter sub-community, so that those in the collective can observe, discuss, and authenticate a potential news peg. Direct mentions and @replies abound during this phase, as the activists talk directly either with each other or with their news audiences. It is in this phase that some witnesses engage in offline conversations also, likely through Twitter's DM function or through emails and text messages on their smartphones. When the activists feel confident that a story is viable, it moves from Black Twitter's enclave to the broader Twitter counterpublic. The activists engage in production, publication, and agitation until their topics engender debate in Twitter's discursive spaces, and beyond.

It is important to note too, that the 15 activists I profiled did not report news under any pretense of objectivity. Their reports were juxtaposed often alongside serialized "call-to-action" tweets that encouraged audiences to telephone an elected official, participate in a rally, or visit an organizational meeting. The news content, for this reason, was unapologetically subjective and often defiant. It was unafraid to challenge legacy reports or statistics that were false or contributing to hegemonic narratives of blackness. As all of these activists admitted receiving death threats, they were aware that they may not be able to stop the powers that be from watching them. They were emboldened, still, at the prospect of looking back. Samuel Sinyangwe, the data scientist, said his reportage "runs circles around the experts," adding that it feels "pretty cool."

In examining the activists' Twitter timelines, I did find evidence that Black Twitter may be stratified along class lines. Many of our 15 activists shared the same educational markers of success, in terms of attaining advanced degrees from prominent universities. This may be a function of my snowball recruitment process, in that the activists recommended those with whom they shared the closest ties in real life. It bears further study, however, to make sure that research about Black Twitter or black social movements that take place via Twitter are not skewed to focus mainly on elite users who have the leisure time to access the platform around the clock.

My last key finding that emerged from the Twitter analysis is that the platform can support an enclaved black public sphere, even though it is a public communication platform. No, it will never be completely private. Twitter's timelines are noisy though, so it is very easy to miss the flow of side conversations that occur between activists. Any conversations that I highlighted in this chapter came as the result of drilling down into individual tweets to find a thread of dialogue within a very small sliver of time. A casual Twitter user may not have the time to mine through threads in this way, so black witnesses work as quietly as the platform's interface allows until they are ready to enter the counterpublic with hashtags, live videos, and poignant images. Many of the activists continue to rely on Twitter to make content "go viral." Others, like Devin Allen, have migrated to Instagram, using the visual platform to post photoessays that celebrate the pain and beauty of being black. In either case, the activists who continue to bear witness to the anti–police brutality movement—even when no particular hashtag is trending—indeed form a Greek chorus of sorts, reminding elected officials and, sometimes, legacy media that the whole world is watching.[23]

PART III
SELFIES

7

Shooting Back

The Making of a Black Visual Public Sphere

"Please don't shoot her," I whispered. Someone had emailed me a clip of Brittany "Bree" Newsome's now-iconic climb to the top of the 30-foot flagpole at the South Carolina state house. I watched the petite, African American woman scale it with apparent ease, then calmly cut down the Confederate flag. She raised the traditional symbol of white nationalism and said: "You come against me with hatred and oppression and violence. I come against you in the name of God. This flag comes down today!"[1]

Newsome made it down the pole safely and into the waiting handcuffs of area authorities. "I am prepared to be arrested," Newsome told the police— one white, the other black—as she unhooked herself from the flagpole. The police helped her over a small fence that surrounded it. "The Lord is my light and my salvation; whom shall I fear?" she said breathlessly as she was taken into police custody. Her partner, James Tyson, who had been filming the protest with his cellphone, was arrested too that Saturday, June 27, 2015.

Newsome's choice of Scripture punctuated a painful realization: just ten days before her protest, Dylann Roof, a white man, had gone into Emanuel AME Church in Charleston, participated in an hour of Bible study, and fatally shot nine black people. Various legacy media outlets reported that he wanted to start a "race war." Pres. Barack Obama traveled down to South Carolina on June 26, 2015, to eulogize the church's senior pastor, Clementa Pinckney, 43, who also served as a State Senator. In a stirring oration, he said:

> Removing the flag from this state's capitol would not be an act of political correctness; it would not be an insult to the valor of Confederate soldiers. It would simply be an acknowledgment that the cause for which they fought—the cause of slavery—was wrong—the imposition of Jim Crow after the Civil War, the resistance to civil rights for all people was wrong. It

Bearing Witness While Black. Allissa V. Richardson, Oxford University Press (2020). © Oxford University Press.
DOI: 10.1093/oso/9780190935528.001.0001

would be one step in an honest accounting of America's history; a modest but meaningful balm for so many unhealed wounds.

Newsome recounted to *Vox*, "I was riding down to Columbia to take the flag down when I was listening to [Pres. Obama's] eulogy and it only confirmed for me that we were doing the right thing—very much in the spirit of the history of civil disobedience and the history of the civil rights movement in this country."

Newsome also told *Vox* that she felt called by God to represent her ancestors who were enslaved in South Carolina. "I recognized just how powerful the symbolism of it all was . . . I could just feel at that moment I really did symbolize the struggle . . . of all these generations of black people to dismantle white supremacy."

The imagery of a black woman with the Confederate flag in her hands—looking *down* at police—indeed activated Twitter that Saturday morning. Hours after her climb, the hashtag #FreeBree began trending. A San Francisco-based organization, called CREDO Action, opened an IndieGogo crowdfunding account to raise money for her bail.[2] Celebrities, such as the National Basketball Association's Dwyane Wade, urged people to donate. The campaign exceeded its goal of $20,000 in less than a day—garnering $70,000 in just seven hours. In the following weeks, Newsome appeared in a round of morning news shows. Artists even rendered her in cartoon form, often as a superhero.[3,4] The movement had a new icon.

In the third, and final, part of this book, I want to explore the powerful, deliberate, and fresh imagery that Black Lives Matter activists have inspired. Whereas the first third of this book focused on theories of rebellious looking, and the second portion recounted the activist's own rhetoric surrounding the price and the process of that looking, the next three chapters analyze what their gazes have meant for us all. How have their sightings made us see *ourselves*? Perhaps the most successful aspect of the Black Lives Matter Movement has been its ability to take the United States by the chin, as an impatient parent would do with a wayward child and exclaim "*Look* at me when I am talking to you!" Forcing a country to regard its Dark History—all that is monstrous, that is shameful, that seethes just below the surface of civility—has been a key tactic of the allied groups that are working in this moment. In this chapter, I illuminate the three strategies that Black Lives Matter activists have used to create a black visual public sphere.

The Movement's Three Semiotic Approaches

The so-called "selfie generation" has responded to the tragic images of black death by creating its own visual vernacular. Devastating images of black death unquestionably propelled the Black Lives Matter Movement forward, as video after video emerged between 2013 and 2018. Frontline witnesses captured heartbreaking footage. Distant witnesses then viewed those videos. That process, as we have discussed it, was credited generally with galvanizing local and national uprisings. What we have not yet discussed, however, is how the imagery from these demonstrations reverberated further throughout the U.S. political imaginary, to create an ever-expanding catalog of relevant iconography: a black visual public sphere. Scholar Kirsten Pullen has surmised, "Public debate now relies heavily on visual images rather than verbal discourse, as traditional news outlets as well as new media traffic in images as much as words." She added, "As cell phone cameras, surveillance videos and self-made digital recordings proliferate, literacy increasingly includes the ability to produce and read images as well as words."[5]

The study of reading symbols for meaning is called semiotics. In terms of television and film, Umberto Eco wrote that messages can be deconstructed from video by focusing on: "(1) the intentions of the sender; (2) the objective structure of the message; and (3) the reactions of the addressee to items 1 and 2."[6] The Eco model can explain the process of black witnessing whereby: (1) frontline black witnesses record fatal encounters with police to hold cops accountable; (2) the footage's "structure" provides video evidence of a killing; and (3) the "addressee" (the distant witness) reacts to that video by participating in some form of protest. I wish to add a step to this process: (4) distant witnesses encapsulate or "freeze frame" their protests by producing a new visual symbol. That symbol is what circulates in the black visual public sphere, alongside the video evidence of the slaying, for debate and remembering. Black Lives Matter activists—and those who have been inspired by them in the broader popular culture—have used three tactics to create freeze frames: historic juxtapositions, symbolic deaths, and satiric memes.

Historic Juxtapositions

All of the activists spoke of police brutality not as isolated incidents captured serendipitously on camera, but as episodic proof of a pattern of abuse that is decades old. The activists depict these temporal arcs between the various eras of police terror by creating historic juxtapositions. Distant witnesses either: (1) remix an old image in a new context or (2) mash-up an old image alongside a new one to compare and contrast timeframes. Distant witnesses who have been inspired by the Black Lives Matter Movement have appropriated images most commonly from the Gunpowder Plot of 1605 and the Civil Rights Movement of the 1950s and 1960s. Images of its two martyrs, Guido "Guy" Fawkes and Dr. Martin Luther King Jr., respectively, serve as popular templates onto which distant black witnesses map new meanings.

Remixing old images of resistance. The Gunpowder Plot of 1605 was a failed attempt to assassinate King James I of England and VI of Scotland. A group of nearly a dozen Catholics, which included Guy Fawkes, planned to bomb the House of Lords during the state opening of England's Parliament on November 5, 1605. They were protesting religious persecution. After an anonymous letter tipped off the heads of state, Fawkes was found guarding the explosives. At trial, Fawkes was convicted of high treason. He was hanged, drawn, and quartered.[7] After Fawkes's death in 1606, Parliament designated November 5 as a day of "thanksgiving." Londoners were encouraged to burn effigies of Fawkes.[8] Parades and fireworks eventually punctuated the holiday. Fawkes got a makeover when the film *V for Vendetta* (2005) became a cult classic.[9] A superhero donning a Fawkes mask took down a fascist regime set in a British dystopia. Thanks to the film, Fawkes's visage suddenly became synonymous with anarchy and rebellion for a new generation.[10]

The Fawkes mask was a prominent fixture in both the global Occupy Movement and the Arab Spring Movement in 2011.[11] When peaceful protests in Ferguson turned violent in August 2014, Fawkes emerged there too. The first time I saw a brown forehead and ears peeking from behind the white Fawkes mask was online, in an August 21, 2014, *TIME* magazine piece.[12] It was jarring. The person appeared to be African American. He was standing next to a black police officer. A sea of black protestors surrounded them. It was Frantz Fanon's *Black Skin, White Masks* come to life. By the end of the *TIME* article, I was thinking of the black poet Paul Laurence Dunbar's famous lines: "We wear the mask that grins and lies/It hides our cheeks and shades our eyes/This debt we pay to human guile;/With torn and bleeding hearts we smile."[13] The Fawkes mask was grinning. I am almost certain that its wearer was not.

The masked protestor, however, remixed what was old to give it new meaning. The presence of Fawkes's white face, rather than the protestor's black face, simultaneously called into question the paucity of white allies in the photograph; the irony of both Fawkes and Mike Brown as controversial martyrs; and the symbolic cloaking in whiteness to render oneself invisible and safe. These three layers of meaning created a complex visual iconography for Ferguson, beyond the burning buildings and clouds of tear gas. To don a plastic, white face amid a predominantly black demonstration would have seemed antithetical to the cause in past social movements for African American civil rights. However, its appropriation in a modern movement for black lives—situated in a neoliberal era that pretended not to *see* color— makes the mask all the more powerful.

The mask functioned to create a visual synecdoche also: to see one masked protestor there in Ferguson was to view a part of a virtual whole.[14] While frontline Ferguson protestors were in the streets, a group of so-called "hacktivists," called Anonymous, joined the movement. Anonymous had been active in Occupy and in the Arab Spring, breaking into the world's top information systems to disrupt the flow of information from governments to the people. In Ferguson, the group vowed to protect all protestors by accessing the town's employee records. If any demonstrator was harmed, the group said in a YouTube video, addresses of Ferguson officials would be made public.[15] Anonymous promised also to hack into the PD's databases to find the name of the officer who killed Mike Brown. The mask, therefore, served as a visual proxy for Anonymous activists who were working clandestinely behind computers.

Mashing up the old and new. Images of Dr. Martin Luther King Jr. commonly provide historical juxtapositions of past black social movements. In chapter 2, I described how Black Lives Matter protestors have crafted their protest placards to resemble the "I am a man!" posters of the 1968 Memphis sanitation worker demonstrations. That was King's final campaign before he was assassinated. Perhaps even more famous than that King remix, however, is that of the kneeling Colin Kaepernick. It had been nearly a month and a half after the back-to-back killings of Philando Castile and Alton Sterling. A summer of nationwide protests was winding down. Football season was gearing up. Kaepernick, the quarterback for the San Francisco 49ers, did not stand for the playing of the national anthem in the third preseason game on August 26, 2016. He went unnoticed, in fact, when he remained seated for the first two preseason games on August 14 and 20.[16] A tweet from Jennifer Lee Chan of Niners Nation changed that. In her post, he was pictured amid his teammates, sitting on the bench in uniform.[17]

He explained after the game in a press conference: "I am not going to stand up to show pride in a flag for a country that oppresses black people and people of color. To me, this is bigger than football and it would be selfish on my part to look the other way. There are bodies in the street and people getting paid leave and getting away with murder."[18]

By September 1, Kaepernick's interview had gone viral. NFL fans tuned in to see if he would continue his silent protest. Instead of sitting, this time he kneeled. His teammate, Eric Reid, joined him. Reid later wrote in a *New York Times* editorial piece: "In early 2016, I began paying attention to reports about the incredible number of unarmed black people being killed by the police. The posts on social media deeply disturbed me, but one in particular brought me to tears: the killing of Alton Sterling in my hometown Baton Rouge, La. This could have happened to any of my family members who still live in the area. I felt furious, hurt and hopeless."[19]

Reid explained further how the symbolic protest evolved. He wrote: "After hours of careful consideration, and even a visit from Nate Boyer, a retired Green Beret and former NFL player, we came to the conclusion that we should kneel, rather than sit, the next day during the anthem as a peaceful protest. We chose to kneel because it's a respectful gesture. I remember thinking our posture was like a flag flown at half-mast to mark a tragedy."

Professional and student athletes from various sports kneeled in solidarity with Kaepernick for more than a year. At the top of the 2017 football season, the silent protest showed no signs of stopping. Pres. Trump said in a September 22, 2017, political rally in Alabama, "Wouldn't you love to see one of these NFL owners, when somebody disrespects our flag, to say, 'Get that son of a bitch off the field right now. Out. He's fired. He's fired!'"

Bernice King, who is Dr. King's youngest child, responded directly to the president on Twitter the next day. She wrote: "The real shame & disrespect is that, decades after the 1st photo, racism STILL kills people & corrupts systems. #America #TakeaKnee @POTUS."[20] She punctuated her tweet with a picture: a visual mashup of Civil Rights Movement protestors kneeling alongside a modern image of Kaepernick assuming the same position. King's tweet was "liked" more than 20,000 times. Within two days, Bernice King had set the narrative agenda, entering this mashed-up image into the black visual public sphere. *TIME* magazine published a retrospective piece on Dr. King's kneeling as protest.[21]

Bernice King's reaction to the NFL players' demonstrations (and the uproar it caused in some circles) inspired her to freeze frame a new visual symbol. The juxtaposition of the two kneeling men grounds the Black Lives Matter Movement historically. It serves as a reminder that while this type of civil disobedience may have been practiced before, it is being made new by a fresh set of dissenters. The passing of several decades between the two pictures makes the cause all the more poignant, since even time has not healed these wounds.

Symbolic Deaths

The start of the communication pathway—from frontline black witness to the eventual, mediated distant witness reaction—begins with death. Media scholar Barbie Zelizer has written extensively about the news media's depiction of people who "are about to die—as a prism for addressing news images more broadly."[22] While such images can be starting points for discussions about sweeping social ills, Zelizer has argued that a picture offers only "flashbulb memories" since the viewer cannot see the person dying in real time. Only the moments before and after one's expiration are visible with a still camera. Video is not limited in this way. The horror of seeing Eric Garner's body go limp; of watching Philando Castile take his last breath; of watching the bodies of Walter Scott and Tamir Rice fall to the earth below them, all were made possible by video. Some distant witnesses who were triggered by this footage have chosen to photograph or film symbolic deaths in the form of die-ins and human chains. Even black America's top musicians have engaged in the practice, feigning death on video to launch a conversation. I call this addition to the black visual public sphere "corporeal iconography."

Staging die-ins. Protestors from the Civil Rights Movement crafted part of its visual messaging around nonviolent lunch counter sit-ins. Today, Black Lives Matter activists stage "die-ins," to enact symbolic deaths. A dozen clergy members fell "dead" to the ground, for example, in a Capitol Hill cafeteria at lunchtime in January 2015 after yelling, "Black lives matter!"[23] Flash mobs of protestors have dropped dead in front of the world's largest Apple stores, at packed train stations, and during high-brow piano concerts.[24] Black bodies even have fallen to the ground in the nation's largest retail center on Black Friday: at the Mall of America in the late Philando Castile's home state of Minnesota.

In December 2014, *BBC News* asked, "When did die-ins become a form of protest?"[25] The news outlet's investigation of the trend featured a picture of a person laying on the ground, face up. The person wore a Guy Fawkes mask. A cardboard box placard was placed over their chest. It read, "I am a human. Don't shoot."

Naima Keith, deputy director of the California African American Museum, explained to *Los Angeles Times*, "It [the die-in] forces people . . . to see and interact with the black body in a way that is very powerful. It's a way of claiming space."

Similarly, Helen Molesworth, the chief curator at the Museum of Contemporary Art has surmised "[T]hey understand that to occupy the public space isn't to only occupy the street—it's to occupy the Internet, the meme, the hashtag. . . . [S]treet activism was designed to be caught on a camera. Black Lives Matter has understood how to be received on the Internet, on social media."

Linking chains. Black Lives Matter activists use their bodies to form human chains in stunning displays of corporeal iconography too. The visual metaphor here is rich, insofar as African American subjugation has been held together literally by chains: shackled Africans at the auction block; black convicts leased to work on railroads in chain gangs; and chained school doors in states like Virginia, which refused to integrate even after the Supreme Court ordered it to do so. Moreover, every new victim of police brutality joins a long, mythical chain of previous martyrs. When the body is used to create a human chain in protest, therefore, it addresses the crisis of witnessing that we explored in chapter 2. Since the slain cannot rise again and protest their untimely deaths, the living stand as intercessors—filling the gaps in time and testimony.

"The idea of people linking arms and closing up the subway train in Oakland in response to the shooting of Oscar Grant—or using bodies to shut down a bridge—it's directly connected to dealing with state violence in our lives," activist Nina Angela Mercer explained to the *Los Angeles Times*. "It's the body being violated, so using the body as part of the movement, I think it's a direct response to that."[26]

Black Lives Matter activists tend to form human chains in some of the world's busiest thoroughfares. They have used their bodies to block the 405 freeway in Los Angeles,[27] Lakeshore Drive in Chicago while the city hosted NFL Draft Day,[28] and even the tarmac at London's Heathrow airport.[29]

Researchers at the Rudin Center for Transportation at New York University counted more than 1,400 protests in nearly 300 U.S. and international cities related to the Black Lives Matter movement from November 2014 through

May 2015, according to the *Washington Post*. Half of these protests involved the formation of a human chain to disrupt traffic at a peak time, in a bustling place.[30]

U.S. urban highways, journalist Emily Badger explained, are "white men's roads through black men's homes." She added "People occupied these spaces long before they felt they had to occupy the roads we built on top of them." Protest at these sites, therefore, are as visually arresting as they are historically symbolic.[31] As highways typically have been built through blighted neighborhoods—allowing the middle-class to zip into a central business district for work and back out to the suburbs in time for dinner—its blockage calls attention to that which we have tried to ignore. Highways allow us *not* to see poverty and its persistent problems. Putting one's body on the line in such a contested space sends the strong message that activists are unwilling to be ignored any longer.

Feigning resurrection. The final kind of symbolic death that distant witnesses have produced for the black visual public sphere is that of the feigned resurrection. Perhaps the most famous examples are from two of black America's top crossover entertainers: the Pulitzer Prize-winning rapper Kendrick Lamar and the Grammy Award-winning songstress Beyoncé Knowles-Carter. Both Lamar and Beyoncé's artistic works provided a popular culture corollary to a nascent national dialogue. In Kendrick Lamar's 2014 song "Alright" he spins a tale of triumph amid an urban backdrop. He famously announces in the refrain: "We gon' be alright!" The simplicity of the message—that despite the struggle black people would emerge victorious—proved to be a balm to Black Lives Matter protestors. Journalists hailed the tune as the "new black national anthem."[32] Viral videos of protestors singing it at rallies flooded the Internet. And Lamar picked up another round of Grammy Awards that year.

What is more notable, perhaps, is that Lamar's music video for "Alright" is just as popular as the song; it has been viewed more than 100 million times on YouTube. The stark, black-and-white footage opens in the Bay Area of California, then progresses south, to Los Angeles. In a year, 2014, when the United States viewed a succession of dead black bodies lying prostrate on the ground, "Alright" dared to show Lamar floating high in the air like a black superhero—even standing on a light pole in one magnificent scene. As quickly as Lamar ascends, however, a white police officer appears in the bottom of the frame. The cop takes aim at the rapper and makes a shooting gesture with his hand. Lamar falls from the light pole, blood spraying from his wound during his descent. It is a jarring scene that does not seem to match the song's jubilance. Lamar hits the ground and lays silently for a beat. Then, he opens his eyes and smiles. Black liberation theologians have argued that Lamar's resurrection in "Alright" symbolizes the freedom that comes with fearing no one but God. "[I]f God got us we then gon' be alright," Lamar indeed says when he opens the song. James D. McLeod Jr. explained further:

> The rap artist Kendrick Lamar, in his masterful record *To Pimp a Butterfly*, seeks to elucidate the black experience in the United States by describing the manner in which the threat of death always affects the way African Americans view their lives. In addition, on the album, Lamar celebrates the ability of members of the African-American community to courageously face this danger while still declaring power and strength within their race.[33]

Lamar's resurrection in "Alright" functions in the black visual public sphere to suggest immortality also. Frontline black witnesses who captured the deaths of victims of police brutality immortalize the slain. Distant witnesses who capture the movement's ongoing works immortalize the struggle. In both instances, neither the people nor the purpose truly ever dies.

Beyoncé's symbolic death in her music video, *Formation*, struck similar notes when it debuted in 2016. Throughout the work the singer pivots between several New Orleans-inspired scenes, such as laughing in a 19th century–style parlor with friends or channeling Voodoo vibes from a front porch. Perhaps the most memorable scene, however, arrives at the end. The New Orleans PD car that Beyoncé lays atop sinks slowly into Hurricane Katrina's rising flood waters. Her eyes close as she drowns. The camera performs a jump cut. Beyoncé reappears, resurrected, in the parlor. She is wearing all white and twirling a parasol like a Southern belle.

Critics of the video claim that it appropriated news images of protest without making any sincere statements about police brutality. Alicia Wallace, for example, seethed:

> The song lyrics and video content are profoundly divergent; they send two different messages, and lack sensitivity toward survivors of traumatic events. The song itself continues to center Beyoncé, alluding to haters, paparazzi, and designer clothing. She ultimately places her stamp of approval on

the same capitalist system that has oppressed generations of the same black people the song is said to empower.[34]

Laura Bertens situated Beyoncé antithetically, stating that *Formation* worked masterfully to create a black visual public sphere for a discrete group of African Americans. She explained:

The video strongly appeals to a sense of shared identity amongst the black community of New Orleans . . . and does so by invoking a sense of group memory, only directly and fully understandable, supposedly, for this specific community. . . . Beyoncé invites those who possess the cultural capital and memory to understand the images and lyrics to step in formation with her.[35]

Somewhere between these two analyses of Beyoncé's video lies the true meaning of her rebirth at the end of the work. I believe that her reaction to the frontline black witnesses' videos, via *Formation*, was a rumination on black death en masse. Beyoncé visually connected police brutality to the federal government's brutality, of leaving poor, black New Orleans to fend for itself in the wake of one of the most catastrophic hurricanes in history. By exploring the deaths that both police brutality and Hurricane Katrina have wrought in the black community, Beyoncé drew historic ties between the various ways that racism has killed African Americans. Still, like Lamar, Beyoncé's resurrection suggested a transcendence from tragedy. Both artists' rebirths, in two different settings, suggest that the Black Lives Matter Movement will neither die with one person nor be confined to one U.S. town.

Satiric Memes

The movement's final semiotic approach to crafting a black visual public sphere involves satiric memes. Lisa Guerrero has argued that black satire "serves to both critique society and legitimate black rage in a society that systematically invalidates black rage."[36] Comedians such as Dave Chapelle, Keegan-Michael Key, and Jordan Peele rose to prominence with namesake sketch comedy shows that lambasted the country's alleged colorblind turn. Similarly, black witnesses to the Black Lives Matter Movement often use biting humor to create visual critiques of racial injustice. Perhaps the most viral memes include "Black Guy on the Phone," #AskRachel, and "BBQ Becky."

Black guy on the phone. When Martin Baker decided to attend a rally in Ferguson to support Officer Darren Wilson (who fatally shot Mike Brown), there is, perhaps, no way he could have known that he would become one of Black Twitter's most infamous icons. According to the *Guardian*, the Republican congressional candidate was the only African American person to participate in the all-white rally on August 17, 2014. A picture of Baker talking on a cellphone surfaced to corroborate his presence. In it, he looked peeved and a bit defensive.[37] He told the *Guardian*, "People are too quick to play the race card. Lawlessness knows no color."[38]

In less than 24 hours, Black Twitter released its fury. An Uproxx blog post described it: "Upon hearing of his presence at the rally and his head-scratching comments, social media tore Baker a new a**hole, calling him everything from an 'Uncle Tom' to comparing him to *Boondocks'* Uncle Ruckus and *Chapelle Show's* Clayton Bigsby. Yeah, he's definitely not the most liked guy right now."[39]

In the most popular macros-style memes, Baker's picture was superimposed with hilarious potential conversations that he could have been having on the phone.[40] Black Twitter continued to produce variations on the joke for nearly six months. Baker earned a reprieve by the year's end but resurfaced in February 2017. Twitter user @Jay_50_Williams tweeted a picture of Baker shopping in a convenience store. He wrote: "I think I just found the guy from the meme in a soda shop lmao."[41] The photograph garnered more than 19,000 likes and 11,000 retweets in less than 48 hours, thereby solidifying Baker's place in the black political imaginary.

The Baker memes highlighted the frustration that many African Americans felt toward a black man who could have become a hashtag himself. By standing on the other side of the political line, Baker conjured old images of black obsequiousness in the face of white terror. As Black Lives Matter is unapologetic in its approach, his participation in the rally created cognitive dissonance for those who supported the frontline demonstrators. Instead of resorting to low insults, Black Twitter elevated his presumed disloyalty to the level of immortal Internet infamy.

#AskRachel. Rachel Dolezal became the next subject of the so-called dragging culture in 2015. In March, Dolezal claimed that she had been sent hate mail. President of the Spokane, Washington, chapter of the NAACP, Dolezal said that someone placed threatening materials in her mailbox. An investigation revealed that no one but Dolezal (or another NAACP staffer) could have accessed the box. Dolezal remained in local news media headlines for the rest of the spring season, championing various Black Lives Matter-inspired initiatives. The *Coeur d'Alene Press* printed an exposé on June 11, 2015, however, that introduced Dolezal to the nation.[42] In the piece, Dolezal's parents claimed that she was a white woman who had been disguising herself as black for more than a decade. When the story broke, a local news outlet, KXLY attempted to interview Dolezal about her race. She walked abruptly off camera. Taylor Viydo, a reporter for the KREM news station in North Idaho, found a childhood picture of Dolezal. She was blonde and smiling. Black Twitter, again, unleashed its anger with a series of ingenious tweets.

The format was deceptively simple: African Americans posted multiple choice "tests" of Dolezal's blackness with the hashtag (#AskRachel). In each iteration of the game, the test "proctor" posed three to four possible answers to a question that presumably only black people would know. The underlying premise, and comical device of the joke, was that if Dolezal truly were black, then she would know the right answers. That was one level of the satire. The deeper level, however, was that the questions posed were very superficial performances of blackness. Black Twitter asked her about the proper way to make potato salad, the names of main characters in iconic black films, and so on. This tongue-in-cheek quiz material reduced blackness to a series of trivia questions—not a complex state of being or seeing. This was, perhaps, the most ironic part of the joke: if one assumed that a "black card" could be earned by merely answering a set of questions, then one truly has never known or appreciated black culture. Blackness, according to the #AskRachel meme, was not a costume or a phase. Although Dolezal never publicly apologized for misrepresenting herself, she resigned from NAACP on June 15, 2015—four days after the scandal broke. The #AskRachel meme dissolved soon after that announcement. Dolezal remained a pariah in the black visual public sphere though. Journalist Hannah Davies explained:

On Twitter and beyond, Dolezal's name is shorthand for anyone brazenly partaking in cultural appropriation, or generally being misguided about race (Kanye West, among others, has been accused of "Dolezaling"). Pictures of the former NAACP president and civil rights activist complete with Afro-style weave often pop up as punchlines where non-wokeness is concerned. (Too much fake tan? Dolezaling. Misunderstanding racial politics? Dolezaling.)[43]

The irony of Dolezal's name becoming a verb is that blackness, indeed, is something people *do*. It is as performed as it is policed. Satire helped black witnesses—especially black women—articulate the insult of invaded corporeal and visual space.

BBQ Becky. The final viral meme that has lampooned contemporary racism is that of so-called "BBQ Becky." Jennifer Schulte, who is white, called the police on two black men who were barbecuing at a lakeside park in Oakland, California, on April 29, 2018.[44] A YouTuber named Michelle Dione Snider posted a video of her confrontation with Schulte. In the video's description she explained:

> At around 11:20 AM a white woman approached a black man named Deacon for having a BBQ grill at Lake Merritt today. She told him he could not BBQ there and called the police. She would not leave Deacon alone. A young black woman [sic] was walking by overheard how the white woman was harassing him telling him he can not [sic] be there, she stopped and asked the woman to leave her alone. The white woman became aggressive with the woman. She started filming the woman's aggressive behavior and has told us it's up on Facebook (probably a live stream). Shortly after that Deacon's friend Kenzie arrived. According to Kenzie, the woman said, "Oh another nigger." She proceeded to tell all three of the people at the BBQ table that she owned the park, and they are not allowed there. She also said them they were going to jail. Kenzie's wife (me) was up the street finishing brunch at Lakeshore Ave. He texted me a picture of the white woman and said: "If I go to jail this who did it to me." So, I walked over to the scene, and that's where the video starts. I arrived 12:50 PM.[45]

A crowd of people surrounded the black men with smartphones, protecting them by bearing witness. Snider shouted at Schulte: "It seems like a new Jim Crow going on because for some reason every time I see it, black people are the ones targeted regarding barbecuing at the lake and you're a perfect example of it right now."

Schulte shrugged and remained on her cellphone.[46] The women continued to argue until the police arrived. Ultimately, the police did not arrest the black men. The video has been viewed more than 2 million times.

Daily Show comedian Roy Wood Jr. tweeted the image of Schulte on the phone alongside the Baker meme on May 11, 2018. He wrote: "Black Twitter Meme Council, I respectful [sic] propose that 'Black Man on Phone' be replaced with 'White Lady Spoils BBQ.'" The tweet garnered more than 37,000 likes and 10,000 retweets in just one day.[47]

Black Twitter sprang to life, photoshopping Schulte's image into various displays of black jubilation. Schulte appeared calling the police on the 1963 March on Washington, on a Beyoncé concert, on Pres. Obama's official swearing-in, and on and on.[48] The memes became national news by mid-May 2018. Local organizers in the Bay Area then seized the moment to take the meme to the next level. A group of several hundred Oaklanders planned a weekend picnic that they dubbed "BBQing while Black."[49] The New York Times covered the meme-within-a-meme. One attendee, Logan Cortez, told the outlet, "It was a sea of love and blackness and food and fun."[50]

The BBQ Becky meme inspired a national conversation on "existing while black." Legacy news media were primed to report further incidents of egregious police calls, in which the black "suspect" proved to be involved in nothing nefarious at all. Without BBQ Becky, the New York Times might not have reported on whites calling the police on an African Yale student who was napping in a dorm lounge, the group of black women playing golf "too slowly," or the two black men who wanted only to have a business meeting in a Philadelphia Starbucks.[51]

As with other satirical memes, black witnesses channeled the humiliation of racist encounters with biting wit. By holding Schulte accountable for her actions—and by reclaiming the site of the humiliation with an ironic, grand display of unity—activists created two new arresting images for the Black Lives Matter Movement. The BBQ Becky meme, after all, truly is about the contested, yet everyday spaces that African Americans must fight to inhabit. By joking about a white person calling the police when black people are doing mundane things, activists forced Americans to check their biases in similar situations.

The Lasting Impact of the Black Visual Public Sphere

We are living in a visual paradigm. That paradigm is not only "read-write"; it is full of opportunities to create or mashup media to invent new symbolic meanings. Distant black witnesses have been masterful at using images to advance the dialogue about Black Lives Matter ideologies. The first images that stirred the public were videos of death in real time. Those images spurred protests. The protests then spawned their own visual iconography. Perhaps even more remarkable, however, is how the movement's visual public sphere continues to evolve now, past imagery of black death to critiques on black *life*. Bree Newsome's undoing of the Confederate flag, Colin Kaepernick's kneeling, and human chains blocking urban freeways all function to remind the viewer that Black Lives Matter is not just about police brutality. It is about the freedom to live and thrive without harassment, or vigilante, or state-sponsored violence. Historic juxtapositions, symbolic deaths, and satiric memes serve as visual shorthand to address systemic racism and the social ills that it inspires. These semiotic approaches contextualize the movement, allowing activists to situate their tactics and messaging on a historic continuum of civil disobedience. At the same time, the collective cathartic laughter at satiric memes, such as BBQ Becky, reinvigorates the movement by offering shared cultural touchstones that strengthen black solidarity. Change can be slow. National news coverage often cools. Memes can sustain a dialogue between crises or major demonstrations, to remind a nation that these issues are always at the fore for marginalized communities of color. Lastly, the black visual public sphere is essential because it marks time to create a collective memory. Historic juxtapositions help activists see when patterns are repeating or when progress is being made. Symbolic deaths, in the form of die-ins or mock resurrections in artistic works, force us to consider the real and existential costs of black lives lost. It would be disingenuous to end here, however. The other caveat of the black visual public sphere is that it can terrify just as much as it can empower distant witnesses. Sometimes the inability to *un*-see binds every fiber of one's being in ways that scholars tend to overlook when they are extolling the virtues of mobile media. In the next chapter, I pull back the veil on the price of witnessing.

8

#NoFilter

Exploring the Trauma of Black Witnessing

Four days before Michael Brown's death galvanized a movement, police gunned down 22-year-old John Crawford III in an Ohio Walmart store. Crawford was on the phone with the mother of his children as he shopped, on August 5, 2014. Ronald Ritchie, who is white, placed a 911 call from the store to report a black man roaming the aisles with a shotgun. The man was pointing it at children and women, Ritchie alleged. Police arrived at the scene and quickly rounded the corner, into the aisle where Crawford was shopping. The police did not Mirandize him. They opened fire almost instantly.

Police reports later stated that an aggressive Crawford advanced at them with a gun. Surveillance footage from the store showed a different story. In the videos that Walmart released, Crawford was shown pointing what turned out to be an air rifle toward the ground.[1] He intended to purchase the BB gun and had taken it off a rack to hold while he continued shopping. At no point did Crawford ever point it at anyone. In fact, Crawford was alone in the aisle when the officers ambushed him. The videos showed a startled Crawford running away from police then falling to the ground, where he lay dying.

"It was horrible. I don't think anyone wants to hear on the phone their child dying, taking their last breath," said Crawford's mother, Tressa Sherrod. Sherrod was home with the mother of Crawford's two young children, Leecee Johnson, while Johnson was speaking to him on the phone.[2]

The police contacted neither Sherrod nor Johnson in the immediate aftermath of the shooting. Instead, they asked Crawford's friend, Tasha Thomas, who was waiting in the car for him, to exit the vehicle. Thomas, 26, was taken in for questioning. The tapes from the recorded session revealed that Det. Rodney Curd threatened Thomas with jail time if she did not tell police where Crawford had gotten the gun. Thomas stated repeatedly that Crawford did not enter Walmart with a firearm. Curd accused Thomas of being intoxicated.

Bearing Witness While Black. Allissa V. Richardson, Oxford University Press (2020). © Oxford University Press.
DOI: 10.1093/oso/9780190935528.001.0001

"I swear to God on my dead brother's grave! I don't know anything," Thomas exclaimed.

Near the end of the 90-minute interrogation, the officer informed Thomas that Crawford was dead. "Unfortunately, John has passed away as a result of this," Det. Rodney Curd said.[3]

Thomas covered her face and sobbed, slumping in her chair.

A grand jury decided not to indict Officer Sean Williams of the Beavercreek PD, less than two months after the incident. No settlements have been reached with the family either, at the time of this book's writing. Ritchie, whose false 911 call led to the killing, was neither fined nor indicted for any crime. It has been five years since Crawford's death.

Perhaps even more heartbreaking than the non-indictment is what happened to those closest to Crawford. In March 2016, Crawford's children were found wandering alone on a Cincinnati city street. Their mother, Leecee Johnson, who listened to him die over the phone, was charged with four counts of fourth-degree child endangerment. She was sentenced to 18 months incarceration at the Ohio Reformatory for Women in Marysville.[4] *She* is serving time while the police who killed her partner are free. Crawford's friend, Tasha Thomas, died in a mysterious car crash with a companion. Eyewitnesses said their car was speeding at 90 miles per hour, at least, when it careened into a tree on New Year's Day 2015.[5] The killing of John Crawford III will forever affect his boys, who will grow up without a father to guide them. His death perhaps rendered the mother of his children mentally unstable and diminished her capacity to care for her children. And Thomas took untold trauma to her early grave.

Even at the level of distant witness, the Crawford killing was incredibly traumatic to some. A bystander to the Walmart shooting died, for example. Angela Williams, 37, suffered a cardiac arrest when the police ran past her in the store, to gun down Crawford.[6] Andrew Hawkins, who was a wide receiver for the Cleveland Browns, was not in the store at the time of the shooting, but felt so moved by the video that he wore a warm-up jersey with Crawford's name on it in a 2014 football game. The shirt also bore the name of Tamir Rice, the 12-year-old boy who was killed by police in Cleveland, roughly three hours away from Beavercreek, where Crawford was fatally shot. When the press asked Hawkins why he decided to bear the names of both slain Ohioans, he fought back tears and said: "The thought of what happened to Tamir Rice happening to my little [son] Austin, scares the living hell out of me."[7]

I write of these events to illustrate that media scholars tend to ignore the ripple effects that *seeing* causes. We opine often about the promises of a democratized and empowered contingent that has the power to topple certain media relationships. But what happens when the witnesses topple *along with* the corrupt systems that they attempt to expose? Or what if the systems never topple at all—they simply sway a bit, as if shoved? This chapter explores those associated traumas. Bearing witness while black, after all, is gazing into forbidden space—the space of vigilante and state-sponsored violence against black bodies. It is a ferocious space that many African Americans always knew existed, even though they never had enough visual evidence to prove that it did. Even Ida B. Wells, who kept a written tabulation of lynching victims, never saw federal legislation to ban its practice in her lifetime. Videos were supposed to change everything. Videos were supposed to be the proof that marginalized communities needed to corroborate their claims of excessive, and often fatal, police force. What happens, then, when black witnessing bears no punitive fruit? The realization that maybe black lives *do not* matter is simply too much for some distant witnesses to bear.

As a result, the movement has lost some of its leaders to suicide, incarceration, or some combination of these. Moreover, activists are beginning to disagree about the whether they should continue to circulate videos of fatal police shootings. In view of these unintended consequences of black witnessing, I analyze its myriad effects here. In this chapter, I wish to explore what it means to absorb a mediated account of a fatal police encounter. I do not expect that scholars will agree any time soon on whether mobile-mediated viewings of black death help or harm race relations in the United States. Instead, I want us to think now about the ways in which news organizations must make different decisions regarding whether to loop such footage on live television, since the black body's mutilation for so many years served as entertainment for white supremacists. When police are not punished for these black deaths, and when news media air these deaths with the casual frequency of a sports highlight, then black witnessing runs the risk of being exploited for capitalist gain.

The Horror, the Horror

Perhaps one of the most poignant moments in Joseph Conrad's controversial novella, *Heart of Darkness*, is when its central character, Kurtz, is on his deathbed. The narrator, Charles Marlow, described his last moments thus: "Anything approaching the change that came over his features I have never seen before and hope never to see again. . . . He cried in a whisper at some image, at some vision—he cried out twice, a cry that was no more than a breath: 'The horror! The horror!' "[8]

Kurtz's final words are meant to give the reader a glimpse into his psyche. Many scholars have written about the profound sense of regret that he must have felt when he regarded a life spent oppressing native people in Africa, in pursuit of colonization. Eighty years later, *Heart of Darkness* was reset during the Vietnam War for the film *Apocalypse Now*. A young Marlon Brando played the role of Kurtz and again sputtered the words—"The horror! The horror!"—as he reflected, presumably, on the senselessness of the war. If the predominately black cities and towns in the United States today were the third imaginative setting for *Heart of Darkness*, would the police officers who committed fatal shootings of black men, women, and children feel a Kurtzian sense of remorse? Or would they feel, after years of media priming, that they were merely upholding "law and order" in their respective communities?

Darren Wilson, for example, has said that he has a "clean conscience" about killing Michael Brown in 2014.[9] Blogger Colette Shade argued accordingly, in 2016, that many of the police shooting videos actually function to reinforce social hierarchy through mediated horror. She wrote: "If hierarchy is order and order is good, then the overturning of hierarchy is inherently disorderly, and inherently bad. Police brutality is a combination of warning and punishment for those at the bottom of the hierarchy."[10]

If we extend this line of thinking, we can reason that some non-black witnesses, who may not have "weighty baggage," might believe that these videos depict the *maintenance* of power. This helps to explain why the videos evoke visceral reactions in activists and aloof responses from those who oppose the Black Lives Matter Movement. This clash—of victims arguing with victim-blamers—has wrought incredible horror in the lives of some Black Lives Matter activists. The mortal ripple effect that a fatal police encounter creates expands the circle of black death often to include many more people than the original victim. Before I compare and contrast how today's smartphone videos teeter on the brink of racial exploitation, I want to explore this concept of related secondary and tertiary deaths further. Black witnessing is not without consequence. It would be disingenuous of me to present this kind of looking as one filled with valor only, and not horror.

The suicides. Ten days after Michael Brown's dead body lay on Canfield Drive in Ferguson, Missouri, for more than four hours, Kajieme Powell walked into a local convenience store in the neighborhood. The 25-year-old man stole a couple of energy drinks and a pastry. Then, he walked out of the store. This is where the video of Powell's last moments begins.[11] As people coming in and out of the market warned him not to taunt the police, whom the shopkeeper had called, Powell paced back-and-forth in front of the establishment.

"This is not how you do it," someone scolded Powell in the video as another onlooker passed by, shaking his head and laughing.

The laughter ended abruptly when the police SUV arrived. Two officers hopped out, their guns drawn.

"Shoot me! Shoot me! Kill me!" Powell screamed.

The police obliged him within 23 seconds of their arrival, firing upon Powell nine times. His body fell to the ground instantly. The police then handcuffed the dead man.

"It does not seem like it should be so easy to take a life," wrote Ezra Klein for *Vox*, noting also, "There was no warning shot, even."[12]

The police report describing the incident stated that Powell advanced on them, holding a knife high above his head. The video, however, showed Powell backing up when the police SUV arrived initially, only to walk toward them slowly with his hands by his sides. He was holding a butter knife. Powell's family explained later that he had experienced a psychotic break, which may have been triggered by Ferguson's ongoing trauma in the aftermath of Michael Brown's killing. One blogger surmised: "As a result of the nation's patchy, frequently inadequate mental-health-care system, police are all too often the first responders to mental-health crises. Powell's death is a worst-case reminder of why this is can be disastrous."[13]

In the days after the Powell video went viral, a new phrase was bandied about, and "suicide by cop" joined the Black Lives Matter lexicon. Still, St. Louis police viewed the video as exculpatory, believing that it cleared both officers of any potential wrongdoing. The city decided not to bring charges against them in November 2015. St. Louis Prosecuting Attorney Jennifer Joyce said: "The officers had a very strong self-defense claim in this case and criminal charges could not be brought."[14]

Powell's family disagreed. Karen Powell, Kajieme's mother, sued both officers who had attended the scene, Nicholas Shelton and Ellis Brown; the police chief, Sam Dotson; and the City of St. Louis for wrongful death.[15]

Her attorney, Jermaine Wooten, said: "I think it's pretty clear that they had a number of options rather than pulling out their guns and start shooting. They had their vehicle as defense; they could have pepper sprayed him. There were a number of citizens out there who didn't feel any threat from Mr. Powell. They were out there laughing and videotaping him."[16] Wooten added: "At the very worst case, they could have Tased him, but I think they could have just talked to him calmly and got the knife from him. He [Kajieme Powell] did not need to go to jail that day, he needed to go to a mental hospital and he would have, if Brown had followed the crisis intervention training."[17]

The Powell case pushed to the fore a fact that many news outlets had not discussed prior to his death. About 50 percent of the unarmed victims of police shootings in 2014 suffered from some form of mental illness.[18] What remains unknown, however, is how many of these deaths were triggered by the consumption of mediated images of police brutality. How many people, in the middle of a mental health episode, replayed a horrific clip of black death in their heads during their own encounter? Moreover, how many people may have exacerbated their experience with police as those images looped in their heads? Media scholars have yet to grapple with such questions, which challenge the normative ideals of journalism as a public service.[19] There is some nascent research, however, in the area of psychology. A 2016 study found that racial profiling by police triggered "race-based traumatic stress" in black men. Dr. Samuel R. Aymer noted that news media play a crucial role when it comes to portraying who needs mental health care and who does not. He wrote:

> For instance, in Newtown, Connecticut (children living in this town were shot and killed by a mass murderer while they were at school), a horde of mental-health experts were brought in to work with surviving children and interviewed by the media, exposing the sequelae of individual and community trauma (pertaining to the mental health of children, their families, teachers, etc.) Unlike this type of media coverage, discussions of police killings of unarmed Black men are usually devoid of any exploration of how racial profiling, brutality, and racial harassment by police and other entities causes traumatic reactions and possibly posttraumatic stress disorder in this population.[20]

Aymer is arguing that both the Newtown massacre and the fatal police shootings across the country have invoked trauma throughout entire communities. Yet, while Newtown was largely white, and since fatal police encounters have occurred disproportionately among communities of color, the former group received swift, thorough therapy while the latter earned another layer of trauma, in the form of expanded (and often militarized) policing. The collective result is a group of people who are triggered at the sight of police, not comforted by them.

This psychological triggering is not limited to police encounters, however. Many Black Lives Matter activists have shared that their everyday encounters with Internet trolls and real-life bigots have driven some among their ranks to take their own lives. MarShawn McCarrel II, for example, was one of the fallen activists that were commemorated most often in my interviews. Activists remembered McCarrel as an outspoken voice in the wake of the George Zimmerman verdict in 2013. At the time, Ohio legislators were considering a "Stand Your Ground" bill that was very similar to the Florida law that had served as Zimmerman's core defense. McCarrel led the Ohio Student Association in a vociferous opposition, which included a die-in at the statehouse. The group was able to stall the legislation.

Additionally, McCarrel led the Ohio Student Association to protest the killings of John Crawford and Tamir Rice. As for the activists I interviewed, McCarrel's visibility inspired repeated cyberbullying and death threats. He shared on Facebook, for example, a message that read: "Were [sic] gonna keep making your life hell until you keep your NIGGER mouth closed."

McCarrel replied on his timeline: "1. I usually don't share these because they're ugly and powerless. 2. I'm usually not petty and don't respond but I'm up today lol #MyBigNiggerMouth." A wave of commenters offered him support. But by January 2016, he tweeted increasingly foreboding messages.[21]

On January 16: I got demons I have to deal with before they deal with me.

On January 19: Kingdom on the outside. Ruin on the inside.

On January 27: I don't want anyone to think my decisions are about them. My path belongs to me.

On January 30: Too many battles on the inside for these battles on the outside.

McCarrel's Facebook timeline was dotted with celebratory pictures after these dark posts. His mood seemed to have shifted when he won the NAACP Image Award in the Hometown Champion category in early February 2016. One photograph showed him beaming on the red carpet at the Los Angeles award ceremony. A week after McCarrel collected his trophy, however, he posted, on February 8, 2016: "My demons won today. I'm sorry."

Just a few hours later McCarrel lay on the steps of the Ohio statehouse—a building that served as a site for many of his demonstrations. He was dead at age 23, from a single gunshot wound to his head. As the news flowed through the network of Black Lives Matter activists on Facebook, a Cleveland activist confessed that he, too, had tried to take his own life. Dozens of other organizers shared stories of their battles with depression and anxiety. And a leader in Oakland, California, shared the suicide prevention hotline phone number on Facebook.[22] Supporters flooded the Black Lives Matter Cincinnati Facebook page to seek solace in the virtual community. Not all discourse online was kind though.

An off-duty police officer, Lee Cyr of Fairborn, Ohio, posted to his social media outlets: "Love a happy ending."[23] Others commenting on the post replied that McCarrel's suicide meant there was "one less to worry about." The Fairborn PD placed Cyr on administrative leave after another officer alerted the force to the Facebook post, and he was fired about a month later for violating the department's social media policy.

Psychologists who have started to study the ideological polarization of Black Lives Matter activists and their detractors have explained that Terror Management Theory (TMT) is responsible for this callous sort of response to black suffering. Jeff Greenberg, Sheldon Solomon, and Tom Pyszczynski explained in their 2015 book, *The Worm at the Core*, that most human actions are driven by the fear of death. The trio built upon Ernest Becker's 1973 work, *The Denial of Death*, to explain that humans' survival instincts have evolved to such a degree that we are horrified by the notion that our eventual death will mean nothing in the grand, cosmic scheme of things. The day after we die, the rest of the world will continue to get up and go to school or to work; society generally presses forward as if nothing significant has occurred. Some people respond to these feelings by insulating themselves with an in-group of people who offer them the feelings of self-importance and value that they seek, so as to not feel so insignificant. This results often in racial prejudice and extreme political polarization. Kirk J. Schneider has explained that polarization "has appeared as bigotry, bullying, tyranny, vengefulness, and arrogance; and it has also manifested as narrowness, rigidity, pedantry, and obsession."[24]

When I read about TMT and the real-world manifestations of ideological polarization, I began to infer a different reading of the fatal police shooting videos. While these images are, for black people, mediated evidence that an African American's right to survive a police encounter was violated, the videos may provide consolation for white supremacists, whose deepest fear is being exterminated by communities of color. Every video, then, can become a digital "attaboy" for the police, who are expected to maintain the system of white supremacy. Any ripple effects, such as activist suicides, are a bonus for this system of domestic terror.

In 2014, the year that McCarrel died, a study by the federal Office of Minority Health found that African American men are four times more likely to commit suicide than African American women. Even though the suicide rate for black men is 70 percent lower than for white men, the suicide rate among black boys, ages 10 to 14, increased by 233 percent between 1980 and 1995—during the Golden Age of the War on Drugs and mass incarceration— as compared to a 120 percent increase among whites. It should be noted also that 2014—when these new black mental health statistics were tabulated— was the year that black boys would have viewed viral police videos of Ersula Ore, the Arizona State University professor who was slammed to the ground by campus police after she was accused of jaywalking; or Marlene Pinnock, the 51-year-old homeless grandmother whom California Highway Patrol punched in the face after she attempted to reach an underpass to go to sleep; or Chris Lollie, who was Tased in Philando Castile's home state of Minnesota as he waited in a public area to pick up his kids from school. These boys, who felt drawn to suicide, also may have seen the 2014 viral videos of Jamal Jones and Lisa Mahone, who had their rear car windows smashed by police during a traffic stop. They may have seen the footage of Levar Jones being shot four times after he reached for his wallet in compliance with a South Carolina officer's request for his driver's license. They would have seen the Kajieme Powell video. The Tamir Rice video. The John Crawford video. The Eric Garner video. They would have seen the photographs of Michael Brown's body laying the street, as blood streamed from his head down the road. The horror.

Brittany Ferrell's wife, Alexis Templeton, told the *Washington Post* accordingly: "There are so many folks in this movement that have serious mental health issues. There are so many people on the brink of killing themselves."[25]

Templeton went on to share that she, too, experienced suicidal ideation at one time. In the months before Michael Brown's killing, she had been a passenger in a deadly car crash that claimed the life of her father, uncle, and partner. Her survivor's remorse was more than she could bear. There were many days, she told the *Post*, when she sat in her room with a loaded gun to her head. August 13, 2014 was one of those days. As she thought about pulling the trigger, she said she could not shake the images of Ferguson rising up against its police. One of her childhood friends was among the first community members to tweet a picture of the protests in her hometown. Templeton said that she remained glued to her smartphone all day, as she watched the force begin to deploy tear gas. "I went outside and I never came back in," Templeton told the *Post*, adding, "Mike Brown saved my life."[26] For other activists, however, their involvement with the Michael Brown protests may have cost them their lives.

Mysterious and untimely deaths. Since Darren Wilson's non-indictment in November 2014, four Ferguson residents who were related to the movement in varying degrees have died under questionable circumstances. Darren Seals, 29, and DeAndre Joshua, 20, were found shot dead in their cars, which then were set ablaze—Seals in 2016 and Joshua in 2014. Seals was, perhaps, one of the most photographed men of the Ferguson uprisings. A *Washington Post* article remembered him this way: "In many ways, Seals was a fitting symbol of the Ferguson protester: a local resident, not a trained activist or organizer, who saw Michael Brown's dead body and the trauma that his death had inflicted on the community, members of which organically poured into the streets—bringing with them their baggage, their contradictions and their humanity."[27] As the Ferguson uprising grew in 2014, Seals was seen standing next to Michael Brown's father, in one photograph and hugging Brown's mother in another, as she collapsed into tears when the Wilson non-indictment was announced. Seals co-founded Hands Up United, which had begun to organize a campaign called Polls Ova Police at the time of his death. Its aim was to transform the organizing power of allied groups in Ferguson into real political power, by backing progressive candidates in key public offices. He died before this dream was realized.

Two years before Seals' death, 20-year-old Deandre Joshua was shot in the head and torched in his car too. Joshua's white Pontiac Grand Prix was found near the Canfield Green Apartments, not far from where Michael Brown died. While rumors swirled online that Joshua was killed because he testified against Darren Wilson in the grand jury hearings, St. Louis County Prosecutor Bob McCulloch denied that Joshua was a witness.[28] Joshua's family added that he had not participated in any of the local demonstrations after Michael Brown's death, even though he knew Dorian Johnson, the man who was with Brown when he died. Police ruled Joshua's death a homicide, yet arrested no one in connection with his gruesome killing.

Then, there was Edward Crawford, 27, who was immortalized in a Pulitzer Prize-winning photo. In the iconic image Crawford lobbed a tear gas canister back at Ferguson police, a bandanna covering his face to protect himself. Crawford was shot dead in a car too, in May 2017.[29] St. Louis police ruled it a suicide. They reported that two unnamed witnesses said Crawford was riding in the backseat when he began telling them that he was having personal problems. The witnesses heard him fumbling for something in a bag. Then, he pulled out a gun and shot himself.

Missouri State Sen. Maria Chappelle-Nadal stated publicly in a May 5, 2017, Twitter thread: "Edward Crawford is dead. Found in his car shot to death. He is #Ferguson's hero. For those of us tear-gassed, he was our local champion. RIP"[30] She added: "It is now not coincidental. There is a murderer targeting activists from #Ferguson. #WeAreNotInvisible #Resist."[31]

Yet another prominent Ferguson activist, Melissa McKinnies, alleged that her 24-year-old son, Danye Jones, was lynched in her backyard on October 17, 2018. Relatives found him hanging from a tree behind their north St. Louis home. McKinnies told the *St. Louis Post-Dispatch* that her son was upbeat before his death, not suicidal. She added that he did not know how to tie the knots that were used in the makeshift noose's ligature, and that the sheets around his neck did not match bed linen from the family home. In her anguish, McKinnies uploaded Jones's postmortem pictures to Facebook and Instagram. In an interview she did with *Rolling Stone* magazine, she seemed to channel Mamie Till Mobley with an uncanny utterance: "I'm sick and losing my mind, but I had to let the world know what they did to my baby!"[32]

I happened upon the Danye Jones photograph in early November 2018, when it appeared in my Instagram timeline without a trigger warning. Jones's fists were clenched, as if he was fighting until his final breaths. His shorts had been pulled down around his ankles to expose his underwear. I scrolled to read the comments underneath the horrifying image. I needed to know what I was looking at, as I had not yet heard of Jones's story. The comments revealed a startling array of weighty baggage. From people seeing themselves as vulnerable, to others feeling helplessly enraged, it was yet another photographic reminder to "stay woke" in a climate that seemed to be punishing black witnesses.

Brittany Packnett Cunningham, one of our Day 1's, tweeted a heartbreaking thread before mainstream media picked up the story: "This is #DanyeJones. His mom, Melissa McKinnies, is a #Ferguson Activist. Danye was found hanging from a tree in his mom's backyard on 10/17. The police didn't investigate, but called it a suicide. But Danye has just bought property to sell & his mother knows this isn't true."[33] Packnett Cunningham added: "#DanyeJones is at least the 4th person related to the #Ferguson uprising to die in more than suspicious circumstances. This is a pattern."[34]

A month after Jones's horrific hanging, a colleague alerted me to yet another Ferguson activist's mysterious death. As I logged on to Twitter to confirm the news, I read that Bassem Masri, 31, was found unresponsive on a bus in Bridgeton, Missouri. The Palestinian American had risen to national prominence among the allied organizations working under the banner of the Black Lives Matter Movement after he live-streamed Ferguson's uprisings faithfully, helping to report from the frontlines. I remembered his mantra that mainstream media "ain't gonna say the truth [about Brown's death.] They ain't gonna never say the truth. They got their own narrative."[35]

Toxicology reports stated that he suffered a heart attack after overdosing on fentanyl.[36] A man named Faizan Syed, who identified himself as Masri's cousin on Facebook, eulogized him on the platform. He wrote: "A gentle man who was fierce when he faced injustice. In his short life he did as much if not more to unite the fight for black liberation and Palestinian liberation. . . . May Allah accept his sacrifices for justice and overlook his flaws and mistakes."[37]

Packnett Cunningham tweeted her own tribute again. She said of Masri: "There are some folks who you wonder if they're all the way in for liberation. You could never wonder that of https://twitter.com/bassem_masri. His investment was real, and his commitment was unwavering. I don't even understand why we keep losing activist family so young. Rest in power."[38]

One of Packnett Cunningham's followers affirmed her post, explaining that Masri's livestreams of the Ferguson uprisings kept her up until 3:00 or 4:00 a.m. at the height of the protests. "Live-streaming changed News Reporting!" the user exclaimed. In addition to documenting the movement in real-time, Masri had plans to run for local office, before he died. He posted on Facebook, eight months before his death, the following promise:

> If Missourians decide to elect me as a state representative in 2020, I will be one of the biggest advocates for ALL people in Missouri. If you know me you know I'm very candid and unfiltered, when i see something wrong or unjust i don't sit idly by, and I certainly won't start anytime soon. My allegiance is not for sale, the people of Missouri have that. #2020 let's start a new chapter, I would like to help out the other state representatives that work tirelessly to get justice for the voiceless.[39]

Masri, like Seals, did not live long enough to see his dream of Ferguson grassroots power translated to traditional political power. For many activists in the movement, it was a chilling reminder that the life cycle of a frontline black witness can be very short. I was reminded of this—very personally—at the end of 2017. Two days before most of the world rang in the New Year, on December 30, my research assistant sent me an urgent email. She told me that Eric Garner's eldest child and namesake, Erica Garner-Snipes, suffered a heart attack on Christmas Eve. Now, she wrote, doctors were declaring the 27-year-old woman "brain dead."

My assistant and I had spent most of 2017 sending Erica emails and Twitter direct messages to schedule an interview with her. We remained hopeful Erica would reply eventually, though we knew she was incredibly involved on the ground. Erica was an outspoken advocate and crusader for her father. When I first saw her emerge as an activist in 2014, I knew I wanted to speak to her. She was different. I was used to seeing the parents of the slain rise up to affect change. The so-called "Mothers of the Movement," for example, delivered a collective keynote address at the 2016 Democratic National Convention (DNC).[40] I had witnessed the same DNC that denied Fannie Lou Hamer a platform to discuss black enfranchisement in 1964 extend its televised dais to Eric Garner's mother, Gwen Carr, more than 50 years later. Still, I had yet to observe a child rallying so prominently on behalf of their deceased parent as the movement's momentum grew. This, in part, may have been due to the fact that many of the movement's victims—such as John Crawford, Korryn Gaines, Philando Castile, and Alton Sterling—left behind such young children. For Erica, however, her age allowed her to be visible and unrelenting. I wanted to talk with her about her die-ins, her endorsement of Sen. Bernie Sanders in the presidential election, and how she kept pace as an activist while being a wife and mother. It hurt to realize that Garner-Snipes had not juggled all of these roles as stoically as I had believed initially. She was now yet another organizer who had succumbed to the horrors of bearing witness while black.

In an interview with the Marshall Project, Garner-Snipes recounted how she learned about her father's death. Her oral history was part of a broader project called *We Are Witnesses*. Garner-Snipes said her sister called her at work to tell her that her dad "stopped breathing." She left work immediately. When she arrived at the place where her father had taken his last breaths, she found a police barricade and news reporters. She said a reporter from the *Daily News* informed her that there was a video of her father's killing. Her brother quickly searched for it on YouTube. They viewed it together.

"Get off of him! Stop it!" Garner-Snipes screamed in vain at the computer screen, recalling also, "My head was spinning. I was hot. Throwing up. That's how we found out."

Five months later, a grand jury declined to indict Officer Daniel Pantaleo, who administered the fatal chokehold. Garner-Snipes said the decision stunned her mother and siblings. As she rode home from her parents' house that night in a taxi, a sea of protesters annoyed her driver as they clogged the Brooklyn Bridge. At first she did not know what the thousands of people were protesting, until she heard chants of her father's name.

She opened the car windows and yelled out: "Thank you! I'm Eric Garner's daughter!"

Some of the demonstrators surrounded the cab. They told her that they loved her and that they were rallying for her family. Their activation, from distant witnesses to active protestors, moved Garner. She told the Marshall Project, "In my saddest moment where I didn't know how to feel, and I saw all of these people out here for my dad, it made me feel empowered in a way." She fought back tears and smiled for the camera. Then, she was gone.

Black Twitter reacted to the news of her passing quickly, despite the holiday season. They shared pictures and self-care tips. The discourse centered black public health issues, such as depression, heart health, and proper postnatal care, as Garner-Snipes had just welcomed a baby boy into the world three months before her death. An even smaller subgroup of Black Twitter users revived the argument about whether African Americans should continue to view fatal police killings caught on video.

When I interviewed Dread Scott, the visual artist who reimagined the iconic NAACP flag, I asked what he thought about not looking anymore. He shook his head ruefully and said:

> The videos have helped increasing numbers of people see the depth of the problem, but left to its own it's just going to be sort of like lynching photos, where those were used by white people to celebrate a job well done and towards black people to terrorize us. Now, I don't watch every single one [cellphone video], but I think it's important to bear witness.

I stared at him on FaceTime when he finished speaking, temporarily unable to formulate a follow-up question. At the time of our interview, Erica Garner-Snipes had not yet died, but I was beginning to hear from lots of

African Americans in my everyday life that the videos were traumatizing. They did not want to look anymore.

Eve Ewing, our Chicago Bard, told me that journalists (and news audiences), for example, have not considered fully the impact that continuous looking has on the psyche. Ewing said that she found it offensive when news outlets or even other black witnesses would post videos of black death online without a disclaimer or an opt-out method. She lamented:

> I've been very vocal about pushing news media outlets to not have auto-play videos because there have been times—like when Philando Castile was killed—that I'm reading an article and then I scroll down and this video starts playing that I didn't consent to watching. . . . I used to know people that really made me feel like if I didn't watch videos of black people dying then I didn't care or that I was somehow sheltering myself from reality when in fact I think that we vastly underestimate the trauma that we endure by watching videos like that and also we overestimate the degree to which those videos actually make a difference.

Ewing explained further that she has sent private, DMs to other Twitter users to ask them to remove police shootings of African Americans from their main Twitter feeds that anyone can encounter while browsing casually. "When the Sandra Bland video came out I was very public about saying, on Twitter, I cannot watch this right now . . . and so many people responded . . . just affirming and saying you don't have to do anything that is unsafe for you emotionally, or saying thank you for saying that because in you saying that I now realize that I have permission to care for myself."

As Ewing spoke, I remembered how the Bland video triggered immediate fear for me when I encountered the customs agents in Milan in July 2016. I nodded silently. How much more horrific would viewing such a video be if it were my family member? Garner-Snipes took those mysteries, of how prolonged stress and depression manifests in the body, to her premature grave.

Touré, writing for the *Daily Beast*, explained: "Eric's death had a transformative impact on Erica's life, and Erica's death will have a profound impact on her children's lives. And on and on, racism metastasizing through black families like a vicious cancer, the deprivations of each generation weighing down the next in a horrible, unavoidable inheritance."[41] In the end, then, did Erica's witnessing matter? Did the witnessing of the thousands who blocked the Brooklyn Bridge matter? Or was the Garner video, as Dread Scott opined, akin to beholding the strange fruit about which Billie Holiday sang? Scott's question, though haunting, bears exploration.

The New Lynching Postcards

To investigate Dread Scott's assertion fully, I researched how other scholars have believed that lynching postcards have communicated power through terror. I found that these types of "stationery" served as more than souvenirs of the ghastly events. These images have reinforced U.S. racial hierarchies; elevated black male killings while obscuring the lynchings of black women and children; and even served as profitable enterprises that deny the dead the right to rest. In these three distinct ways, smartphone footage from black witnesses also has the potential to toe the line between digital tyranny that upholds white supremacy and visual evidence that galvanizes change.

The "uncontested truth." Many of my students at the elite Southern California university where I teach now have asked me how white people could have remained silent at the sight of charred black bodies, swinging from trees. I paused before I answered this question for a pensive student during a lecture one afternoon. Then I asked whether she, as a white woman, ever had posted public support for the Black Lives Matter Movement after viewing a fatal police shooting video. "No," she answered. I then asked if she had attended any recent protests. "Yes," she replied with a small smile. She said she had attended the Women's March in Los Angeles in January 2017. When I asked why she had not attended any number of the anti-police brutality protests in the city she nodded slowly, her eyes beginning to brim with tears. She answered slowly: "Because, I know what it is like to be a woman. I don't know what it is like to be black. I didn't feel like it was my fight."

I remember her deep sigh. It was a very difficult and brave admission to make in our incredibly diverse class, in which she was the minority. As her classmates nodded, she seemed to pull from their silent support to add: "Until your class, I probably would have assumed that the police were always right—just doing their jobs—and that the African Americans in the videos must have done something wrong."

I nodded. Those assumptions, I explained, of inherent black deviance, are what allowed U.S. lynchings to persist too. Many white viewers may have believed that the black people we see in those photographs deserved their fatal punishments, I explained to the class. Or, they may not have viewed anti-lynching efforts as their concern. Moreover, the people committing the lynchings were often law enforcement officers, which gave the act another layer of extrajudicial business as usual, rather than mere mob rule. Lastly, the presence of a photographer in this context elevated the killings to the level of news events. Taken together, this partnership of police and ad-hoc "photojournalists" formalized and sanctioned the affair, perhaps silencing would-be activists, I told my students.

Historian Amy Louise Wood has explained similarly: "[Lynching postcards] served as visual proof for the uncontested 'truth' of white civilized morality over and against supposed black bestiality and savagery."[42] She added:

> To be sure, many white Americans would have derived satisfaction from these images out of their racist sensibilities about innate black depravity and their own fears about black crime. . . . For these Americans, a photograph of an actual lynching might have borne no more meaning than representations of fictional lynchings they encountered in motion pictures or in pictorial magazines—as a gory and thrilling but distant "local custom."[43]

For non-black, would-be allies—like many of my current students—it may be difficult to look at lynching photographs without feeling guilty. To view black death in this way creates a paradox, after all. If one looks away from a lynching photograph today, even out of respect for the dead, there may be feelings of avoiding an ugly U.S. history. If one does peer at the photos, Dora Apel has claimed, some people still experience conflicting emotions since: "the pictures are hard to see, and they are made all the more so by the presence of death, already difficult to look at but here having occurred so excruciatingly in an atmosphere of self-righteous cruelty and gloating."[44] This is a crucial distinction to make. Whereas the white supremacists in the most infamous lynching postcards often pointed triumphantly to the black body hanging overhead—posing fearlessly in groups of several hundred people— today's lynch mobs hide online. Instead of an entire town coming out to bear witness then, the whole world can view state-sanctioned killings of African Americans in the comfort of their own homes. The horror, therefore, expands beyond a small town to a global village of seers. The footage becomes more powerful than a lynching postcard in that it terrorizes potentially a larger audience of black distant witnesses and reifies ideas of white supremacy for international audiences.

For these reasons, I argue that the footage that frontline black witnesses produce be treated with care by legacy news media. Like the lynching postcards of old, overexposure to these horrific images could have a numbing effect on the very audiences that black witnesses hope to galvanize. When news media privilege the private last moments of some groups of people and not others, the implied message is that the hidden group is human and deserving of such cultural shrouding, while the visible group is inhuman and worthy of a public death, like a deer on the side of a road.

In August 2015, for example, a lone gunman, Bryce Williams, shot two journalists on live television in Moneta, Virginia. Alison Parker, 24, was conducting an interview on-air as her cameraman Adam Ward, 27, filmed the broadcast for WDBJ-TV, a CBS affiliate. In subsequent reports of the chilling double murder all of the major news networks I observed made the same decision: to freeze the frame of Parker during the interview just before she was shot. The unedited audio still rolled, allowing news audiences to hear her final screams amid the gunshots. The footage is horrific even without it rolling in real time. Thus, the freeze frame provides a respectful, yet effective way to report the tragic event. It is a deliberate news decision.

Philando Castile did not receive this treatment in July 2016. On the day he died, I observed countless 24-hour cable news networks looping videos of his demise. Instead of blurring Castile's face, cutting away from the footage of him dying, or freezing the frame to a moment just before his death, CNN (and many other outlets) replayed the raw footage of his horrified face and bleeding body.[45] I should note that Parker and Ward, the journalists who were slain in Virginia, were white. While it is unfair to surmise that news networks made the decision to edit out the moment of the journalists' deaths solely because of their race, suffice it to say that black victims of fatal police shootings often do not receive such thoughtful framing before televised reports air.

One need look no further than YouTube to see raw footage of Alton Sterling struggling in a Baton Rouge parking lot, while two police officers attempted to straddle him. As one pressed a gun into his chest, the other shot him, point blank, in rapid succession.[46] There was no blurring of his face. There was no freeze frame. In McKinney, Texas, Officer Eric Casebolt's efforts to break up a suburban pool party culminated into him slamming Dajerria Becton, a 15-year-old black girl, onto the concrete.[47] She was unarmed, wearing only her bathing suit. As he pinned her to the ground with his knee in her back, there was no blurring of the minor's face. There was no freeze frame. If we venture back to Oscar Grant even—to the first time that the *Los Angeles Times* reported the release of the infamous cellphone videos in June 2010—there was no blurring of his face. There was no freeze frame.[48] In these cases, and many more, I observed that it has become de rigueur to air images of black people in the throes of police brutality on television like GIFs. Future research should center on why newsrooms continue to make such decisions. All of the victims named here—and the many others whose last moments were captured on camera—deserve news coverage that feels respectful and not exploitative. When news managers fail to present the fatal police encounter videos with the same care that they would extend for fallen journalists, then these images begin to function as something more sinister.

Decentering male victims. Another similarity I found between fatal police encounter videos and lynching photographs is that both genres elevate the plight of men, while obscuring the women and children who are vulnerable to state-sponsored violence too. The National Memorial for Peace and Justice opened its doors in April 2018 in Alabama. It commemorates the more than 4,000 documented cases of lynching in the United States with hundreds of steel columns suspended from beams to symbolize the ritualistic hangings.[49] It is the first museum of its kind. It is also one of the few places that commemorates Mary Turner and her unborn baby, who arguably suffered one of the most brutal lynchings in U.S. history.

In May 1918, in Brooks County, Georgia, a week of mob rule claimed the lives of more than a dozen African Americans, many of whom were women and children. It all began with a killing. A black worker, Sydney Johnson, murdered a white plantation owner, Hampton Smith, for whom he worked. Smith had such a terrific reputation for abusing his employees that many local African Americans would not work for him willingly. He relied, therefore, on debt peonage, bailing black men out of jail, then forcing them to repay their debts by working his land. In this way, he hired Sydney Johnson, 19, who was arrested for "rolling dice" and fined $30. Smith and Johnson were involved in an altercation within only a few days of the new hire. Johnson was upset about not being paid his wages, and Smith beat him for protesting such treatment. Johnson fatally shot Smith, which kicked off a weeklong, town-wide manhunt for him.

During the mob's rampage, the townsmen killed Hayes Turner, husband of Mary Turner, then eight months pregnant, who vowed publicly to press charges against Hayes's killers. Local newspapers declared that Mary had made "unwise remarks."[50] Soon, she found herself trying to flee town to save her life and that of her unborn baby. The townspeople caught her, however, and took her to the edge of Brooks County, just beyond their neighborhood. Men from the mob tied Mary Turner's ankles and hung her upside-down from a tree. Then, they poured gasoline on her and burned off her clothes. They cut open her stomach and let her unborn child drop to the ground. Local newspapers reported that the child cried twice before the men stomped fatally on the baby's head and body.[51] Before leaving the scene, the mob unleashed a hail of bullets at Turner's body. They left her, and the baby, there until nightfall. A few members of the mob returned later to bury both bodies a few feet away from where they were murdered. Their graves were marked with little more than a whiskey bottle and a cigar.

The reign of terror ended three days later for other blacks in the community, when police engaged Sydney Johnson in a shoot-out in Valdosta, Georgia. Newspapers reported that more than 700 people joined the fray to mutilate his dead body. Members of the mob castrated him. Then, they tied a rope around his neck and dragged his corpse for nearly 20 miles to a town called Morven, where they burned what remained of his body. More than 500 African Americans are thought to have fled the area during these events. When they scattered, their story made its way to a group called the Anti-Lynching Crusaders, who proposed one of the first laws, the 1922 Dyer Bill, which would make lynching a federal crime. The NAACP learned of Mary Turner and her neighbors too.[52] Walter White, the group's lead investigator, wrote a scathing piece in their official magazine, the *Crisis*, to recount the events.[53] This is where the media coverage of Mary Turner ends typically. Since her killing was not photographed, she is not remembered in the way that Emmett Till would be, nearly 50 years later.

Without pictures, Turner fights to be centered as an example of black women's vulnerability in the face of white supremacy. If we think about the Black Lives Matter Movement, we can observe some parallels. We do not have video footage to document the deaths of Rekia Boyd in 2012 in Chicago or Sandra Bland in 2015, inside the Waller County Jail in Texas. Though Korryn Gaines tried to provide a livestream of her fatal standoff with Baltimore County police in 2016, Facebook temporarily suspended her account, so we have no full record of that either. In just these three cases, black witnessing failed to highlight sufficiently that women can be victims of fatal police encounters too—just as lynching photographs may have led us to assume that only Jewish men or men of color suffered this horrific fate. Leigh Raiford has explained: "Such strategies, while making visible the crimes committed against black men, obscure the extent of violence practiced against black women and children, almost never documented by a camera. . . . Lynching and its narratives completely silenced and erased black women, leaving them vulnerable to violence outside of the public eye."[54]

This is one of the weaknesses of modern black witnessing too. A consequence of the anti–police brutality movement is that people look online now for proof of death, for better or worse. Since the preponderance of fatal police shootings have featured black men and boys, they dominated the headlines, hashtags, and hearts of many Americans. This is why Kimberlé Crenshaw's parallel #SayHerName movement was a brilliant addition to the public discourse in 2015. By highlighting state-sponsored violence against women, Crenshaw and her team helped prevent fatal police shooting videos emulate the male-centered lynching photographs that galvanized movements past. Though there may not be as much video to corroborate police brutality against black women, it does exist. And, as Mary Turner's story indicates, this kind of gendered violence is old, persistent, and pervasive.

The problem of profit. Lynching photographs are similar to fatal police shooting videos in one more way: both genres inspire a macabre commercial element that disallows the forgetting of the victim. Walter Benjamin has called lynching photographs, for example, "a certain type of fashionable photography" that "makes misery into a consumer good."[55] Lynching postcards, I should note, were sold for money. Even though it was illegal to mail them, people still traded the postcards like baseball cards, Dora Apel has explained. Everyone from the photographer, to the postcard printer, to the shopkeeper who sold the cards made money from these grotesque souvenirs. Likewise, many African American journalists working for legacy media outlets have bemoaned the increasing profitization of black suffering at the expense of our collective numbing to the images. Touré wrote in the *Daily Beast*, for example:

There's [Eric] Garner and Tamir Rice and Walter Scott and Philando Castile and John Crawford and on and on, together forming one giant snuff film— like that gory old compilation *Faces of Death*—where officers are predators and blacks are gunned down in vicious modern-day lynchings.[56]

Indeed, *Faces of Death* was, and still is, a shocking collection of brutal human and animal deaths caught on video. When it was released in 1978 it was billed as a horror film, although it contains amateur footage that includes home videos. As of October 2018 the film is banned in 46 countries, yet remains on YouTube with nearly 500,000 views and counting.[57] It grossed $35 million at the box office when it debuted in 1978—worth roughly $142 million today. It may be the earliest viral video. John Fecile, writing for the *Guardian*, commented on the film's cultural endurance: "Even today, in the age of police body cameras and Islamic State execution videos, it retains its power." I offer these quick statistics to illustrate how so-called "gore pornography" became big business into the early 1980s.[58]

It is worth researching how much legacy media companies have gained from capitalizing on black death during the ongoing anti–police brutality movement. April Reign, the creator of the #OscarsSoWhite hashtag, has decried, for example, how "The media is complicit in this morbid voyeurism when it chooses to be. . . . In the same way that we do not show the lethal executions of prisoners, one wonders how the media justifies depicting the death of non-imprisoned citizens at the hands of the same system."[59] Reign called the looping of fatal police shootings a "sick sort of voyeurism." Where is the line though? I am calling on researchers to investigate this further.

For every person like Devin Allen, who told me that he does not wander around Baltimore looking for pictures, there are still black trauma opportunists afoot—like the ones who took advantage of his students. They are looking for a quick, emotional sale to a media outlet, which is also looking to captivate readers, viewers, and listeners in today's attention economy.[60] How do we reconcile these tensions, between the need to populate U.S. top news feeds quickly, with real updates on substantive problems, all while bringing in new voices that may have been marginalized until now? Again, I believe that the answer lies in making black witnesses the subject matter experts on their own communities. People who are living in Ferguson, Baltimore, or Baton Rouge can tell you exactly what local conditions killed Michael Brown, Freddie Gray, and Alton Sterling. News media, therefore, must regard the fatal police shooting video from these local experts as a notification system. These videos are meant to alert journalists of a deeper problem that bears investigation. They are not meant to stand on their own.

I offer a brief example. One night, I was fast asleep when my home security system began blaring. The panel said to me: "Back door glass break," in its robotic tone. I jumped up and ran to my window to see if I could see anyone in the backyard. Then I went into my son's room and grabbed him, bringing him into my daughter's room to barricade us all in while I called the police. Her room had a window that was lower to the ground, I reasoned, and if we needed to jump out, we would. When the officers came, both of them had their guns drawn low at their sides. They were polite and nodded at me reassuringly, but I was terrified still. In the end, one of the helpful officers discovered that the sensor on my back door had loosened. It had caused the system to trip. Such a tiny detail activated an entire system to make so much noise. Black America is very much like this, I think. What seem like tiny details to outsiders activate an entire system of oppression for many African Americans. To an outsider, a parking ticket or a local fine may be a minor inconvenience to be paid off quickly. In Ferguson, petty ticketing is a system that punishes the poor, making jail time a reality if one cannot afford to pay.[61] To an outsider, the year a building was erected may be a fact reserved only for architecture history buffs. In Baltimore, it can mean the difference between being exposed to toxic lead paint, which has cognitively impaired children like Freddie Gray, or not.[62]

Finding these small details, and explaining how they work to create a complex web of structural inequality in the United States, must be the work of legacy media. This is how we honor black witnessing. Just as we would expect an emergency medical technician (EMT) to help stabilize a patient before taking her to the hospital, we can consider black witnesses to be our first responders—before major media outlets arrive. When legacy media do come to the scene, they should work increasingly with willing black witnesses to develop a richer profile of what happened—just as the EMT may work with a hospital's medical team to begin patient care. These kinds of partnerships seem to be starting among some of the activists that I interviewed. Brittany Ferrell, for example, told me that she relies on a network of journalists that she trusts when she wants to break news. Ferrell has come to respect their work, she said, and trusts that what she tells them will be conveyed properly. Activists like Ferrell are helping to build a collective memory of fatal police encounters, just like Ida B. Wells' tabulation of lynchings informed a national memorial more than 100 years later. This is important work and, incidentally, the final similarity that lynching photographs and black witnessing videos share.

The Shadow Archive

Lynching photographs, in all of their horror, helped galvanize the early 20th century civil rights movements. Leigh Raiford has explained that these images built a "shadow archive" that fueled membership in the NAACP. Lawrence Beitler took the first such picture in August 1930. It is arguably the most infamous lynching photograph, as it features a white man pointing at three dead black men hanging from a tree. His eyes seem wild with delight. The killing took place in Marion, Indiana. Two African American men, Thomas Shipp and Abram Smith, were arrested and charged with armed robbery of a white factory worker, Claude Deeter, and the rape of his partner, Mary Ball. On the night that Shipp and Smith were taken to jail, a mob of nearly 1,000 people broke into the jail with sledgehammers and crowbars to pull the young men out of their cells. Shopkeepers printed and sold thousands of postcards that featured the men's dead bodies. The photograph inspired Abel Meeropol to write a poem/song, "Strange Fruit," which Billie Holiday recorded in 1939.

Similarly, the dragging, hanging, and burning of Jesse Washington in Waco, Texas, impelled W.E.B. Du Bois to bear witness in NAACP's magazine, *Crisis*, in July 1916.[63] Du Bois and his team sent a white ally, Elisabeth Freeman, to travel to Texas in search of postcards or photographs from the black man's hanging. What she brought back was ghastly. The image of the dismembered and charred corpse shocked NAACP's news audiences. Circulation for the *Crisis* grew by 50,000 during the next two years. Moreover, the organization raised $20,000 (nearly $500,000 today) in the months after publishing the lynching photograph. The group used some of the proceeds to purchase the flag—"A man was lynched yesterday"—which Dread Scott reimagined in 2015.

Khalil Gibran Muhammad notes rightfully: "The arc of history that connects lynching's past to policing's present runs through the bodies of black unarmed men, women, and children—Eric Garner, Sandra Bland, Tamir Rice—whose names might one day be added to the weathered steel columns of the National Memorial."[64]

By linking the bygone victims of lynching to today's victims of fatal police force, Muhammad highlights how much these intertwined histories have relied on the shadow archive to make its case. The pictures punctuate Ida B. Wells' painstaking census. In the same way, I argue that while frontline videos from black witnesses are painful to watch, they help build a catalog of proof. One does not have to view every viral video that emerges to understand that this problem of police brutality is systemic. Yet, having a growing body of cases is part memorial and moral suasion. In filming these moments and treating them with subsequent care, just as we would a lynching photograph, we can address the horror that the footage contains in ways that are progressive and not exploitative.

Solidifying a black critical memory. Marcus Wood has argued that slavery's black visual culture is "not necessarily preserved within conventional archives, in boxes and glass cases, or framed on museum walls."[65] Similarly, since there are few spaces to memorialize black victims of police brutality—outside of so-called "dead man's T-shirts" and crude roadside altars—then the call to save all footage of these deaths becomes all the more urgent, perhaps.

A curator of a traveling lynching exhibition, Joseph Jordan, asserted once:

> If we put these photographs back into the trunks, or slide them back into the crumbling envelopes and conceal them in a corner of the drawer, we deny to the victims, once again, the witness they deserve. We deny them the opportunity to demand recognition of their humanity, and for us to bear witness to that humanity. That is exactly what happened in those terrible moments; people who considered themselves decent and devout turned their heads and averted their eyes so they wouldn't have to see. And thousands died because they did so.[66]

The activists I interviewed for this book did not agree about whether they would continue to view every video. Even black journalists working for mainstream media outlets seem flummoxed by the choice they are given: to either honor the dead by bearing witness or protect their own psyches by looking away. Touré, for example, wrote: "I watch all the killing videos I can find because I have to know. What happened exactly? I'm unable to shy away from the pain—I have to know."[67]

This is a theme I hear regularly now, that there is an obligation to view the horror at least once. I argue that when we continue to look, we help secure a stronger future—one that has marked time and taken a tally of all that we have lost and all that we have left to gain. For African Americans, Leigh Raiford wrote, "the persistence of peril and renewed forms of racial inequity and sub-jugation"[68] require an ever-present vigilance. America needs records of her wrongdoings, read back to her writ large, when oppression mutates. It is the only way we will be able to compare and contrast how we have marginalized black people before and what that looks like now. Memory also offers a set of facts around which to organize. This is important for African Americans, who typically were not granted historical spaces to document their cultural trajectory. Consider that the Smithsonian's National Museum of African American History and Culture only opened in 2016 in Washington, DC. The town had long welcomed every other kind of museum, from an Air and Space Museum to the Holocaust Museum decades before then.

History has been, for many African Americans, passed down orally or curated and saved from trusted black sources, just as African American elders were known for saving every copy of *Jet* or *Ebony* magazines. The horror was, and is, not a figment of the black imagination. These things—these killings of men, women, and children—happened, even if a library book or a museum did not record it. Black people have had to be Wikipedia, therefore, before there was a Wikipedia—crowdsourcing all that they knew about a relative who may have disappeared in the night so that they would not be forgotten. This is the true legacy of the lynching photograph. It is not relevant because it is monstrous—even though it is. It is not relevant because it depicts the use of an emergent technology—even though it does. The lynching photograph is record. Part of the *Red Record*. Fatal police shooting videos that feature black people pick up this mantle of service, to black critical memory and so-cial organizing. I am reminded of this when my research assistant sent me a different kind of frantic email just before we ushered in 2019. She wrote to tell me that the Senate unanimously passed legislation that made lynching a federal crime on December 19. The Justice for Lynching Act was Ida B. Wells' unfinished work, continued by Sens. Cory Booker, Kamala Harris, and Tim Scott, who are all African American. As of this book's writing, the House of Representatives has not passed the bill, which would then put it in the hand of the president. And so, in the name of honoring the dead, we wait—and fight—still.

9

Black Witnessing, Body Cams, and the Enduring Fight for the Whole Truth

The room was silent, save for the rapid clicks of camera shutters.

Lesley McSpadden took a deep breath then greeted the Missouri Senate Committee from her seat at an oversized cherry wood table.

"It has been 557 days and I'm still left with the mystery surrounding what really happened to my son on August 9 [2014]," McSpadden said as she fought back tears. She added, "On August 9th, there was no recorded account of my son's last moments in life. I still do not have closure. Please let police-worn body cameras be a voice of truth and transparency in Missouri communities."

McSpadden acknowledged during her 2016 testimony that police "body cams," as they are referred to colloquially, are not a substitute for strong policing. Still, the right to bear witness to a loved one's demise should be the new way forward, she said. She supported Missouri Senate Bill 628 for that reason, she told her legislators.[1]

A year before McSpadden's speech, Walter Scott's brother, Anthony Scott, drafted the "Pass the Police CAMERA Act of 2015" petition on Change.org. He wrote: "The officer who killed Walter wasn't wearing a body camera. Had he been wearing one that was recording his actions, he might not have chosen to commit murder knowing that he'd be held accountable."[2] Scott's campaign garnered more than 120,000 signatures.

Both McSpadden's and Scott's arguments—that police-worn body cameras illuminate more than they obscure—add a final layer of complexity to black witnessing. Thousands of civilians have died during police encounters between 2005 and 2014, yet only 54 officers were charged criminally during this time period.[3] The common argument is that body cams would have saved these lives. Body cams, the logic goes, discourage police misconduct and lead to more accountability. In many of the controversial cases that propelled the anti–police brutality movement, however, body cams merely have complicated the pursuit of officer convictions. In the case of Korryn Gaines,

Bearing Witness While Black. Allissa V. Richardson, Oxford University Press (2020). © Oxford University Press.
DOI: 10.1093/oso/9780190935528.001.0001

for example, police said the officers involved were not wearing body cams as they stormed into her Maryland apartment and shot her in front of her five-year-old son.[4] In the case of Alton Sterling, police said that their body cameras "fell off." Two years after the incident, however, body cam video indeed emerged after an intensive federal investigation.[5,6]

Indeed, body cams have been a part of policing since at least 2010, but the national focus on excessive force after the Ferguson uprisings inspired their widespread adoption across the country. After Michael Brown died, body cam sales spiked 154 percent. Taser International, which leads the industry in stun gun sales, said that its Axon cameras are outfitted on more than 200,000 officers across the United States—and counting.[7] Body cams now capture more than a black witness ever could see. Black witnesses most often have caught precipitating incidents with police in the middle of the action and in a public place. Police body cams, however, film people in their most vulnerable moments. "Dying moments, crying moments, scared silent and unresponsive moments. Mixed in with everyday travails. Warring neighbors, exes, family members; hit-and-runs; and the steady drumbeat of calls about someone dealing drugs, on a residential street, in the corner store, or at the park where children play ball,"[8] legal scholar Mary Fan has noted. That the body cam has become the response to the fatal police encounter is then, perhaps, the greatest irony of black witnessing. Bearing witness while black is, after all, an act that is borne of a desire to be seen as human. Body cams can dehumanize, in that they rob everyday people of privacy. Moreover, body cams restore the power of "veillance" to police. For these reasons, body cams alone will not save us.

Three Problems with Police Body cams

Legal scholars have described the rise of police body cams as a "singular policy response" amid a "moral panic." In December 2014, for example, one month after a St. Louis grand jury decided not to indict Darren Wilson for killing Michael Brown, Pres. Obama asked Congress to allocate $75 million toward outfitting police across the nation with body cams.

Howard M. Wasserman noted that year: "As society's elites coalesce around the idea that some problem poses an existential threat to their values and interests and demands a response, they also coalesce around one bold quick-fix solution endorsed as the comprehensive answer to the problem, even if that solution is rushed, not fully considered, and often ineffective."[9]

In a May 2015 speech from the Roosevelt Room, Pres. Obama acknowledged that his plan to direct federal dollars to state and local law enforcement agencies to buy body cams was far from a complete answer. He cautioned:

> There's been a lot of talk about body cameras as a silver bullet or a solution. I think the task force concluded that there is a role for technology to play in building additional trust and accountability, but it's not a panacea, and that it has to be embedded in a broader change in culture and a legal framework that ensures that people's privacy is respected and that not only police officers but the community themselves feel comfortable with how technologies are being used.

The invasion of privacy, as Obama recognized, is the top legal concern that body cams pose. It is, however, not the only issue.[10] Three other dilemmas that police body cams introduce include (1) first-person viewership bias, (2) narrative fragmentation, and (3) naïve realism. All three of these problems steep the body cam's gaze in white supremacy and obfuscate all that black witnesses try to elucidate.

First-person viewership bias. A generation that came of age in the era of first-person shooter video games—and lives now amid the rise of immersive virtual reality games—might view the police officer's perspective from the body cam as heroic by default. In games such as *Call of Duty*, for example, a player sees the gaming environment from the perspective of the main character. The digitized, outstretched arms, which are seen wielding a gun most often, are meant to be an extension of one's own. Scholars have found such framing incredibly fraught. In 2009, for example, Dmitri Williams and a team of researchers conducted a video game census. The team found a "systematic over-representation of whites" and a "systematic under-representation of females, Hispanics, Native Americans, children and the elderly."[11] The cumulative effect of marginalizing diverse video game characters is that virtual worlds privilege the immersion of only one type of imagined player: "young, white males who want to be powerful white adults," the team concluded.[12]

Other video game scholars have found that even when racially diverse avatar creation options are available, "white avatars remain the 'default' option" or pigeonhole ethnic groups to specific game genres.[13] In this manner video games are "simulating oppression," cloaking white supremacist ideologies in gameplay, and leaving a lasting impact on social identity formation in the same way television is thought to have cultivation effects.[14,15,16] This legacy of gaming—of privileging one group's immersive viewing experiences over another's—is imperative to consider when we dissect how police body cams function. Viewers of body cam footage are placed into a world of unruliness and threat, from a distance. This positionality may lead some viewers—especially those who do not carry weighty baggage—to believe that police are ever the protagonists in a game of law and order. Just as in video games, the people on the opposite side of the gun are enemies.

Some scholars have ventured further still, arguing that the goal of gaming, increasingly, is to annihilate anything non-white. The turn of the 21st century ushered in a slew of post-apocalyptic games that featured "crumbling dominant Western narratives of progress" and "whiteness in crisis," Soraya Murray has written.[17] Games such as *The Last of Us* and *Tomb Raider*, Murray explained, feature "victimized white protagonists in hostile circumstances." In these virtual environments, players are encouraged to kill the zombies, aliens and all manner of grotesque threats, thereby positing the white avatar as the "new oppressed group," Murray wrote.

Gaming's emergent narratives of imperiled whiteness produce real attitudes about race relations in the United States. In 2014, the year of the Ferguson uprisings, a team of researchers found that "white study participants who played a violent video game as a black avatar displayed stronger implicit and explicit negative attitudes toward blacks than did participants who played a violent video game as a white avatar or a nonviolent game as a black or white avatar."[18] Moreover, white participants "who played a violent video game as a black (vs. white) avatar displayed stronger implicit attitudes linking blacks to weapons."[19]

We need more research to state definitively whether this first-person viewership bias of video games occurs when people watch police body cam footage too. It is an essential inquiry to make at a time when videos of fatal police encounters enter more frequently into evidence for juries to consider. Legal scholar Caren Myers Morrison has explained: "[W]e are primed to read body camera footage as even more legitimate than ordinary video evidence. In fact, there is such strong association between handheld movements and documentary aesthetics that fiction filmmakers have sometimes used them just to add a realistic quality to their images."[20]

Media scholars should investigate, therefore, whether non-black people see themselves in police body cam videos either as avatars that uphold law and order, as avatars that benefit from protection against "encroaching black chaos and lawlessness," as both of these, or as something else.[21] Doing so could help explain why the cases of police misconduct that do make it to trial end up in hung juries so often, as in the case of Freddie Gray or Walter Scott.

Further studies about the role of police body cam footage in the white mind might investigate how such footage predisposes viewers to believe that crime happens only in urban communities of color too. While much of the viral video that fueled the Black Lives Matter Movement between 2014 and 2018 featured the overexposed, disinvested landscapes of West Baltimore, Ferguson, or Baton Rouge, white-collar crimes happen every day in some of the United States' most pristine neighborhoods—and it is largely invisible. One of the biggest academic admissions scandals ever to be brought before U.S. federal courts occurred while I wrote this book, for example, yet no viral police body cam footage video exists of it. Some of the 50 people indicted on charges of bribery, mail fraud, and other related crimes included A-list celebrities and Ivy League admissions counselors and athletic coaches alike, yet one would be hard pressed even to find a body cam video of these alleged criminals being handcuffed.

When police do not film themselves enforcing these types of crimes, it gives the crime itself an air of exclusivity.[22] It may be perceived as an exception and not the rule—a case of a few bad apples that got greedy, sloppy or irresponsible. White-collar crime underexposure from police body cams may add also to existing stereotypes about inherent black criminality and aberrant white criminality. Morrison has written, accordingly, that racialized underexposure is: "borne out by the civilians we see in videos of violent encounters—typically people of color, motorists, people engaged in petty crimes, or mentally disturbed people acting erratically. . . . Again, this reflects a general conception of the poor, the disenfranchised, or simply the non-white as the enemy."[23] Taken together, police body cams perform two functions in service of whiteness: they either create a protagonist's space to observe the work of law enforcement as a heroic avatar or simply look away from wealthy white people behaving badly. In both instances, the gaze is disingenuous.

Narrative fragmentation. On blogs, on Twitter, and at academic conferences, I have heard people state that black witnesses' videos do not tell a complete story. I argued then, and now, that *all* filmed accounts of events include some things in the frame while excluding others. The direction of the gaze determines what is captured and what is not. I have agreed that the horrific snippets of death that looped at the height of the Black Lives Matter Movement were gathered during moments of extreme duress. Very few of the viral police shooting videos—save for that featuring Kajieme Powell in Ferguson perhaps—have shown what happened before police arrived at the scene.

Police body cams, therefore, could be effective if they helped viewers fill in the gaps. Most often, however, police do not release these videos immediately. Some departments have claimed that the body cam footage in question is part of an ongoing police investigation, as it did during the Philando Castile trial. Other departments have delayed video releases for political reasons, as former Chicago Mayor Rahm Emanuel is thought to have done in the case of 17-year-old Laquan McDonald. Critics accused Emanuel of embargoing the Chicago PD videos of McDonald's fatal shooting during a heated election season where he was seeking another term.[24] Yet other departments never release entire videos. There are inexplicable gaps in the Waller County Jail surveillance footage, for example, that haunt the family of Sandra Bland. In a HBO documentary about Bland's fatal incarceration in July 2015, her sister noted that portions of the footage appear to have incongruous timestamps or entire frames missing.[25] For all of these reasons, relying upon body cam footage to hold police accountable has proved futile at times, as many departments control whether the footage ever will see the light of day.

When law enforcement agencies do cooperate to release body cam footage quickly—as in the case of Stephon Clark in Sacramento, California—police still can contribute to narrative fragmentation. In the Clark case, officers Terrence Mercadal and Jared Robinet responded to a 911 call about car break ins in March 2018. They cornered Clark, 22, in his grandmother's backyard. Clark reached into his pocket for what police presumed was a gun. The officers shot more than two-dozen bullets at him. Six of the eight bullets that hit him were fired into his back, an autopsy revealed. In his hand, Clark held a cellphone. The Sacramento police chief released body cam and police helicopter camera footage in record time to Clark's family—within 30 days. The problem, however, was that just after the officers shot Clark fatally they muted the audio on their devices at least 16 times, according to the *Washington Post*. For many people, this generated more questions than answers.

This is the paradox of the police body cam. When its footage is not released in a timely manner, we are reminded that the police control the filming and archiving of potentially damning evidence in a misconduct case. When footage is released quickly, manipulated audio or video quality could leave potential jurors more confused than ever. All of this creates a new power struggle to prove whose filmed interpretation—that of the black witness or the police—is right. Naïve realism makes us all believe that we have the singular, right viewing. This is the third problem with police body cams.

Naïve realism. Throughout this text I have been careful not to present black witnesses' reportage about the anti–police brutality movement as the only interpretation of the events that led up to the deaths of this generation's civil rights martyrs. Instead, I have positioned the activists' work as a counternarrative to mainstream media's accounts of the events that led up to the deaths of so many black men, women, and children between 2014 and 2018. Within this frame there was more than one way to report on Black Lives Matter too; be it through poetry, like Eve Ewing, through music, like David Banner, or through the practice of law, like Chris Stewart. The crux of this study, therefore, has been to investigate what people bring "with them" when they engage in black witnessing. I have emphasized that this kind of looking is incredibly subjective and fraught with identity politics, African American history, and concepts of historic oppression and activism. Naïve realism is the opposite of all these ideas.

Naïve realism states that the camera is an impartial gatherer of imagery, and dismisses any references to critical race theory, which would analyze someone's gaze based on their implicit cultural biases. Wasserman has explained: "video is seen as a truthful, unbiased, objective, and unambiguous reproduction of reality, deserving of controlling and dispositive weight."[26] As I have argued here, however, video is incomplete. Without context, viewers can, and will, fill in the blanks, based on their own life experiences and biases. The problem is that when we fill in these blanks, we believe that everyone is filling in the gaps with the same assumptions and conclusions that we make. When we are confronted with a different viewpoint, "we conclude that the difference of opinion is due to a lack of information, intelligence, or objectivity on their part," Morrison has claimed.[27]

Police body cams may complicate further this issue of naïve realism. A recent Pew survey showed a stark racial divide in perceptions of how African Americans are treated by the police. Only half of the white respondents said they believed that African Americans are treated less fairly, while 84% of black respondents said they did.[28] The study did not mention whether the people surveyed trusted police body cams or black witnesses' smartphone videos more. This is a ripe area for research. Is this divide due to strictly implicit biases that viewers may have, or is it due to the viewing source to which the person was exposed? In other words, do people now favor the police's body cam footage over the civilian's cellphone? Is the body cam footage regarded as more objective than a person's cellphone footage? If so, then why is this? Both media sources can contain biased gazes. We need additional research into naïve realism and its effects, therefore, before saturating communities with more cameras. If we do not explore this concept further then we will arrive at a point where more cameras equal only more gazes, more questions, and less justice for the families of the slain victims.

Telling the Truth, the Whole Truth, and Nothing but the Truth

On the morning of October 15, 2018, I drove along the same California freeway that Rodney King traveled that night in March 1991. I was sitting on the 210, crawling along in the legendary Los Angeles traffic, and thinking about what I would say to a room full of community activists in about an hour. The Los Angeles Sheriff's Department had invited me to its first-ever Civilian Oversight Commission community policing conference.[29] The commission, formed in 2016, was the hard fought for byproduct of Patrisse Khan Cullors' activism. As one of the three founders of the Black Lives Matter Movement, she had woven her decades-long activism to end police brutality into her newfound international platform with incredible results.[30] The same city that was once home to one of the nation's most brutal police departments now led the nation in the establishment of a first-of-its-kind, citizen-led group that was designed to evaluate police misconduct. I was intrigued by the idea, even while I thought the phrase "civilian oversight" was a misnomer. I did not think we needed more looking from on high—it was the gazing from below that fascinated me.

As I entered the venue that day and waited in the green room with the other panelists, I felt inexplicably uneasy. Although I traveled many of the infamous streets where the LA riots took place on my way into work at the University of Southern California every day, I had managed to compartmentalize my historical references of the Los Angeles Police Department (LAPD) and Rodney King to old memories of myself sitting with my family watching the city go up in smoke on television. That I would one day be sitting in a room full of officers from that same police force felt incredibly overwhelming. On this day, the LAPD was not an abstract concept, or even something I could view from afar. The LAPD that day, and every day, was real people walking around, talking, laughing, and getting coffee from the refreshments table in the back of the room. Holding the door open for me. Smiling at me. I excused myself from the green room and found a restroom. I felt a heaviness in my chest, yet could not cry. At the risk of sounding hyperbolic, I felt at that moment that everything I had witnessed—as a black witness myself—had brought me into a space where I could speak finally to police and activists at the same time, in hopes of making change.

At nine years old, I did not know that the compassion I felt for Rodney King would one day lead me to teach journalism in the very city where he nearly lost his life. At nine years old, I did not know that my first job after graduate school would be at *Jet* magazine, the publication that printed Emmett Till's tragic photograph. At nine years old, I did not know that I would one day win a grant, which would buy iPods for hopeful black journalism students in Baltimore. I did not know that I would lovingly call these students MOJOs. I did not know that I would tell my MOJOs that smartphones were their newsrooms and their weapons. I did not know, at nine years old, that this style of journalism would take me to Africa, to teach HIV-positive girls how to bear witness. I did not know that one of these girls would die from her illness shortly after I returned home. I did not know that Michael Brown would die the same year my own son was born—the year when I started my doctoral studies, in 2014. I did not know that his death would stay with me through every lecture and assignment. I did not know that Alton Sterling would die. That Philando Castile would die. That Sandra Bland would die. I did not know, at nine years old, that I would one day find a way to add my voice to a problem so persistent and painful. That I would find a way to weave my love of journalism into an activist space—and find others who were leveraging imaginative forms of smartphone journalism to tell the truth too.

Something shifted during that Civilian Oversight Commission conference for me. When I emerged from the restroom, and gazed upon the activists and victim's families wearing "dead man's T-shirts," I realized that black witnessing is something that we must protect. As police body cams vie for the role of the "official record," and as black witnesses increasingly are intimidated or punished for looking, the United States must continue to consider the message and the footage from the people who put themselves in harm's way to capture an alternative story. This is an old story, after all. It is a story that was told long before me—through slave narratives, black newspapers and magazines, urban radio, televised civil rights–era news broadcasts, black blogs and websites and, now, by witnesses with smartphones. For so many decades, African Americans have leveraged the storytelling technologies of the day to create a brand of advocacy journalism that has impelled change—even if the instigators did not live to see it happen.

As I prepared my notes at the dais I readied myself to tell the audience of activists and officers that there is a dual revolution now, which blossomed at the height of the Black Lives Matter Movement. Just when African Americans wielded smartphones to reimagine protest journalism, police added another vantage point. Body cams became the latest evolution in the visual arsenal of policing, rounding out the collective gaze offered by their helicopters, dash cams, surveillance footage, and street-corner blue light cameras. It is a small wonder scholars deem this the era of "toutveillance," where everyone is watching someone.[31]

This war of the gazes will be resolved neither readily nor easily, I told the Civilian Oversight Commission that day. I am inspired, however, by the 15 activists I interviewed for this book. They know that the same city of Baltimore, which blessed Frederick Douglass with freedom, also extinguished the light that was Freddie Gray. They know that the same city of New York, where Ida B. Wells sought refuge from *Southern Horrors*, also shook its Brooklyn Bridge with rage over Eric Garner. They know that Florida, which was home to the first all-black town of Eatonville, also allowed Trayvon Martin's killer to go free. They know that Ohio, which was a bastion of black prosperity during the Great Migration, also snuffed out the lives of Tamir Rice, John Crawford, and MarShawn McCarrel. They know these things.

But they also know that the same city of Oakland that took Oscar Grant also birthed the Black Panther Party for Self-Defense. They know that the same Chicago that killed Laquan McDonald also boasts a street bearing the name of Ida B. Wells. They know that the Emanuel AME church in Charleston, which buried nine of its congregants after a heinous hate crime, was founded by Denmark Vesey—an organizer of one of the largest slave revolts that almost was. They know these things also. They told me so. The 15 activists told me that they will not look away, even when their hearts are broken. They will not look away, even when the movement's progress comes in fits and starts. They will not look away, even when the hashtags stop trending or the videos threaten to make us numb. They will not look away, even when the convictions do not come.

When they continue to bear witness to police brutality, they create a shadow archive for future generations. When they continue to bear witness, they help all of us connect historic dots between human rights injustices then to human rights injustices now. When they continue to bear witness, they will the kind of world they want into existence. It is in this unbroken, historic chain of looking that I now find the ready answer when people ask me if bearing witness while black still matters. If *seeing* still matters. If filming still matters. For the sake of the record, in the name of the dead, and in honor of those who are still living—and still fighting for change—the answer is, simply, yes.

Epilogue

The Evidence of Things Not Seen

I had a hard time finishing this book, because books should have endings. The story of the anti–police brutality movement is still being written though. Just as I was getting ready to submit the final copy of this text to my editor, three major developments happened. First, an unsealed report from BART revealed that one of the officers who had been involved in the Oscar Grant killing—Anthony Pirone—had escalated the incident by hurling racial epithets at Grant. The report revealed also that Officer Johannes Mehserle, who dealt Grant the fatal shot, had a history of excessive force. He had used force "six times in 2008, more than any other officer on the platform that day, and more than most other BART police officers that year," the *Mercury News* reported in May 2019.

As I reeled from the Grant revelations, Black Twitter exploded that same week with news of a "lost" Sandra Bland cellphone video. For the previous four years, #SayHerName supporters had believed that the only footage capturing Bland's encounter with Officer Brian Encinia was from his cruiser dash cam. Moreover, the seemingly edited Waller County Jail surveillance footage remained a heartbreaking mystery. But now, here was evidence that Bland *did* attempt to bear witness to her own case of excessive force. That it had been buried sent a chill through Black Twitter—especially since it came on the heels of a similar revelation that spring.

Just two months prior, in March 2019, the Baton Rouge PD admitted that the police body cams had not fallen off the offending officers during their fatal scuffle with Alton Sterling. The department released disturbing new footage that depicted Officer Salamoni yelling at Sterling almost as soon as he arrived at the convenience store. After the fatal encounter, one of the officers called the dead man a "stupid motherf—er." These disclosures—that both the Bland and Sterling stories had been incomplete for the previous three years— infuriated some members of Black Twitter. Clint Smith, one of our Bards, tweeted on May 7, 2019: "The woman who said Emmett Till came onto her lied about what he said. The officer who killed Oscar Grant lied about what he did. The police withheld video of Sandra Bland that tells a different story.

There's a long history of black ppl being killed based on someone else's lie."[1] More than 80,000 people "liked" this comment.

How does one end a book then, knowing that there may be even more relevant news somewhere that will resurface at any given time? Similarly, what does one tell future generations of potential black witnesses about the power of looking when there are forces working to thwart their right to see, and working harder still to destroy or discredit what they have recorded already? These questions haunt me as a scholar and as a mother.

I began this book by sharing the birth story of my son, explaining what his entry into the world during the Ferguson uprisings meant for my work. I want to end by reflecting on my daughter, who is my first-born child. At age seven, she is a deeply perceptive girl already—and a prize-winning orator to boot. She has a way of sensing shifts in my moods by searching my countenance and vocal inflections intensely. This is why I could not fool her in early July 2016. I did not hear her come up behind me in my home office as I watched Dae'Anna Reynolds comfort her mother, Diamond, in the backseat of a police cruiser. My daughter heard Dae'Anna say, from my computer: "It's okay. I'm right here with you," as her mother sobbed.

"Who's that, Mommy?" my daughter asked. I wiped away tears hurriedly, but not fast enough.

"A girl your age," I told her. Both she and Dae'Anna were four at the time.

"Why is her mommy crying?" she asked as she wiped my face too.

"Because something very bad happened," I said.

My daughter paused and stared at the frozen frame onscreen. "Are you going to write about it?" she asked, wise beyond her years.

"I am going to try," I told her.

"What's going to happen?" she asked, laying her head on my chest.

"I don't know," I remember answering, adding, "What would you like to happen?"

She smiled at me. "I would like to play with that little girl on the computer. And I want you to write about what all the grown-ups did to make her mommy feel better."

In keeping with my daughter's advice, I will end by sharing the hope that the Movement for Black Lives, as it is now called, has inspired. All of the 15 activists who were interviewed for this book have done incredible things with their media platforms since we last spoke.

Alicia Garza, one of three co-founders of Black Lives Matter, launched a new initiative in Black History Month 2018, called Black Futures Lab, which aims to engage black voters year round. Garza wants to help African Americans affect change at the local and state level of government especially, by supporting exciting candidates and helping with community organizing and fundraising. Garza helped Stacey Abrams canvas the state of Georgia, for example, in her 2018 bid to become its first-ever black woman governor. Garza also became a guest editor for *Marie Claire*.

Marissa Johnson co-created the Safety Pin Box in 2017, a media company offering ally training for white people who want to help advance racial justice. In the year that it sold subscriptions for upwards of $100 per month, Johnson and her business partner, Leslie Mac, raised $250,000 that they sowed back into black women organizer efforts around the country. The company dissolved in 2018.

Shellonnee Chinn continues her fight to prove that her former employer, Elmwood Franklin School in Buffalo, New York, discriminated regularly against students and faculty of color. She is representing herself in the case before federal court and even has begun to convene her own press conferences to set the agenda for the reporting of the case.

Brittany Ferrell returned to graduate school to earn a master's in public health at Washington University in St. Louis. She is studying maternal and reproductive health, public policy, and race—issues that drove the mournful conversations that surrounded Erica Garner's untimely death in 2017. Ferrell is developing her own documentary and photo memoir about black maternal mortality. She works also on the staff of Garza's Black Futures Lab.

Brittany Packnett Cunningham has launched a multimedia brand since Pres. Obama tapped her to join the President's Task Force on 21st Century Policing in 2014. She started a clothing line, Love + Power. She co-hosts a popular podcast, *Pod Save the People*, with fellow activists Clint Smith and Sam Sinyangwe. She is an ambassador for Pantene and BET. She was a fellow for the prestigious Harvard Kennedy School Institute of Politics fellowship. She has graced the cover of *Essence*. She gave a TED talk in 2019. She joined MSNBC as a contributor in 2020. And she still serves as Teach for America's vice president of national community alliances.

Samuel Sinyangwe published two more works of data journalism after creating his comprehensive database of fatal police encounters. *Our States* quantifies the political voting power necessary to push progressive agendas through state governments. And *Restore the Vote* visualized a real-time map of petitions that his nonprofit, StayWoke, filed in support of restoring voting rights to Floridians with felony convictions. On November 6, 2018, voters in his home state approved a constitutional amendment that re-enfranchised 1.4 million formerly incarcerated people.

Devin Allen can add "best-selling author" to his list of accomplishments. He published *A Beautiful Ghetto* in 2017, which garnered an NAACP Image Award nomination in the category of Outstanding Literary Work—Debut Author. Allen launched *Through Their Eyes*, a photojournalism program for Baltimore youth in 2017. He became a Gordon Parks Foundation fellow too, that same year.

Dread Scott delivered a well-received TED talk in 2018. More than 1 million people have viewed his presentation, "How Art can Shape America's Conversation about Freedom." Scott launched a new art project too: he and 500 people re-enacted the largest rebellion of enslaved people in North America. The 2019 performance involved hundreds of re-enactors marching 26 miles over two days.

Lincoln Mondy began publishing a monthly social justice newsletter called the *Assembly* in February 2019. Additionally, he is the senior manager of strategic projects at Advocates for Youth, where he crafts the messaging for young people's sexual and reproductive health rights campaigns.

Eve Ewing had a banner year in 2018, when her book *Ghosts in the Schoolyard: Racism and School Closings on Chicago's South Side* debuted. She was profiled in the *New York Times* and appeared on the *Daily Show with Trevor Noah*. She began penning *Marvel* comics and children's books too, to engage the next generation of activists.

Clint Smith earned two prized fellowships since our interview, from the Art for Justice Fund and the National Science Foundation. His book of Black Lives Matter-themed poetry, *Counting Descent*, won the 2017 Literary Award for Best Poetry Book from the Black Caucus of the American Library Association. He is completing a new work of narrative nonfiction, *How the Word is Passed*. He promises that it will be an intergenerational examination of how different places throughout the United States reckon their legacies of slavery.

David Banner is enjoying his newfound role as an activist and public speaker. He has appeared regularly on all of the major cable news networks as a commentator. His interview on the urban radio program, the *Breakfast Club*, is one of its most-watched episodes, with nearly 800,000 views and 13,000 "thumbs up" ratings on YouTube. He has launched an eponymous podcast.

L. Chris Stewart is still an award-winning civil rights attorney, based in Atlanta. He helped form the state's first-ever Conviction Integrity Unit, which will ensure that those who were imprisoned wrongfully may be exonerated quickly. Stewart appears on CNN frequently now as a legal analyst.

Ieshia Evans appeared on an MTV news program in 2017 to criticize Pepsi's controversial commercial, in which model Kendall Jenner handed a white police officer a soda to quell a protest. Pepsi pulled the advertisement when Black Twitter lampooned it. Since then Evans, as she promised, has been very selective about the press she does.

Lastly, Mark Luckie left Facebook in November 2018. His open letter that explained his departure ran in *USA Today* shortly thereafter. Then, he testified before the House Energy and Commerce Committee at an "Inclusion in Tech" hearing. He told Congress that racism was built into the platforms of many tech companies. He promised to keep illuminating the need for diversity in his future work.

In all of these instances, bearing witness while black opened the doors for these activists to do their work on a bigger scale. Whether it was landing an appearance on a mainstream television show, publishing a book, or appearing before the country's top legislators, all of the organizers I interviewed have shifted from their roles as media producers on the frontlines of protests, to become more deliberate thought leaders who infiltrate traditional public spheres. It will be interesting to see what their protest journalism will look like in a few years. It is too early to determine whether the traditional press—with its big financial payouts and built-in systems of validation—will lure many of these indie media makers away from their grassroots.

What I do hope to see is the continued partnership between these journalist-activists and reporters for legacy media. It was that kind of coalition that brought California's Senate Bill No. 1421 to fruition in September 2018. The California Public Records Act now requires a state or local agency to make public records of police misconduct available for inspection. Journalists were able to leverage SB 1421 for the first time in early 2019, to investigate the 10-year-old Oscar Grant case. It is this kind of transparency that will help black witnesses, and their legacy newsroom allies, to tell different stories about policing in the United States. I hope to see other states in the nation adopt police misconduct transparency laws similar to California's trailblazing legislation. Above all, I hope to one day tell the story of how the fight against police brutality was won.

When my daughter witnessed me weeping that day in 2016 she was searching my face for clues in the same way that I had searched my dad's face in 1991, as he watched the Rodney King video. Whether my daughter knew it or not, she was binding bits of my gaze into her own nascent visions of black history and black memory—just as I did—knitting and weaving an ongoing narrative that will be passed on to future generations. As I smiled down re-assuringly at my daughter in my lap, I promised her that I would write about the things the grown-ups did to make the world a little better. I did not have the heart to tell her that I did not know how the story would end. Maybe it was not my story to conclude, I thought to myself that day. Maybe the ending belonged to her and to all of the littlest black witnesses. Maybe their looking would shift the world seismically again someday, in ways that are as yet un-seen. That is the hope we have. This is the heritage we have. This is the faith we have.

Glossary

Black Lives Matter A global network of chapter-based groups that aims to end police brutality and vigilante violence against black people.

Black public sphere A digital or physical gathering space for African Americans to engage in political or cultural dialogue.

Black Twitter A dynamic subgroup of black users on Twitter that creates and shares culturally relevant news and social critique.

Black witnessing A leveraging of the latest news production technology in order to document human rights injustices against black people.

Blacktag A hashtag that signals its cultural relevance to people of African descent, by virtue of its spelling or its reference to black icons.

Corporeal iconography The act of creating an indelible image of protest with the body, as seen during Black Lives Matter die-ins or highway obstructions.

Counternarrative A news frame that challenges stereotypical representations of race, class, gender, and other identity markers.

Counterpublic An oppositional discursive space that forms when dominant dialogues marginalize or stereotype groups that hold less power.

Critical race theory A way of thinking about the world that examines how race, law, and power work together to form systems of oppression.

Die-in A form of corporeal protest that involves large groups of people feigning death in public places.

Discourse Written or oral communication, especially in the sense of a public debate.

Distant witness A person who views secondhand footage of a fatal police encounter and by doing so, may be moved to action.

Enclave A black discursive sphere that organizes and dialogues privately until it has gained enough political power to speak out.

Ethnocentric A focus on the culture of a people, which helps define its values and mores.

First-person viewership bias The act of fusing a gaming avatar's identity with one's own, so that the player assumes its point of view.

Framing A news storytelling technique that relies on thematic shortcuts to describe individuals, groups of people, or complex topics.

Frontline witness A person who records an incident of police brutality with a smartphone.

Greek chorus A storytelling device in ancient dramas that relied on a small group of singers to offer moral interludes.

Hacktivist A person who seeks unauthorized access to social networks, servers, or computer files to further a social movement.

Historic juxtaposition The intentional mash-up of old social movement iconography with new, yet similar, images of protest.

Intersectionality The exploration of how race, class, gender and sexuality overlap to create layered, systemic disadvantages for certain groups of people.

Legacy media The traditional press, which includes mainstream television networks, newspapers, magazines, radio stations, and websites.

Livestream The act of broadcasting a video in real time to one's followers within a social network.

Marginality An involuntary socioeconomic status that is assigned to a person, or groups of people, when denied access to political resources.

Mobile journalism A form of journalism that relies on only smartphones and tablets for the gathering, production, and distribution of news.

Movement for Black Lives A nationwide coalition of more than 100 allied groups that are working to foster racial equality in the United States.

Naïve realism The belief that everyone interprets media, such as a photograph or a video, in the same way.

Narrative analysis An interpretation of the stories that interviewees share during a research study.

Narrative fragmentation The failure of video to tell a complete story either by virtue of its start time or because of heavy tampering or editing.

News myths The unchallenged, and often stereotypical, frames on which journalists rely to tell stories.

Panopticon A circular prison, as described by Jeremy Bentham, in which officers can watch inmates at all times.

Phenomenology The study of one's lived experiences as a means to understanding intentions and actions.

Post-racialism A mythical, "colorblind" state of being that claims that racism is a relic of the past.

Protest #journalism A form of social media enabled, advocacy based news making that attempts to connect historic arcs of human rights injustices.

Public sphere A digital or physical space where people meet to discuss cultural and political issues.

Satellite A form of the black public sphere that does not engage or negotiate with the broader mainstream.

Satiric meme A subgenre of online humor that pokes fun at problematic cultural or political issues.

Semiotics The exploration of symbols and signs for deeper, embedded meaning.

Sousveillance The act of looking from below—from a less powerful social position—to observe the actions of authority figures.

Stingray The brand name of a military-grade cellphone surveillance tool, which has been used without a search warrant in the United States.

Symbolic death The manufacture of images of feigned death to depict large-scale social ills, such as police brutality.

Toutveillance A modern condition where filming is both bottom-up and top-down; where everyone is watching everyone else.

Weighty baggage The identity markers that inform ways of looking and the interpretations of what is seen.

Woke To be in a state of actively calling out and dismantling structural inequalities—especially pertaining to race.

Chronology

This book provides an historical snapshot of anti–police brutality activism and the protest journalism that it inspired, from 2013 to 2017. Many of the precipitating events highlighted in this text coincided with civilian hate crimes and with civil disobedience from movement supporters. This chronology offers a brief timeline of the contemporary racial climate in the United States during the zenith of Black Lives Matter.

YEAR	DATE	TIPPING POINT
2013	July 13	George Zimmerman, 28, was acquitted of the second-degree murder of 17-year-old Trayvon Martin in Sanford, Florida.
	July 14	Alicia Garza wrote a love letter to black people, which contained the sentence, "I continue to be surprised at how little Black Lives Matter." Her friend and colleague, Patrisse Khan Cullors, converted her post to a hashtag, #BlackLivesMatter, which began trending on Twitter.
	July 20	Demonstrators stage a massive sit-in in New York City's Times Square, to protest Zimmerman's acquittal.
2014	July 17	Officer Daniel Pantaleo, of the New York City Police Department, approached Eric Garner, 43, in Staten Island on the suspicion of selling loose cigarettes. Ramsey Orta began filming the exchange. When Garner denied the sales, Pantaleo tried to handcuff him. Garner moved his hands away. He was unarmed. Pantaleo placed him in an illegal chokehold. Garner rasped "I can't breathe," 11 times. He died an hour after losing consciousness. His refrain became the rallying cry for the Black Lives Matter Movement. Garner's daughter, Erica, vowed publicly to seek justice.
	August 5	Ronald Ritchie, who is white, was shopping in an Ohio Walmart when he called 911 to report a black man pointing a gun at other shoppers. That man was 22-year-old John Crawford III. Officer Sean Williams, of the Beavercreek Police Department, rounded the aisle where Crawford was shopping minutes later. Williams fatally shot Crawford within seconds. Store surveillance footage later showed that Crawford never pointed the open-box BB gun at shoppers. Instead, the video showed him on his cellphone with the air rifle at his side.

August 9   Officer Darren Wilson, of the Ferguson Police Department, fatally shot 18-year-old Michael Brown. Brown was unarmed. Wilson later testified to a grand jury that Brown was combative after being confronted about allegedly stealing cigarillos from a nearby convenience store. A witness who lived in a nearby apartment filmed Brown's body in the street as police converged on the scene. Brown lay on Canfield Drive, uncovered, for more than four hours.

August 10   Uprisings in Ferguson, Missouri, began. Black Lives Matter evolved from a hashtag to physical protests. Chapters sprang up around the nation. So-called Freedom Riders from all corners of the country chartered buses to Ferguson to join the protest. Ferguson police responded by deploying its force in armored vehicles and riot gear, and armed with sniper rifles. The demonstrations lasted for nearly one month.

August 18   Gov. Jay Nixon deployed the National Guard in Ferguson as fiery riots continued. Law enforcement officials brutalized members of the press, such as CNN news anchor Don Lemon, who was shoved on live television. Allied Black Lives Matter protests grew in other US cities, to show solidarity with Ferguson.

August 20   Attorney General Eric Holder attempted to quell the protests by visiting Ferguson. He announced the launch of a federal probe into the Ferguson Police Department.

August 23   The cellphone video of Eric Garner's death continued to go viral, inspiring a peaceful march through Staten Island. More than 2,500 people participated, many of them wearing tape over their mouths that read, "I can't breathe."

August 30   Ferguson protestors stopped traffic in St. Louis for more than four hours, to symbolize the length of time Brown's body lay on Canfield Drive.

October 20   Officer Jason Van Dyke, of the Chicago Police Department, responded to a call about a teenager breaking into cars in a parking lot. Van Dyke initially stated that Laquan McDonald, 17, lunged at him with a knife. Dashcam footage revealed that McDonald was walking away from Van Dyke's car when Van Dyke fatally shot him—16 times. The Chicago chief of police was forced to resign when journalists discovered that the department buried the footage to hide it from the public.

November 16   Massive die-ins took place across the United States, as Black Lives Matter protestors commemorated the 100 days that had passed since Brown's death. Demonstrators lay down in public places, as if dead, creating mock mass graves.

November 23   Officer Timothy Loehmann, of the Cleveland Division of Police, fatally shot 12-year-old Tamir Rice, who was playing with a toy gun in a local park. Police reported that the department received a 911 call about a "guy" pretending to shoot people. Municipal surveillance footage captured the encounter.

November 24   One day after Tamir Rice was shot, a Ferguson grand jury decided not to indict Officer Darren Wilson for killing Michael Brown.

November 25   Black Lives Matter demonstrators marched to the Department of Justice, in Washington, DC, and to New York's Times Square to protest Ferguson's decision not to indict Officer Darren Wilson.

November 26   Black Lives Matter protestors shut down the 101 freeway—a major thoroughfare—in Los Angeles. On the east coast, demonstrations in Manhattan continued for nearly 24 hours.

November 28   On the day after Thanksgiving, Black Lives Matter organizers created the #blackoutblackfriday campaign, urging African Americans not to shop. Die-ins were staged at several major US malls.

November 30   Professional athletes began to use their platforms to enter the national dialogue on police brutality. Five players from the St. Louis Rams ran onto the field for a televised game with their hands up, in solidarity for Ferguson.

December 3   A grand jury in Staten Island decided not to indict Officer Pantaleo for choking Eric Garner to death. Attorney General Eric Holder called for a federal investigation into Garner's death.

December 4   Black Lives Matter protestors shut down the Brooklyn Bridge and major thoroughfares in Manhattan to protest the Pantaleo non-indictment.

December 8   LeBron James and scores of other NBA players donned "I Can't Breathe" T-shirts during their televised warm-up exercises, in support of the movement.

December 11   Members of the Congressional Black Caucus stage a "walk-out" to support the Mike Brown and Eric Garner protests.

December 18   In the face of several high-profile non-indictments of police who were involved in fatal shootings, the White House announced a new task force to increase law enforcement accountability. The Task Force on 21st Century Policing was charged with compiling a report on the state of police-citizen relations and official data on fatal police encounters, since there was no such federal database.

	December 22	Black Lives Matter protestors filled the largest shopping center in the United States, the Mall of America in Minnesota.
2015	January 1	#BlackLivesMatter averaged 10,000 Tweets per day, according to *Mother Jones* magazine.
	February 1	The African American Policy Forum launches the #SayHerName Movement, to highlight police brutality against black women.
	March 4	The Department of Justice released its Ferguson report, which revealed that the city's police received financial incentives for targeting black residents with nuisance citations and also engaged regularly in a pattern of racial profiling.
	April 4	North Charleston police officer Michael Slager shot Walter Scott in the back as Scott attempted to flee from a routine traffic stop. Slager planted a Taser next to Scott's body after he fell to the ground and claimed later that Scott tried to take his gun. A bystander, Feidin Santana, filmed the encounter, unbeknownst to Slager.
	April 12	Six officers from the Baltimore City Police Department arrested Freddie Gray, 25, for allegedly possessing an illegal knife. Gray attempted to flee the police on foot. The police caught Gray and loaded him into a police van. During the ride to the station, Gray's spine was 80 percent severed at his neck. Police denied abusing Gray. Gray fell into a coma.
	April 19	Freddie Gray died from his injuries. Massive riots and looting began in Baltimore, prompting Maryland Governor Larry Hogan to declare a "state of emergency." Black witnesses captured Gray's last moments and the city's anguished response to his death on cellphones.
	June 5	Eric Casebolt, an officer for the McKinney Police Department in Texas, slammed 15-year-old Dajerria Becton onto the pavement in an attempt to disperse a pool party of predominantly black children. Casebolt pinned down Becton with his knee in her back. She was unarmed and wearing only a swimsuit. In the cellphone video that captured the assault, Becton begged for her mother through tears. Becton survived but #McKinneyPoolParty trended on Twitter for days.
	June 17	Dylann Roof entered Emanuel African Methodist Episcopal Church for an evening service. He shot eight members of the congregation and their senior pastor while their eyes were closed in prayer. The parishioners became known as the Charleston Nine. Erika Totten's hashtag, #IfWeAintSafeinChurch, began trending.

June 26	President Barack Obama delivers a eulogy for State Sen. Clementa Pinckney, one of the slain Charleston Nine. In it, he calls for South Carolina to remove the Confederate flag from its statehouse.
June 27	Brittany Ann "Bree" Newsome, an African American woman, seemingly answered Pres. Obama's call. She scaled the flagpole at the South Carolina state house to remove the Confederate flag. When she reached the bottom of the pole, officials arrested her immediately. The crowdfunding website, Indiegogo, raised more than $125,000 for her bail and legal fees within a matter of hours.
June 29	Black Lives Matter activists staged a die-in at a general assembly meeting of the United Nations in New York City.
June 30	The Pulitzer Prize-winning rapper, Kendrick Lamar, released his song, "Alright," to radio stations around the world. The music video, which featured police fatally shooting Lamar, has been viewed more than 100 million times on YouTube. "Alright" became the unofficial theme song for the Black Lives Matter Movement, accompanying numerous peaceful marches and demonstrations around the world.
July 10	Texas State Trooper, Brian Encinia, pulled over Sandra Bland, 28, for failure to signal a lane change. During the exchange, Encinia asked Bland to put out a cigarette. She refused. Encinia threatened to Tase her. Bland was arrested and taken to Waller County Jail. Police dash cam footage captured the encounter.
July 13	Sandra Bland was unable to post her $5,000 bond. She died in police custody at Waller County Jail. Her death was ruled a suicide. Bland became the unofficial martyr for the #SayHerName movement to end police brutality against women.
July 19	Then-presidential hopeful Donald J. Trump became the official nominee for the Republican Party. His campaign slogan was "Make America Great Again."
August 12	Pres. Trump said Sen. Bernie Sanders showed weakness when facing #BlackLivesMatter protestors who interrupted his rally. "That will never happen with me," he said. "I don't know if I'll do the fighting myself or if other people will, but that was a disgrace." Numerous incidents of violence against Black Lives Matter protestors erupted at Trump rallies after his comments.
November 9	Donald Trump won the US election for the highest public office in the nation in a stunning upset over Sec. Hillary Clinton—who won the majority of the popular vote, but failed to clinch the electoral college.
2016 January 20	Donald J. Trump was sworn in as the 45th president of the United States.

February 7   Police unions around the country called for a boycott of pop singer Beyoncé after she performed a Black Panther Party-themed rendition of her song, "Formation," at the Super Bowl 50 halftime show. The song's video featured a black boy in a hoodie dancing in front of a line of police wearing riot gear.

February 24   Black Lives Matter activists continued to disrupt presidential hopefuls on their campaign trails. One group confronted Sec. Hillary Clinton backstage at an event, calling for her to apologize for calling African Americans "super-predators" during her husband's controversial "three strikes" campaigns in the 1990s.

May 26   Police unions around the country celebrated a major victory as Louisiana became the first state to pass a "Blue Lives Matter" law, which made assaulting an officer a hate crime.

June 23   Officer Caesar Goodson, who drove the van during Freddie Gray's fatal "rough ride," was acquitted of second-degree depraved-heart murder, second-degree assault, misconduct in office, and involuntary manslaughter.

July 5   Officer Blane Salamoni, of the Baton Rouge Police Department, fatally shot Alton Sterling outside of a local convenience store. Sterling was selling DVDs. Several witnesses, including the store owner, filmed the killing with cellphones.

July 6   Jeronimo Yanez, an officer with the Saint Anthony Police Department, fatally shot Philando Castile, 32, during a routine traffic stop. Castile's four-year-old daughter and his fiancée, Diamond Reynolds, were in the car. Reynolds livestreamed the encounter and posted it to Facebook. The footage went viral within hours, prompting Black Lives Matter protests around the world.

July 7   National narratives around Black Lives Matter demonstrations began to shift following fatal shootings at a Dallas protest. Micah Xavier Johnson—a lone, black gunman—killed five police officers and then hid in a parking garage. The Dallas police force killed Johnson with a robot that detonated a bomb near him.

July 12   Pres. Obama defends Black Lives Matter publicly during a eulogy for the slain Dallas police officers.

July 17   Gavin Eugene Long, a black military veteran, posted a rant to Facebook, lamenting the string of acquittals of police in high-profile shootings. Then, he fatally shot three police in Baton Rouge, where Alton Sterling had been killed just a few days earlier.

July 18   Milwaukee Sheriff David Clarke, who is black, declared at the Republican National Convention, "Blue lives matter." He further denounced Black Lives Matter as the United States' true "enemy." African Americans began to split—ideologically and politically—about the movement's tactics and way forward.

July 27   Another officer was acquitted in the Freddie Gray trial and the state attorney for Baltimore, Marilyn Mosby, made the difficult decision to drop all other charges against the remaining four officers.

August 1   Officers from the Baltimore County Police Department attempted to serve Korryn Gaines, 23, a bench warrant at her home for failing to appear in traffic court. Gaines refused to let them into her apartment and quickly took up arms to defend her family. She livestreamed the six-hour standoff to Facebook and Instagram, which showed her cradling a shotgun and a child. Police contacted both social networks to have Gaines's accounts disabled. Then, they raided Gaines's home. Officer Royce Ruby Jr. fatally shot her. Stray bullets struck her five-year-old son, Kodi, in the face and arms. He survived.

August 14   Colin Kaepernick, a star football player for the San Francisco 49ers, began his controversial "Take a Knee" protest. During the national anthem Kaepernick kneeled, rather than stood, with his hand over his heart. Many players in the coming months followed his lead. Kaepernick's silent protest is pictured in the National Museum of African American History and Culture in Washington, DC.

September 16   Officer Betty Jo Shelby of the Tulsa Police Department fatally shot Terence Crutcher, 40, while responding to a call about an unattended vehicle that was blocking the road. Shelby told investigators that Crutcher was not following instructions when she encountered him. She believed he was intoxicated with PCP. Crutcher was unarmed, with his hands in the air, when he began to walk away from Shelby. Police dash cam and helicopter camera footage captured the killing.

September 20   Brentley Vinson, an officer for the Charlotte-Mecklenburg Police Department, fatally shot Keith Lamont Scott, 43, while attempting to serve a warrant to someone else. Scott's wife filmed the exchange, and was heard begging police not to shoot him, since her husband was unarmed and suffering from a traumatic brain injury, which often disoriented him.

| 2017 | February 28 | US Attorney General Jeff Sessions announced that the Department of Justice would "pull back" on the federal scrutiny of police departments for civil rights violations against people of color. |
| | December 30 | Erica Garner, 27, daughter of Eric Garner and key activist in the Black Lives Matter Movement, died of a massive heart attack. Her death followed a non-indictment of her father's killer. |

Notes

Preface

1. Garza, A. (2014). A herstory of the #BlackLivesMatter movement. In Hobson, J. (Ed.), *Are all the women still white? Rethinking race, expanding feminisms*, pp. 23–28. Albany, NY: SUNY Press.

2. Kast, S. (2010, June 23). Morgan State finds its MOJO. *Maryland Morning: NPR*. Retrieved from https://mdmorn.wordpress.com/2010/06/22/623102-morgan-state-finds-its-mojo/.

3. Carey, N. (2011, August 23). Special report: In Libya, the cellphone as weapon. *Reuters*.com. Retrieved from https://reut.rs/2L8Kn9N.

4. Mortensen, M. (2011). When citizen photojournalism sets the news agenda: Neda Agha Soltan as a Web 2.0 icon of post-election unrest in Iran. *Global Media and Communication*, 7(1), 4–16.

5. Tufekci, Z., & Wilson, C. (2012). Social media and the decision to participate in political protest: Observations from Tahrir Square. *Journal of Communication*, 62(2), 363–379.

6. *See*: http://www.slavevoyages.org to view the database of 36,000 known transatlantic slave voyages. These data estimate that between 10 million and 12.5 million Africans were forced into bondage between the 16th and 19th centuries. Most were taken to Brazil and the Caribbean islands.

7. *See*: http://www.monroeworktoday.org to view a comprehensive database and data visualization of lynching in the United States from 1865 to 1964. The site gives a home at last to the intellectual labor of Monroe Work, who was a premiere sociologist, data activist, and rigorous keeper of lynching tallies. Work served as the director of records and research at the Tuskegee Institute.

8. At press time for this book, the total number of 2.2 million people in the United States are incarcerated, of whom 56 percent are either African American or Latino. African Americans and Latinos make up only 30 percent of the US population though. To see the complete racial analysis of the US prison population, read the Sentencing Project's 2015 report: *Black Lives Matter: Eliminating Racial Inequity in the Criminal Justice System*.

9. Freelon, D., McIlwain, C. D., & Clark, M. (2016). Beyond the hashtags: #Ferguson, #Blacklivesmatter, and the online struggle for offline justice. *Center for Media & Social Impact, American University*. Retrieved from http://creativecommons.org/licenses/by-nc-sa/4.0/.

10. Lartey, J. (2018, Jan. 28). We've ignited a new generation: Patrisse Khan-Cullors on the resurgence of black activism. *The Guardian*. Retrieved from https://www.theguardian.com/us-news/2018/jan/28/patrisse-khan-cullors-black-lives-matter-interview.

11. Gentzkow, M., Glaeser, E. L., & Goldin, C. (2006). The rise of the Fourth Estate. How newspapers became informative and why it mattered. In Glaeser, E. L., & Goldin, C. (Eds.), *Corruption and reform: Lessons from America's economic history*, pp. 187–230. Chicago, IL: University of Chicago Press.

12. Mann, S., & Ferenbok, J. (2013). New media and the power politics of sousveillance in a surveillance-dominated world. *Surveillance & Society*, *11*(1/2), 18.

13. Denvir, D. (2016, July 11). Criminalizing the hustle: Policing poor people's survival strategies from Eric Garner to Alton Sterling. *Salon*. Retrieved from https://www.salon.com/2016/07/08/criminalizing_the_hustle_policing_poor_peoples_survival_strategies_from_erin_garner_to_alton_sterling/.

14. Benkler, Y. (2011). A free irresponsible press: Wikileaks and the battle over the soul of the networked Fourth Estate. *Harvard Civil Rights-Civil Liberties Law Review*, *46*, 311.

Chapter 1

1. Young, R. (2017). The viral video that set a city on fire. *CNN*. Retrieved from https://cnn.it/2LbM72h.

2. Frosh, P., & Pinchevski, A. (Eds.). (2008). *Media witnessing: Testimony in the age of mass communication*. New York, NY: Springer.

3. Ibid, p. 1.

4. Peters, J. (2001). Witnessing. *Media, Culture & Society*, *23*(6), 707–723.

5. Bal, H. M., & Baruh, L. (2015). Citizen involvement in emergency reporting: A study on witnessing and citizen journalism. *Interactions: Studies in Communication & Culture*, *6*(2), 213–231.

6. Allan, S., & Peters, C. (2015). Visual truths of citizen reportage: Four research problematics. *Information, Communication & Society*, *18*(11), 1348–1361.

7. Paschalidis, G. (2015). Mini cameras and maxi minds: Citizen photojournalism and the public sphere. *Digital Journalism*, *3*(4), 634–652.

8. Gregory, S. (2016). Human rights in an age of distant witnesses: Remixed lives, reincarnated images and live-streamed co-presence. In Eder, J., & Klonk, C. (Eds.), *Image operations: Visual media and political conflict*, p. 184.

9. This trademark has since expired, but its official entry in the US Patent and Trademark Office can be found online at http://uspto.gov. Use "bearing witness" as the search term.

10. Felman, S., & Laub, D. (1992). *Testimony: Crises of witnessing in literature, psychoanalysis, and history*. New York, NY: Routledge.

11. Chavez, N., Grinberg, E., McLaughlin, E. (2018, Oct. 31). Pittsburgh synagogue gunman said he wanted all Jews to die, criminal complaint says. *CNN*. Retrieved from https://www.cnn.com/2018/10/28/us/pittsburgh-synagogue-shooting/index.html.

12. Price, W. (2014, Aug. 11). Ferguson protest: "I am a man." Retrieved from http://www. stlamerican.com/gallery/wiley_price_photojournalism/ferguson-protest-i-am-a-man/image_056c85f8-2181-11e4-842b-001a4bcf887a.html.

13. Estes, S. (2006). *I am a man!: Race, manhood, and the Civil Rights Movement.* Chapel Hill, NC: The University of North Carolina Press.

14. Honey, M. K. (2011). *Going down Jericho Road: The Memphis Strike, Martin Luther King's last campaign,* p. 255. New York, NY: W. W. Norton & Company, Inc.

15. Carson, C., & Shepard, K. (2001). *A Call to Conscience: The landmark speeches of Dr. Martin Luther King, Jr.,* pp. 234–244. New York, NY: Hachette Book Group.

16. Davis, A. Y. (1994). Afro images: Politics, fashion and nostalgia. *Critical Inquiry,* 37–45.

17. Wiggins, D. K. (1992). "The year of awakening": Black athletes, racial unrest and the Civil Rights Movement of 1968. *The International Journal of the History of Sport, 9*(2), 188–208.

18. Yesko. P. (2018). Acquitting Emmett Till's killers. *American Public Radio.* Retrieved from https://www.apmreports.org/story/2018/06/05/all-white-jury-acquitting-emmett-till-killers.

19. Huie, W. B. (1956). The shocking story of approved killing in Mississippi. *Look, 20*(2), 46–50. Retrieved from https://www.pbs.org/wgbh/americanexperience/features/till-killers-confession/.

20. Alexander, E. (1994). "Can you be BLACK and look at this?": Reading the Rodney King video(s). *Public Culture, 7*(1), 77–94.

21. Ibid., p. 89.

22. Ibid., p. 88.

23. Laurent, O. (2015, April 30). Go behind TIME's Baltimore cover with aspiring photographer Devin Allen. *TIME Lightbox Photo Blog.* Retrieved from http://time.com/3841077/baltimore-protests-riot-freddie-gray-devin-allen//.

24. I tested out many of the ideas in this first chapter in an academic journal article. I have since added to my original musings, but you can find that initial article here: Richardson, A. V. (2016). Bearing witness while black: Theorizing African American mobile journalism after Ferguson. *Digital Journalism, 17*(4), 398–414.

25. Schwartz, I. (2014, Nov. 17). Eric Holder likens Michael Brown to Emmett Till: "The struggle goes on." *Real Clear Politics.* Retrieved from https://www.realclearpolitics.com/video/2014/11/17/eric_holder_likens_michael_brown_to_emmett_till_the_struggle_goes_on.html.

26. Peters, J. (2001).

27. Exodus 20:16 (King James Version).

28. Alexander, E. (1994).

29. Ogletree, C. (2012). *The presumption of guilt: The arrest of Henry Louis Gates, Jr. and race, class and crime in America.* New York, NY: St. Martin's Press.

30. Alexander, E. (1994), p. 85.

31. Collins, P. H. (2009). *Another kind of public education: Race, schools, the media, and democratic possibilities,* p. 42. Boston, MA: Beacon Press.

32. Teague, M., & Laughland, O. (2016, July 7). Alton Sterling shooting: New footage appears to show police taking gun from body. Retrieved from https://www.theguardian.com/us-news/2016/jul/06/alton-sterling-gun-baton-rouge-new-video.

33. The original Twitter threads that announced Michael Brown's killing live are online still. *See*: https://twitter.com/TheePharoah/status/498152622012907520 and https://twitter.com/TheePharoah/status/498152874312867840.

34. Crilly, R. (2014, Aug. 16). Dramatic pictures emerge of Michael Brown shooting in Ferguson, Missouri. *The Telegraph*. Retrieved from https://www.telegraph.co.uk/news/worldnews/northamerica/usa/11038527/Dramatic-pictures-emerge-of-Michael-Brown-shooting-in-Ferguson-Missouri.html.

35. Java, A., Song, X., Finin, T., & Tseng, B. (2007). Why we twitter: Understanding microblogging usage and communities. Paper included in Proceedings of the 9th WebKDD and 1st SNA-KDD 2007 workshop on Web mining and social network analysis, pp. 56–65.

36. Armstrong, C. L., & Gao, F. (2010). Now tweet this: How news organizations use Twitter. *Electronic News*, 4(4), 218–235.

37. Pew Research Center. (2018, Feb. 5). *Mobile fact sheet*. Retrieved from http://www.pewinternet.org/fact-sheet/mobile/.

38. Ibid.

39. Sicha, C. (2009). What were black people talking about on Twitter last night?" *The Awl*. Retrieved from https://medium.com/the-awl/what-were-black-people-talking-about-on-twitter-last-night-4408ca0ba3d6.

40. Brock, A. (2012). From the blackhand side: Twitter as a cultural conversation. *Journal of Broadcasting & Electronic Media*, 56(4), 529–549.

41. Manjoo, F. (2010, Aug. 10). How black people use Twitter. *Slate.com*. Retrieved from https://slate.com/technology/2010/08/how-black-people-use-twitter.html.

42. Sharma, S. (2013). Black Twitter? Racial hashtags, networks and contagion. *New Formations*, 78(78), 46–64.

43. Clark, M. (2014). *To tweet our own cause: A mixed-methods study of the online phenomenon Black Twitter*. Chapel Hill, NC: The University of North Carolina at Chapel Hill.

44. Laughland, O., and Swaine, J. (2015, August 17). "I dream about it every night": What happens to Americans who film police violence? *The Guardian*. Retrieved from https://www.theguardian.com/us-news/2015/aug/15/filming-police-violence-walter-scott-michael-brown-shooting.

45. Victor, D., & McPhate, M. (2016). Critics of police welcome Facebook Live and other tools to stream video. *The New York Times*. Retrieved from https://www.nytimes.com/2016/07/08/us/critics-of-police-welcome-facebook-live-and-other-tools-to-stream-video.html.

46. Habermas, J. (1991). *The structural transformation of the public sphere: An inquiry into a category of bourgeois society*. Cambridge, MA: The MIT Press.

47. Gunaratne, S. A. (2006). Public sphere and communicative rationality: Interrogating Habermas's Eurocentrism. *Journalism & Communication Monographs*, 8(2), 93–156.

48. Linke, U. (1999). Formations of white public space: Racial aesthetics, body politics and the nation. *Transforming Anthropology*, 8(1–2), 129–161.

49. Gregory, S. (1994). Race, identity and political activism: The shifting contours of the African American public sphere. *Public Culture*, 7(1), 147–164.

50. Pough, G. D. (2015). *Check it while I wreck it: Black womanhood, hip-hop culture, and the public sphere.* Boston, MA: Northeastern University Press.

51. Collins, P. H. (2000). Gender, black feminism, and black political economy. *The Annals of the American Academy of Political and Social Science*, 568(1), 41–53.

52. Folami, A. (2007). From Habermas to 'get rich or die tryin': Hip hop, the Telecommunications Act of 1996, and the black public sphere. *Michigan Journal of Race & Law, 12*, 235.

53. Baker, H. A. (1994). Critical memory and the black public sphere. *Public Culture*, 7(1), 3–33.

54. Fraser, N. (1990). Rethinking the public sphere: A contribution to the critique of actually existing democracy. *Social Text*, (25/26), 56–80.

55. Ibid., p. 77.

56. Collective, B. P. S. (Ed.). (1995). *The black public sphere: A public culture book*, p. 3. Chicago, IL: University of Chicago Press.

57. Harris-Lacewell, M. (2004). Barbershops, bibles, and BET: Everyday talk and black political thought. Princeton, NJ: Princeton University Press.

58. Squires, C. R. (2002). Rethinking the black public sphere: An alternative vocabulary for multiple public spheres. *Communication Theory*, 12(4), 446.

59. Harris-Lacewell, M. (2004), xxi.

60. Du Bois, W. E. B. (1903). *The souls of black folk*, p. 7. New York, NY: Oxford University Press.

61. Squires, C. (2002), p. 458.

62. Ibid.

63. Ibid., p. 459.

64. LeMelle, T. J. (2002). The HBCU: Yesterday, today and tomorrow. *Education, 123*(1), 190.

65. Ross, L. C. (2001). *The Divine Nine: The history of African American fraternities and sororities.* New York, NY: Kensington Books.

66. Dawkins, W. (1997). *Black journalists: The NABJ story.* Merrillville, IN: August Press.

67. Squires, C. (2002), p. 460.

68. Khan-Cullors, P. (2018). *When they call you a terrorist*, p. 215. New York, NY: St. Martin's Press.

69. Mills, Q. T. (2013). *Cutting along the color line: Black barbers and barber shops in America*, p. x. Philadelphia: University of Pennsylvania Press.

70. Akom, A. A. (2003). Reexamining resistance as oppositional behavior: The Nation of Islam and the creation of a black achievement ideology. *Sociology of Education*, 305–325.

71. Squires, C. (2002), p. 464.

72. Ibid., p. 462.

73. Benson, T. W. (1974). Rhetoric and autobiography: The case of Malcolm X. *Quarterly Journal of Speech*, *60*(1), 1–13.

Chapter 2

1. Frederick Douglass' family gave two black activists, Shaun King and Ben Dixon, permission to re-launch his *North Star* newspaper. The duo have pledged to publish a website and a series of podcasts on social justice issues. To hear King and Dixon discuss the revamped publication *see*: https://buildingthenorthstar.com.
2. Four black journalists launched the Ida B. Wells Society in 2016. Nikole Hannah-Jones, Ron Nixon, Corey Johnson, and Topher Sanders aim to provide high-quality investigative journalism training to reporters of color. For their creation story *see*: http://idabwellssociety.org/about/our-creation-story/.
3. For a fascinating frame-by-frame comparison of Kendrick Lamar's music video *ELEMENT* to the photojournalism of Gordon Parks *see*: https://www.thefader.com/2017/06/27/kendrick-lamar-element-video-gordon-parks-photos.
4. Haygood, C. (2017). The influence of Zora Neale Hurston's films on Beyonce's *Lemonade*. *Kenyon Review*. Retrieved from https://www.kenyonreview.org/2017/12/influence-zora-neale-hurstons-films-beyonces-lemonade/.
5. Goldstein, M. (2006). The other beating. *The Los Angeles Times*. Retrieved from http://articles.latimes.com/2006/feb/19/magazine/tm-holiday8.
6. Djan, O. S., & Cockin, M. S. (1942). Drums and victory: Africa's call to the empire. *Journal of the Royal African Society*, *41*(162), 29–41.
7. Curtis, M. V. (1988). Understanding the black aesthetic experience. *Music Educators Journal*, *75*(2), 23–26.
8. Bluett, T. (1734). *Some memoirs of the life of Job, the son of Solomon, the high priest of Boonda in Africa; who was a slave about two years in Maryland; and afterwards being brought to England, was set free, and sent to his native land in the year 1734*, p. 53. London: Richard Ford. Retrieved from http://docsouth.unc.edu/neh/bluett/bluett.html.
9. Douglass, F. (1960). *Narrative of the life of Frederick Douglass, an American slave*, p. 73. London: Oxford University Press.
10. Blassingame, J. W. (Ed.). (1977). *Slave testimony: Two centuries of letters, speeches, interviews, and autobiographies*. Baton Rouge: LSU Press.
11. McBride, D. A. (2001). *Impossible witnesses: Truth, abolitionism, and slave testimony*, p. 157. New York, NY: NYU Press.
12. Hurston, Z. N. (1979). The Eatonville anthology. *Folklore, Memoirs, & Other Writings*, pp. 813–826.
13. *Born in slavery: Slave narratives from the Federal Writers' Project, 1936–1938*. Digital Collections. Library of Congress. Retrieved from https://www.loc.gov/collections/slave-narratives-from-the-federal-writers-project-1936-to-1938/about-this-collection/.
14. Vassell, O., & Burroughs, T. S. (2014). "No other but a Negro can represent the Negro": How black newspapers "founded" Black America and Black Britain. *Journal of Pan African Studies*, *7*(4), 256–268.

15. Squires, C. R. (2009). *African Americans and the media*. Cambridge, UK: Polity Press.
16. Ibid., p. 15.
17. Blackmon, D. A. (2009). *Slavery by another name: The re-enslavement of black Americans from the Civil War to World War II*. New York, NY: Anchor.
18. Gressman, E. (1952). The unhappy history of civil rights legislation. *Michigan Law Review, 50*(8), 1323–1358.
19. NAACP. (2019). *History of lynchings*. Retrieved from https://www.naacp.org/history-of-lynchings/.
20. Wells, I. B. (1892/2014). *Southern horrors: Lynch law in all its phases*. The Floating Press. Retrieved from http://readingsinjournalism.pbworks.com/f/Ida%20B.%20Wells,%20Southern%20Horrors%20%20SHORT%20PAMPHLET—%20READ%20THIS.pdf.
21. Ibid., p. 36.
22. Curry, T. J. (2012). The fortune of Wells: Ida B. Wells-Barnett's use of T. Thomas Fortune's philosophy of social agitation as a prolegomenon to militant civil rights activism. *Transactions of the Charles S. Peirce Society: A Quarterly Journal in American Philosophy, 48*(4), 456–482.
23. Wells, I. B. (2014). *The light of truth: Writings of an anti-lynching crusader*. New York, NY: Penguin.
24. Richardson, A. (2016). The Platform: How Pullman porters used railways to engage in networked journalism. *Journalism Studies, 17*(4), 398–414.
25. Washburn, P. S. (2006). *The African American newspaper: Voice of freedom*, p. 185. Evanston, IL: Northwestern University Press.
26. Ibid.
27. Ransby, B. (2015). The class politics of Black Lives Matter. *Dissent, 62*(4), 31–34.
28. Tyson, T. B. (2017). *The blood of Emmett Till*, p. 68. New York, NY: Simon & Schuster.
29. Although *Jet* magazine published the infamous Emmett Till photograph in 1955, I accessed it from TIME magazine's online collection, *100Photos*. The staff curated what it deemed "the most influential photos of all time." To view the Till photograph within this visual anthology *see*: http://100photos.time.com/photos/emmett-till-david-jackson.
30. Johnson, J. H., & Bennett, L. (1989.) *Succeeding against the odds: The inspiring autobiography of one of America's wealthiest entrepreneurs*, p. 116. New York, NY: Warner Books.
31. Stange, M., & Vogel, T. (2001). Photographs taken in everyday life: Ebony's photojournalistic discourse. In Marcus, J., & Levine, R. S. (Eds.), *The black press: New literary and historical essays*, pp. 188–206. New Brunswick, NJ: Rutgers University Press.
32. Tait, D. (2009). Reading the "Negro Bible": Online access to *Jet* and *Ebony*. *Resources for American Studies, 62*, 1–9.
33. Johnson, R. E. (1991, March). Backstage. *Jet*. Retrieved from https://tinyurl.com/y2ex6a6r.
34. Frazier, E. F. (1997). The Negro press and wish-fulfillment. In *Black bourgeoisie*, pp. 174–94. New York, NY: Free Press Paperbacks.
35. Stange, M., & Vogel, T. (2001), p. 206.

36. Penrice, R. R. (2014, February 14). Why Malcolm X rifle image still strikes a chord. *The Grio*. Retrieved from http://on.thegrio.com/1XDbdBq.

37. Smith, C. (2006). Moneta Sleet Jr. as active participant: The Selma march and the Black Arts Movement. In Collins, L. G., & Crawford, M. N., (Eds.), *New thoughts on the Black Arts Movement*, 210–226. New Brunswick, NJ: Rutgers University Press.

38. Parks, G. (1966). *A choice of weapons*. New York, NY: Berkley Publishing Corporation.

39. Squires, C. R. (2009).

40. Dingle, D. (2017). 45 Great moments in black business—No. 36: Essence sale continues debate over black ownership. *Black Enterprise*. Retrieved from https://www.blackenterprise.com/great-moments-in-black-business-no-36-essence-sale-continues-debate-over-black-ownership/.

41. Bates, K. G. (2016). Private equity firm buys *Ebony* and *Jet* magazines. *NPR*. Retrieved from: https://www.npr.org/2016/06/16/482279802/private-equity-firm-buys-ebony-and-jet-magazines.

42. Garcia, S. (2018, January 4). With sale, *Essence* is once again a fully black-owned magazine. (National Desk). *New York Times*.

43. Washburn, P. S. (2006).

44. Phillips, J. (2016). Caliver, Ambrose: 1894–1962. *Black Past*. Retrieved from http://www.blackpast.org/aah/caliver-ambrose-1894-1962.

45. Squires, C. R. (2009).

46. Ibid., p. 161.

47. Barlow, W. (1999). *Voice over: The making of black radio*, p. 294. Philadelphia, PA: Temple University Press.

48. Jackson, J. L., & Alvite, D. (2012). Unlikely hero: Rapping with Petey Greene. *Journal on African Philosophy*, 6. Retrieved from https://www.africaknowledgeproject.org/index.php/jap/article/view/1511.

49. Isaksen, J. L. (2012). Resistive radio: African Americans' evolving portrayal and participation from broadcasting to narrowcasting. *Journal of Popular Culture*, 45(4), 749–68.

50. Ibid.

51. Vincent, R. (2013). *Party music: The inside story of the Black Panthers' band and how Black Power transformed soul music*. Chicago, IL: Lawrence Hill Books.

52. CBS News. (2011). Media, MLK and the Civil Rights Movement. Retrieved from https://youtu.be/pll_5s10ils?t=68.

53. Raiford, L. (2007). "Come let us build a new world together": SNCC and photography of the Civil Rights Movement. *American Quarterly*, 59(4), 1129.

54. Raiford, L. (2011). *Imprisoned in a luminous glare: Photography and the African American freedom struggle*. Chapel Hill: UNC Press Books.

55. NBC Staff. (2015). #Selma50: What the media and Hollywood got wrong about Bloody Sunday. *NBC News*. https://www.nbcnews.com/news/nbcblk/media-studies-selma-n319436.

56. Roberts, G., & Klibanoff, H. (2007). *Race Beat: The press, the Civil Rights struggle, and the awakening of a nation*. New York, NY: Vintage Books.

57. Norris, P. (2001). *Digital divide: Civic engagement, information poverty, and the Internet worldwide.* Cambridge, UK: Cambridge University Press.

58. Compaine, B. M. (2001). *The digital divide: Facing a crisis or creating a myth?* Cambridge, MA: MIT Press.

59. Watts, Jenisha. (2011). BlackPlanet's founder talks MySpace, why he was skeptical of Twitter, and if Facebook may have peaked. *Complex.* Retrieved from https://www.complex.com/pop-culture/2011/03/interview-blackplanet-founder-talks-myspace-twitter-facebook.

60. Ibid.

61. Greenwell, A. V. (2012). Twentieth-century ideology meets 21st-century technology: Black news websites and racial uplift. *Fire!!!: The Multimedia Journal of Black Studies, 1*(2), 111–138.

62. Schoetz, D. (2008). Cops cleared in groom's 50-shot slaying. *ABC News.* Retrieved from https://abcnews.go.com/US/story?id=4725206&page=1.

63. Olumhense, E. (2019). 20 years after the NYPD killing of Amadou Diallo, his mother and community ask: What's changed? *Intelligencer.* Retrieved from http://nymag.com/intelligencer/2019/02/after-the-nypd-killing-of-amadou-diallo-whats-changed.html.

64. Schoetz, D. (2008).

65. Hirschfield, P. J., & Simon, D. (2010). Legitimating police violence: Newspaper narratives of deadly force. *Theoretical Criminology, 14*(2), 155–182.

66. CNN Staff. (2008). Close-up: Jesse Jackson crying. *CNN.* https://www.youtube.com/watch?v=CKWKlDznDPE.

67. Leonard, J. (2010, June 24). Court releases dramatic video of BART Shooting. Retrieved from https://youtu.be/Q2LDw5l_yMI.

68. Antony, M. G., & Thomas, R. J. (2010). "This is citizen journalism at its finest": YouTube and the public sphere in the Oscar Grant shooting incident. *New Media & Society, 12*(8), 1280–1296.

69. Winfrey, O. (2013). Why Michael B. Jordan says black males are America's pitbulls. *Oprah's Next Chapter.* Retrieved from http://www.oprah.com/own-oprahs-next-chapter/why-michael-b-jordan-says-black-males-are-americas-pit-bulls-video.

70. McKinley, Jesse. (2009, January 8). In California, protests after man dies at hands of transit police. (National Desk)(Oscar Grant III). *The New York Times,* p. A10.

71. La Ganga, Maria L., & Dolan, Maura. (2009, January 15). Oakland shooting protest ends in violence: Some of those protesting the death of Oscar J. Grant III damage businesses and cars, a former transit police officer is charged in the case. *The Los Angeles Times,* p. 1.

72. Weinstein, A. (2013, July 12). This, courtesy of MSNBC, is Trayvon Martin's dead body. Get angry. *Gawker.* Retrieved from https://gawker.com/this-courtesy-of-msnbc-is-trayvon-martins-dead-body-753370712/.

73. Coates, T. (2012). Florida's self-defense laws and the killing of Trayvon Martin. *The Atlantic,* pp. 7–10. Retrieved from https://www.theatlantic.com/national/archive/2012/03/floridas-self-defense-laws-and-the-killing-of-trayvon-martin/254396/.

74. Cobb, J. (2013). Rachel Jeantel on trial. *The New Yorker*. Retrieved from https://www.newyorker.com/news/news-desk/rachel-jeantel-on-trial.

75. Abad-Santos, A. (2013). My star witness is black: Rachel Jeantel's testimony makes Trayvon a show trial. *The Atlantic*. Retrieved from http://www.thewire.com/national/2013/06/rachel-jeantel-testimony-trayvon-martin-trial/66652/.

76. Samara, R. (2013). What white people don't understand about Rachel Jeantel. *GlobalGrind*. Retrieved from https://bit.ly/2NDRMuT.

77. Fryer, R. G., Jr. (2018). Reconciling results on racial differences in police shootings. *American Economic Review Papers and Proceedings, 108*, pp. 228–233.

78. Lind, D. (2015, December 17). There are huge racial disparities in how US police use force. *Vox*. Retrieved from https://www.vox.com/cards/police-brutality-shootings-us/us-police-racism.

79. Khazan, O. (2018, May 8). In one year, 57,375 years of life were lost to police violence. *The Atlantic*. Retrieved from https://www.theatlantic.com/health/archive/2018/05/the-57375-years-of-life-lost-to-police-violence/559835/.

80. Fogel, R. W., & Engerman, S. L. (1995). *Time on the cross: The economics of American Negro slavery* (Vol. 1), p. 125. New York, NY: W. W. Norton & Company.

81. Apple reported the sale of its one millionth iPhone in an official corporate press release. *See*: https://www.apple.com/newsroom/2007/09/10Apple-Sells-One-Millionth-iPhone/.

82. Samsung reported the sale of its one millionth Galaxy in a corporate press release too. *See*: https://news.samsung.com/global/from-zero-to-infinity-the-five-year-journey-of-the-samsung-galaxy-s.

83. Pew Research Center. (2018). *Mobile fact sheet*. Retrieved from http://www.pewinternet.org/fact-sheet/mobile/.

84. De Bruijn, M. (2009). *Mobile phones: The new talking drums of everyday Africa*. Oxford, UK: African Books Collective.

Chapter 3

1. My Facebook Live discussion about the role of black witnessing in excessive force cases is public. *See*: https://www.facebook.com/nbcwashington/videos/10154413415478606/. At the time of this writing, the video had upward of 17,000 views—even though both deaths took place outside of the Washington, DC, area where this NBC affiliate station is based. Those metrics indicate just how much the Alton Sterling and Philando Castile deaths struck a nerve throughout the United States—especially among black people.

2. CNN Staff. The Disruptors. *CNN*. Retrieved from http://www.cnn.com/interactive/2015/08/us/disruptors/.

3. Laurent, O. (2015, April 30). Go behind *TIME*'s Baltimore cover with aspiring photographer Devin Allen. *TIME*. Retrieved from http://time.com/3841077/baltimore-protests-riot-freddie-gray-devin-allen/.

4. Luckie, M. (2015, September 18). What it's really like being black in Silicon Valley. *USA Today*. Retrieved from https://www.usatoday.com/story/tech/columnist/2015/09/18/silicon-valley-diversity-being-black-in-tech-companies-mark-luckie/72399254/.

5. To read Mark Luckie's entire open letter to Facebook, *see*: https://www.facebook.com/notes/mark-s-luckie/facebook-is-failing-its-black-employees-and-its-black-users/1931075116975013/.

6. Peters, J. (2015, April 28). Where are the police? When cities spasm with violence for complicated reasons, that's the only question CNN wants to ask. *Slate*. Retrieved from https://slate.com/news-and-politics/2015/04/baltimore-freddie-gray-riots-why-cnn-is-incapable-of-understanding-why-violence-erupts-in-cities.html.

7. Ciccariello-Maher, G. (2015, May 4). Riots work: Wolf Blitzer and the *Washington Post* completely missed the real lesson from Baltimore. *Salon*. Retrieved from https://www.salon.com/2015/05/04/riots_work_wolf_blitzer_and_the_washington_post_completely_missed_the_real_lesson_from_baltimore/.

8. Craven, J. (2015, April 29). Wolf Blitzer fails to goad protester into condemning violence. *The Huffington Post*. Retrieved from https://www.huffingtonpost.com/2015/04/29/wolf-blitzer-baltimore-protests_n_7168964.html.

9. Lund, J. (2015, April 29). CNN and Baltimore: A crossfire with 100 percent casualties. *RollingStone.com*. Retrieved from https://www.rollingstone.com/tv/tv-news/cnn-and-baltimore-a-crossfire-with-100-percent-casualties-72812/.

10. Doggett, J. A. (2015, April 29). Five code words the media needs to stop using to describe black people. *Essence*. Retrieved from http://www.essence.com/2015/04/29/5-code-words-media-needs-stop-using-describe-black-people.

11. Elkouby, S. (2015, May 1). A quick lesson on Baltimore: What they're not showing you. *JetMag*. Retrieved from https://www.jetmag.com/talk-back-2/quick-lesson-baltimore/.

12. Fanon, F. (1952). *Black skin, white masks*, p. 93. New York, NY: Grove Press.

13. Ibid.

14. Hall, S. (2001). The spectacle of the other. In Wetherell, M., Taylor, S., & Yates, S. J. (Eds.), *Discourse theory and practice: A reader*, p. 243. Los Angeles, CA: SAGE Publications.

15. Omi, M., & Winant, H. (2014). *Racial formation in the United States*, pp. 9–15. New York, NY: Routledge.

16. Hall, S. (2001), p. 243.

17. Brown Givens, S. M., & Monahan, J. L. (2005). Priming mammies, Jezebels, and other controlling images: An examination of the influence of mediated stereotypes on perceptions of an African American woman. *Media Psychology*, 7(1), 87–106.

18. Schudson, M. (2001). The objectivity norm in American journalism. *Journalism*, 2(2), 149–170.

19. Tuchman, G. (1972). Objectivity as strategic ritual: An examination of newsmen's notions of objectivity. *American Journal of Sociology*, 77(4), 660–679.

20. Ibid., pp. 84–85.

21. For Attorney Stewart's original Tweet on the multiracial Deaundre Phillips protest, *see*: https://twitter.com/chrisstewartesq/status/830503442187710464.

22. Gilroy, P. (2008 [1982]). The myth of black criminality. In Spalek, B. (Ed.), *Ethnicity and crime: A reader*, pp. 113–127. New York, NY: Open University Press.

23. Stratton, J. (2014). Ob-la-di ob-la-da: Paul McCartney, diaspora and the politics of identity. *Journal for Cultural Research*, 18(1), 5.

24. Powell, E. (1968, April 20). Rivers of blood. Speech at Birmingham. Retrieved from http://www.toqonline.com/archives/v1n1/TOQv1n1Powell.pdf.

25. Gilroy, P., 2008[1982], p. 47.

26. Entman, R. M. (1992). Blacks in the news: Television, modern racism and cultural change. *Journalism Quarterly, 69*(2), 341–361.

27. Entman, R. M. (1994). Representation and reality in the portrayal of blacks on network television news. *Journalism & Mass Communication Quarterly, 71*(3), 509–520.

28. Ibid.

29. Chiricos, T., & Eschholz, S. (2002). The racial and ethnic typification of crime and the criminal typification of race and ethnicity in local television news. *Journal of Research in Crime and Delinquency, 39*(4), 400–420.

30. Dixon, T. L., & Linz, D. (2000a). Race and the misrepresentation of victimization on local television news. *Communication Research, 27*(5), 547–573.

31. Dixon, T. L., & Linz, D. (2000b). Overrepresentation and underrepresentation of African Americans and Latinos as lawbreakers on television news. *Journal of Communication, 50*(2), 131–154.

32. Poindexter, P. M., Smith, L., & Heider, D. (2003). Race and ethnicity in local television news: Framing, story assignments, and source selections. *Journal of Broadcasting & Electronic Media, 47*(4), 533.

33. Buchholz, K. (2014). Colorado underreports officer-involved shootings. *CU News Corps.* Retrieved from https://cunewscorps.com/1261/gun-dialog-project/colorado-underreports-officer-involved-shootings/.

34. Campbell, C. P. (1995). *Race, myth and the news*, p. 69. Los Angeles, CA: Sage Publications.

35. Ibid., p. 57.

36. Wilson, C. C., & Gutierrez, F. (1985). *Minorities and the media*, p. 139. Los Angeles, CA: SAGE Publications.

37. Campbell, C. P. (1995), p. 38.

38. Sanders, J. (2015). *How racism and sexism killed traditional media: Why the future of journalism depends on women and people of color*, p. 134. Santa Barbara, CA: ABC-CLIO.

39. Ibid.

40. Neville, H. A., Coleman, M. N., Falconer, J. W., & Holmes, D. (2005). Color-blind racial ideology and psychological false consciousness among African Americans. *Journal of Black Psychology, 31*(1), 27–45.

41. Campbell, C. P. (1995), p. 38.

42. LeDuff, K. M. (2012). National news coverage of race in the era of Obama. In Campbell, C. P., LeDuff, K. M., Jenkins, C. D., & Brown, R. A. (Eds.), *Race and news: Critical perspectives*, pp. 43–63. New York, NY: Routledge.

43. Ibid.

44. Pesca, M. (2005, September 5). Are Katrina's victims 'refugees' or 'evacuees?'" *NPR.* Retrieved from https://www.npr.org/templates/story/story.php?storyId=4833613.

45. Garfield, G. (2007). Hurricane Katrina: The making of unworthy disaster victims. *Journal of African American Studies, 10*(4), 55–74.

46. Heusel, J. (2015). Postracial justice and the trope of the "race riot." In *Impact of communication and the media on ethnic conflict*, pp. 195–213. Hershey, PA: Information Science Reference.

47. For the complete transcript of Pres. Donald Trump's taped conversation about women, *see*: https://www.nytimes.com/2016/10/08/us/donald-trump-tape-transcript.html.

48. Sumlin, T. (2015, June 24). Charleston shooting suspect's Burger King meal gets national attention. *The Charlotte Observer*. Retrieved from https://www.charlotteobserver.com/news/local/article25394389.html.

49. Healy, J., & Turkewitz, J. (2015, July 16). Guilty verdict for James Holmes in Aurora attack. *The New York Times*. Retrieved from https://www.nytimes.com/2015/07/17/us/james-holmes-guilty-in-aurora-movie-theater-shooting.html.

50. Schildkraut, J. V. (2014). *Mass murder and the mass media: An examination of the media discourse on US rampage shootings, 2000–2012*, p. 169. San Marcos, TX: Texas State University.

51. Heitzeg, N. A. (2015). "Whiteness," criminality, and the double standards of deviance/social control. *Contemporary Justice Review, 18*(2), 198.

52. Iyengar, S., & Hahn, K. S. (2009). Red media, blue media: Evidence of ideological selectivity in media use. *Journal of Communication, 59*(1), 19–39.

53. Gilliam Jr., F. D., & Iyengar, S. (1998). The superpredator script. *Nieman Reports, 52*(4), 45.

54. Gilliam, F. D., Iyengar, S., Simon, A., & Wright, O. (1996). Crime in black and white: The violent, scary world of local news. *The Harvard International Journal of Press/Politics, 1*(3), 6–23.

55. Lubbers, M., Scheepers, P., & Vergeer, M. (2000). Exposure to newspapers and attitudes toward ethnic minorities: A longitudinal analysis. *Howard Journal of Communication, 11*(2), 127–143.

56. Arendt, F., Steindl, N., & Vitouch, P. (2015). Effects of right-wing populist political advertising on implicit and explicit stereotypes. *Journal of Media Psychology, 27*, 178–189.

57. Abraham, L., & Appiah, O. (2006). Framing news stories: The role of visual imagery in priming racial stereotypes. *The Howard Journal of Communications, 17*(3), 183–203.

58. Jackson, R. (2016). If they gunned me down and criming while white: An examination of Twitter campaigns through the lens of citizens' media. *Cultural Studies? Critical Methodologies, 16*(3), 313–319.

59. Schiappa, J. (2015). #IfTheyGunnedMeDown: The necessity of "Black Twitter" and hashtags in the age of Ferguson. *ProudFlesh: New Afrikan Journal of Culture, Politics and Consciousness, No. 10*. Retrieved from https://www.africaknowledgeproject.org/index.php/proudflesh/article/view/2144.

Chapter 4

1. Lichtblau, E., & Flegenheimer, M. (2017). Jeff Sessions confirmed as Attorney General, capping bitter battle. *The New York Times*. Retrieved from https://www.nytimes.com/2017/02/08/us/politics/jeff-sessions-attorney-general-confirmation.html.

2. Liebelson, D., & Reilly, R. J. (2015, October 9). Inside Hillary Clinton's meeting with Black Lives Matter. *The Huffington Post*. Retrieved from https://www.huffingtonpost.com/entry/black-lives-matter-hillary-clinton_us_56180c44e4b0e66ad4c7d9fa.

3. Liebelson, D., & Reilly, R. J. (2015, September 16). Black Lives Matter activists meet with Bernie Sanders to make sure he is on board. *The Huffington Post*. Retrieved from https://www.huffingtonpost.com/entry/bernie-sanders-black-lives-matter_us_55f9ca9ce4b00310edf57b02.

4. Luckie, Mark S. (2018, November 27). Facebook is failing its black employees and its black users. *Facebook*. Retrieved from https://www.facebook.com/notes/mark-s-luckie/facebook-is-failing-its-black-employees-and-its-black-users/1931075116975013/.

5. Ibid.

6. For Facebook CEO Mark Zuckerberg's post about Diamond Reynold's tragic livestream, *see:* https://www.facebook.com/zuck/posts/10102948714100101?pnref=story.

7. McCorvey, J. J. (2016, August 3). Before the police killed Korryn Gaines, Facebook deactivated her account. *Fast Company*. Retrieved from https://www.fastcompany.com/4015851/before-the-police-killed-korryn-gaines-facebook-deactivated-her-account.

8. Domonoske, C. (2016, August 3). During fatal standoff, police asked Facebook to deactivate woman's account. *NPR*. Retrieved from https://www.npr.org/sections/thetwo-way/2016/08/03/488500830/during-fatal-standoff-police-asked-facebook-to-deactivate-womans-account.

9. Noble, S. U. (2018). *Algorithms of oppression*, p. 1. New York, NY: NYU Press.

10. Facebook CEO Mark Zuckerberg testified before the Senate Committee on the Judiciary and its Committee on Commerce, Science, and Transportation on April 10, 2018. To read the transcripts, or to view the hearing in its entirety, *see:* https://www.judiciary.senate.gov/meetings/facebook-social-media-privacy-and-the-use-and-abuse-of-data.

11. For data scientist Christopher Wylie's entire exposé with the *Guardian, see: Cambridge Analytica whistleblower: "We spent $1m harvesting millions of Facebook profiles"* at https://www.youtube.com/watch?v=FXdYSQ6nu-M.

12. Stovall, C., & Phillips, E. (2016). Today in Black Twitter: An actual black person who worked at Twitter speaks his mind. *BET.com*. Retrieved from https://www.bet.com/news/lifestyle/2016/15/today-in-black-twitter—an-actual-black-person-who-worked-at-twi.html.

13. Korryn Gaines' family has not yet received the $37 million settlement that it won in February 2018, since Baltimore County requested an appeal of the case immediately after the ruling. This story remains ongoing and has the potential to set great legal precedent in the state of Maryland for its handling of fatal police encounters.

14. Howard, P. N., Duffy, A., Freelon, D., Hussain, M. M., Mari, W., & Maziad, M. (2011). *Opening closed regimes: What was the role of social media during the Arab Spring?* Project on Information Technology & Political Islam.

15. Khondker, H. H. (2011). Role of the new media in the Arab Spring. *Globalizations, 8*(5), 675–679.

16. Lotan, G., Graeff, E., Ananny, M., Gaffney, D., & Pearce, I. (2011). The revolutions were tweeted: Information flows during the 2011 Tunisian and Egyptian revolutions. *International Journal of Communication, 5,* 31.

17. Halverson, J. R., Ruston, S. W., & Trethewey, A. (2013). Mediated martyrs of the Arab Spring: New media, civil religion, and narrative in Tunisia and Egypt. *Journal of Communication, 63*(2), 312–332.

18. Harlow, S., & Johnson, T. J. (2011). The Arab Spring: Overthrowing the protest paradigm? How the *New York Times*, Global Voices and Twitter covered the Egyptian revolution. *International Journal of Communication, 5*(16), 1359–1374.

19. Toch, H. (2012). *Cop watch: Spectators, social media, and police reform.* Washington, DC: American Psychological Association.

20. Brucato, B. (2015). Policing made visible: Mobile technologies and the importance of point of view. *Surveillance & Society, 13*(3/4), p. 455.

21. hooks, b. (2014b). *Black looks: Race and representation*, p. 168. Boston: South End Press.

22. Ibid., p. 116.

23. Currier, J. (2018, July 26). Race for St. Louis County prosecutor focuses on experience, criminal justice reform. *St. Louis Post-Dispatch*. Retrieved from https://www.stltoday.com/news/local/crime-and-courts/race-for-st-louis-county-prosecutor-focuses-on-experience-criminal/article_a364b660-6f7a-5be0-83b9-2e78c889a6c0.html.

24. Goodman, J. D. (2014). Man who filmed fatal police chokehold is arrested on weapons charges. *The New York Times*. Retrieved from https://www.nytimes.com/2014/08/04/nyregion/after-recording-eric-garner-chokehold-ramsey-orta-gets-charged-with-gun-possession.html.

25. Goldenberg, S. (2016, September 12). Records show increased earnings for officer involved in Garner death. *Politico*. Retrieved from https://www.politico.com/states/new-york/albany/story/2016/09/officer-in-eric-garner-death-boosts-overtime-pay-105359.

26. Lopez, C. E. (2018, November 11). Here's why Jeff Sessions' parting shot is worse than you thought. *The Marshall Project*. Retrieved from https://www.themarshallproject.org/2018/11/19/here-s-why-jeff-sessions-parting-shot-is-worse-than-you-thought.

27. Sessions. J. (2018). Memorandum: Principles and procedures for civil consent decrees and settlement agreements with state and local governmental entities. Office of the Attorney General. Retrieved from https://www.justice.gov/opa/press-release/file/1109621/download.

28. Levenson, E. (2017, December 31). Activist Erica Garner, 27, dies after heart attack. *CNN*. Retrieved from https://www.cnn.com/2017/12/30/us/erica-garner-eric-death/index.html.

29. Fields, R. (2017, November 15). New York City launches committee to review maternal deaths. *ProPublica*. Retrieved from https://www.propublica.org/article/new-york-city-launches-committee-to-review-maternal-deaths.

30. Parks, G. (1966). *A choice of weapons.* St. Paul, MN: Minnesota Historical Society Press.

31. Basu, T. (2015, February 25). The Guantanamo-like torture warehouse of Chicago. *The Atlantic*. Retrieved from https://www.theatlantic.com/national/archive/2015/02/behind-the-disappeared-of-chicagos-homan-square/385964/.

32. Clifton, D. (2016, August 9). How protests in Ferguson inspired the occupation of "Freedom Square." *Chicago Reader*. Retrieved from https://www.chicagoreader.com/chicago/freedom-square-homan-square-occupation-ferguson/Content?oid=23089791.

33. To read Eve Ewing's original Twitter thread on what the anti–police brutality movement needs, *see*: https://twitter.com/eveewing/status/758381013911343104.

34. Clabaugh, J. (2018, March 5). 2 DC ZIP codes among nation's "most gentrified." *WTOP*. Retrieved from https://wtop.com/real-estate/2018/03/most-gentrified-zip-codes-dc/.

Chapter 5

1. Cullors, P., & Bandele, A. (2018). *When they call you a terrorist. A Black Lives Matter memoir*, p. 15. New York, NY: St. Martin's Press.

2. At the time of my first traffic stop in 2001, my hometown of Prince George's County, Maryland, was in its heyday. The renowned Brookings Institute even issued a formal economic report of the region, as blacks migrated there in droves to raise their families in affluence. White flight made the county 60 percent black by the time I went to college, according to the Brookings report. The study explained further: "In contrast to the District, Prince George's County had virtually no neighborhoods with concentrated poverty in 2000." Many black residents in Prince George's County believe that its brutal police force was forged as a backlash to the region's success, but I have only anecdotal evidence of this. At any rate, for the Brookings Institute report that launched a thousand ships, *see*: http://citeseerx.ist.psu.edu/viewdoc/download?doi=10.1.1.501.5986&rep=rep1&type=pdf.

3. Dr. Kimberle Crenshaw, who coined the term intersectionality in 1994, is the founder of the African American Policy Forum (AAPF), which launched the #SayHerName campaign in 2015. In the month that Sandra Bland died, AAPF issued the report *Say Her Name: Resisting Police Brutality against Black Women*. The statistics I cited on black women leading the number of traffic stops in New York can be found on page 5 of the online version of the report. *See*: http://static1.squarespace.com/static/53f20d90e4b0b80451158d8c/t/560c068ee4b0af26f72741df/1443628686535/AAPF_SMN_Brief_Full_singles-min.pdf.

4. Angela Rye, the outspoken political commentator for CNN and BET, coined the #WorkWoke mantra in 2018. She explained in numerous interviews that staying woke urged black millennials to educate themselves on pressing political matters, such as police brutality. To "work woke," however, meant to put that knowledge to use, to become engaged in the political process at every level.

5. For testimony before the credentials committee by Fannie Lou Hamer, *see*: Say it plain. American Public Radio. Retrieved from http://americanradioworks.publicradio.org/features/sayitplain/flhamer.html.

6. Wells-Barnett, I. B., & Douglass, F. (1894). *A red record: Tabulated statistics and alleged causes of lynchings in the United States, 1892–1893–1894. Respectfully submitted*

to the nineteenth century civilization in "the land of the free and the home of the brave." Chicago, IL: Donohue & Henneberry.

7. When Ms. Packnett mentions SNCC, SCLC, NAACP, Core, and the Panthers, she is talking about the Student Nonviolent Coordinating Committee, Southern Christian Leadership Conference, National Association for the Advancement of Colored People, Congress of Racial Equality, and the Black Panther Party for Self-Defense, respectively. All of these organizations worked under the banner of the Civil Rights Movement in the 1950s and 1960s and, later, within the Black Power Movement of the 1970s, to varying degrees. She likens the conflation of today's many anti–police brutality groups as all "Black Lives Matter" groups to the way different civil rights groups in the latter half of the 20th century were lumped together.

Chapter 6

1. For the official petition to have Black Lives Matter activists listed as terrorists, *see*: https://petitions.whitehouse.gov/petition/formally-recognize-black-lives-matter-terrorist-organization.

2. To read Gordon Parks' full interview with Dean Brierly, where he explains how a camera can be a weapon, *see*: http://photographyinterviews.blogspot.com/2010/05/gordon-parks-voice-in-mirror-i-have.html.

3. May, P. (2014, December 4). https://twitter.com/may20p/status/540705615329239040.

4. CBS staff. (2014, December 6). Activists say Chicago police used 'Stingray' technology during protests. *CBS Chicago*. Retrieved from https://chicago.cbslocal.com/2014/12/06/activists-say-chicago-police-used-stingray-eavesdropping-technology-during-protests/.

5. In this audio clip, purported members of the Chicago PD discussed the use of a Stingray smartphone hacking device at a local Black Lives Matter protest in December 2014. To listen to the exchange, *see*: https://clyp.it/sv23cozu.

6. Smith, B., Gottinger, P., and Klippenstein, K. (2014, December 7). Anonymous: Chicago police surveilled activists, including politician's daughter. *Reader Supported News*. Retrieved from https://readersupportednews.org/news-section2/318-66/27362-focus-anonymous-chicago-police-surveilled-activists-including-politicians-daughter.

7. Anon. (2014, December 8). Looks like Chicago PD had a stingray out at the Eric Garner protest last night. *Privacy SOS*. Retrieved from https://privacysos.org/blog/looks-like-chicago-pd-had-a-stingray-out-at-the-eric-garner-protest-last-night/.

8. Dodge, J. (2014, October 1). After denials, Chicago Police Department admits cell-phone spying devices. *CBS Chicago*. Retrieved from https://chicago.cbslocal.com/2014/10/01/chicago-police-department-admits-purchase-of-cell-phone-spying-devices/.

9. The Chicago-based civil rights law firm, Loevy & Loevy, posted the CPD Stingray invoices, which reflect purchases of nearly $150,000, online. On its homepage, the law firm lauds itself as a team of "whistleblower attorneys," which protects those that bear witness against powerful entities. To view the invoices, *see*: https://www.loevy.com/content/uploads/2014/09/CPD-Stingray-Purchase-Records.pdf/.

10. Cherney, E. (2017, January 13). Chicago lawyer files federal lawsuit over police cell-phone tracking system. *Chicago Tribune*. Retrieved from https://www.chicagotribune.com/news/local/breaking/ct-chicago-police-stingray-lawsuit-0113-20170112-story.html.

11. Ibid.

12. To read the full text of Jerry Boyle's federal lawsuit against Chicago police, in connection with its use of Stingray technology, *see*: https://www.chicagotribune.com/news/local/breaking/ct-chicago-police-stingray-suit-20170113-htmlstory.html.

13. Joseph, G. (2015, July 24). Exclusive: Feds regularly monitored Black Lives Matter since Ferguson. *The Intercept*. Retrieved from https://theintercept.com/2015/07/24/documents-show-department-homeland-security-monitoring-black-lives-matter-since-ferguson/.

14. COINTELPRO was established by the FBI in 1956 to "disrupt the activities of the Communist Party of the United States" according to its official website. In the 1960s, the FBI expanded its efforts to surveil, infiltrate, and dismantle white hate groups, Puerto Rican grassroots groups, the Black Panther Party for Self-Defense, and other socialist and extreme leftist parties. To view the historic FBI vault on "black extremism," *see*: https://vault.fbi.gov/cointel-pro.

15. https://vault.fbi.gov/cointel-pro.

16. Leopold, J. (2015, June 24). Fearing a "catastrophic incident," 400 federal officers descended on the Baltimore protests. *VICE News*. Retrieved from https://news.vice.com/en_us/article/8x393b/fearing-a-catastrophic-incident-400-federal-officers-descended-on-the-baltimore-protests.

17. To view Shellonnee Chinn's Casebook, *see*: https://www.facebook.com/sbchinnlawsuit/.

18. Bruns, A., & Stieglitz, S. (2013). Towards more systematic Twitter analysis: Metrics for tweeting activities. *International Journal of Social Research Methodology*, 16(2), 91–108.

19. Garza, A. (2016, May 18). https://twitter.com/aliciagarza/status/733093166794997761.

20. Clifton, D. (2018, January 30). Russian trolls stoked anger over Black Lives Matter more than was previously known. *Mother Jones*. Retrieved from https://www.motherjones.com/politics/2018/01/russian-trolls-hyped-anger-over-black-lives-matter-more-than-previously-known/.

21. Audio podcasts were very rarely used for breaking news stories, perhaps since many of the protests were noisy and difficult to narrate without accompanying images. I should note that the Day 1's took up podcasting after leaving the frontlines.

22. To read the entire Twitter exchange between Alicia Garza and her detractors, on the night of the 2016 Republican National Convention, *see*: https://t.co/ETw6QbxNfL.

23. This chapter gets its name from a viral hashtag that Black Youth Project (BYP) 100 coined in 2015. When the dashcam footage of Officer Jason van Dyke shooting 17-year-old Laquan McDonald surfaced that year, a wave of weary outrage rolled through Black Twitter. The graphic video inspired an uprising in McDonald's native Chicago, but also marked the first time that black witnesses included a spoiler

warning with footage. Poet and co-chair of BYP100 Chicago Chapter, Malcolm London tweeted: "Before you watch this, I want you to know you are loved. And no matter what is on this video, your life matters. Before you watch this, people will tell you to be calm in your righteous anger. And I say in the words of Frederick Douglas, the only thing worse than a rebellion, is the reason for it."

Chapter 7

1. The Tribe CLT. (2015). *#KeepitDown Confederate flag takedown.* Retrieved from https://www.youtube.com/watch?v=gr-mt1P94cQ.

2. The crowdsourced bail fund for Bree Newsome has been closed since 2015, but it remains on the Indiegogo website. *See:* https://www.indiegogo.com/projects/bail-for-bree-newsome#/.

3. Ramsey, F. (2015). She left the flagpole in handcuffs. Now artists reimagine her as a superhero. *Upworthy.* Retrieved from https://www.upworthy.com/she-left-the-flagpole-in-handcuffs-now-artists-reimagine-her-as-a-superhero.

4. Moreno, J. (2015). People are making badass art of the woman who removed the Confederate flag. *Buzzfeed.* Retrieved from https://www.buzzfeed.com/javiermoreno/bree-newsome-confederate-flag-art?utm_term=.hamz8kjK5D#.acMYwgZkq5.

5. Pullen, K. (2011). If ya liked it, then you shoulda made a video: Beyoncé Knowles, YouTube and the public sphere of images. *Performance Research, 16*(2), 145–146. https://doi.org/10.1080/13528165.2011.578846.

6. Eco, U. (1965). Towards a semiotic inquiry into the television message. *Television: Critical concepts in media and cultural studies 2,* 3–19.

7. Sharpe, J. A. (2005). *Remember, remember: A cultural history of Guy Fawkes Day.* Cambridge, MA: Harvard University Press.

8. Ibid.

9. The film, *V for Vendetta,* is based on the graphic novel of the same name by Alan Moore.

10. Anon. (2014). Guy Fawkes and the protest mask: An album. *Getty Images.* https://www.gettyimages.com/album/guy-fawkes-and-the-protest-mask-a-look-at-the—WcPVlZg1o0i-3VXXbxrhtQ#demonstrators-wearing-guy-fawkes-masks-as-they-block-traffic-during-a-picture-id459536504.

11. Kohns, O. (2013). Guy Fawkes in the 21st century. A contribution to the political iconography of revolt. *Image & Narrative, 14*(1), 89–104.

12. Rogers, A. (2015). What is Anonymous doing in Ferguson? *TIME.* Retrieved from http://time.com/3148925/ferguson-michael-brown-anonymous/.

13. Dunbar, P. L. (1896). We wear the mask. *Poets.org.* Retrieved from https://www.poets.org/poetsorg/poem/we-wear-mask.

14. Bry, D. (2014). Dear fellow white people: Keep protesting police violence. Just don't throw bottles from the back. *The Guardian.* Retrieved from https://www.theguardian.com/commentisfree/2014/dec/27/white-people-protesting-police-violence-black-lives-matter.

15. For the Anonymous video, where the organization threatened to release Ferguson government officials and police officer data, *see*: https://youtu.be/eOSRQ-c1XW0.

16. Sandritter, M. (2017). A timeline of Colin Kaepernick's national anthem protest and the athletes who joined him. *SBNation*. Retrieved from https://www.sbnation.com/2016/9/11/12869726/colin-kaepernick-national-anthem-protest-seahawks-brandon-marshall-nfl.

17. Chan, J. L. (2016). Colin Kaepernick did not stand during the national anthem. *Niners Nation*. Retrieved from https://www.ninersnation.com/2016/8/27/12669048/colin-kaepernick-did-not-stand-during-the-national-anthem.

18. Wyche, S. (2016). Colin Kaepernick explains why he sat during the national anthem. *NFL*. Retrieved from http://www.nfl.com/news/story/0ap3000000691077/article/colin-kaepernick-explains-why-he-sat-during-national-anthem.

19. Reid, E. (2017). Why Colin Kaepernick and I decided to take a knee. *The New York Times*. Retrieved from https://www.nytimes.com/2017/09/25/opinion/colin-kaepernick-football-protests.html.

20. For Bernice King's original tweet, *see*: https://twitter.com/BerniceKing/status/911603501968642049.

21. Rhodan, M. (2017). This photo of MLK kneeling has power amid the NFL protests. Here's the story behind it. *TIME*. Retrieved from http://time.com/4955717/trump-protests-mlk-martin-luther-king-kneeling/.

22. Zelizer, B. (2010). *About to die: How news images move the public*, p. 1. New York, NY: Oxford University Press.

23. Bogado, A. (2015). Clergy stage a die-in at Congressional cafeteria for Black Lives Matter. *Colorlines*. Retrieved from https://www.colorlines.com/articles/clergy-stage-die-congressional-cafeteria-black-lives-matter.

24. Miranda, C. (2016). "It hasn't left me": How Black Lives Matter used performance to create unforgettable 2016 moments. *The Los Angeles Times*. Retrieved from http://www.latimes.com/entertainment/arts/miranda/la-ca-cm-year-end-black-lives-matter-artists-20161218-story.html.

25. Anon. (2014). When did die-ins become a form of protest? *BBC News Magazine Monitor Blog*. Retrieved from https://www.bbc.com/news/blogs-magazine-monitor-30402637.

26. Miranda, C. (2016).

27. Plevin, R. (2016). Black Lives Matter rally blocks 405 freeway in Inglewood. *KPCC*. Retrieved from https://www.scpr.org/news/2016/07/11/62495/black-lives-matter-rally-blocks-405-freeway-in-ing/.

28. Hayes, K. (2016). Black organizers in Chicago get in "Formation" for Black Lives and public education. *TruthOut*. Retrieved from https://truthout.org/articles/inspired-by-beyonce-black-organizers-get-in-formation-to-disrupt-nfl-draft/.

29. Anon. (2018). Black Lives Matter 'human chain' protest on Heathrow Road. *BBC News*. Retrieved from https://www.bbc.com/news/video_and_audio/headlines/36983828/black-lives-matter-human-chain-protest-on-heathrow-road.

30. Badger, E. (2016, July 13). Why highways have become the center of civil rights protest. *The Washington Post*. Retrieved from http://link.galegroup.com.libproxy1.usc.edu/apps/doc/A457904179/AONE?u=usocal_main&sid=AONE&xid=ebc18072.

31. Ibid.

32. Harris, A. (2015). Has Kendrick Lamar recorded the new black national anthem? *Slate*. Retrieved from http://www.slate.com/articles/arts/culturebox/2015/08/black_lives_matter_protesters_chant_kendrick_lamar_s_alright_what_makes.html.

33. McLeod Jr, J. D. (2017). If God got us: Kendrick Lamar, Paul Tillich, and the advent of existentialist hip hop. *Toronto Journal of Theology*, *33*(1), 123–135.

34. Wallace, A. (2017). A critical view of Beyoncé's "Formation." *Black Camera*, *9*(1), 189–196.

35. Bertens, L. M. (2017). Okay ladies, now let's get in formation!": Music videos and the construction of cultural memory. *Open Cultural Studies*, *1*(1), 91.

36. Guerrero, L. (2016). Can I live? Contemporary black satire and the state of post-modern double consciousness. *Studies in American Humor*, *2*(2), 266–279.

37. Anon. (n.d.) Black guy on the phone. *Know your meme*. Retrieved from https://knowyourmeme.com/memes/black-guy-on-the-phone.

38. Swaine, J. (2014). Ferguson police officer was "doing his job," say supporters. *The Guardian*. Retrieved from https://www.theguardian.com/world/2014/aug/18/ferguson- supporters-police-killed- teenager-protest.

39. Word. (2014). Martin Baker gets blasted for being the lone black guy at a pro-Darren Wilson rally. *Uproxx*. Retrieved from https://web.archive.org/web/20140918021916/http://uproxx.com/smokingsection/2014/08/martin-baker-memes/.

40. Anon. (2014.) Black guy on the phone. *Know your meme*. Retrieved from https://knowyourmeme.com/memes/black-guy-on-the-phone.

41. Ibid.

42. Selle, J., & Dolan, M. (2015). Black like me? Civil rights activist's ethnicity questioned. *Coeur d'Alene/Post Falls Press*. Retrieved from http://www.cdapress.com/archive/article-385adfeb-76f3-5050-98b4-d4bf021c423f.html.

43. Davies, Hannah. (2018). *The Rachel Divide* won't make you like Rachel Dolezal, but it might help you understand her. *Refinery29*. Retrieved from https://www.refinery29.uk/the-rachel-divide.

44. Cleary, T. (2018). Jennifer Schulte, "BBQ Becky": 5 fast facts you need to know. *The Heavy*. Retrieved from https://heavy.com/news/2018/05/jennifer-schulte-bbq-becky/.

45. Snider, M. D. (2018). White woman called out for racially targeting black men having BBQ in Oakland. *YouTube*. Retrieved from https://youtu.be/Fh9D_PUe7QI.

46. Ibid.

47. *See*: https://twitter.com/roywoodjr/status/995030135454789632.

48. Anon. (2018). BBQ Becky. *Know your meme*. Retrieved from https://knowyourmeme.com/memes/bbq-becky.

49. *See*: https://twitter.com/BlakeDontCrack/status/994802724125454341.

50. Holson, L. M. (2018). Hundreds in Oakland turn out to BBQ while black. *The New York Times*. Retrieved from https://www.nytimes.com/2018/05/21/us/oakland-bbq-while-black.html.

51. Victor, D. (2018). When white people call the police on black people. *The New York Times*. Retrieved from https://www.nytimes.com/2018/05/21/us/oakland-bbq-while-black.html/.

Chapter 8

1. Swaine, J. (2014). Ohio Walmart video reveals moments before officer killed John Crawford. *The Guardian*. Retrieved from https://www.theguardian.com/world/2014/sep/24/surveillance-video-walmart-shooting-john-crawford-police.

2. Swaine, J., & Ryan, M. (2014). Police officer who shot black man in Walmart lied, victim's mother says. *The Guardian*. Retrieved from https://www.theguardian.com/world/2014/sep/30/police-officer-shot-john-crawford-walmart-lied-victims-mother-says/.

3. Swaine, J. (2014). Video shows John Crawford's girlfriend aggressively questioned after Ohio police shot him dead in Walmart. *The Guardian*. Retrieved from https://www.theguardian.com/us-news/2014/dec/14/john-crawford-girlfriend-questioned-walmart-police-shot-dead.

4. Govaki, M. (2016). Mother of Crawford's sons in prison for child endangerment. *Dayton Daily News*. Retrieved from https://www.daytondailynews.com/news/crime—law/mother-crawford-sons-prison-for-child-endangerment/q6F0AIs3GsOwQpSu0PosVK/.

5. Swaine, J. (2015). Girlfriend of John Crawford, man killed by police in Walmart, dies in car crash. *The Guardian*. Retrieved from https://www.theguardian.com/us-news/2015/jan/02/girlfriend-john-crawford-dies-car-crash-tasha-thomas.

6. NewsOne Staff. (2014). Angela Williams: Woman's death following Walmart shooting ruled homicide. *NewsOne*. Retrieved from https://newsone.com/3056226/angela-williams-womans-death-following-walmart-shooting-ruled-homicide/.

7. CNN Staff. (2014). Cops kill man at Walmart carrying a BB gun. *CNN*. Retrieved from https://youtu.be/BtPt6GrnE6s.

8. Conrad, J., Knowles, O., & Simmons, A. (2018). *Heart of darkness*. Cambridge, UK: Cambridge University Press.

9. Hall, A. V., Hall, E. V., & Perry, J. L. (2016). Black and blue: Exploring racial bias and law enforcement in the killings of unarmed black male civilians. *American Psychologist*, 71(3), 175.

10. Shade, C. (2016). Police violence and the American caste system. *Literary Hub*. Retrieved from https://lithub.com/police-violence-and-the-american-caste-system/.

11. RT News. (2014, August 21). GRAPHIC: St. Louis police officer shoots Kajieme Powell. *YouTube*. Retrieved from https://www.youtube.com/watch?v=sEuZiTcbGCg&t=41s.

12. Klein, E. (2014). Did the St. Louis police have to shoot Kajieme Powell?" *Vox*. Retrieved from https://www.vox.com/2014/8/20/6051431/did-the-st-louis-police-have-to-shoot-kajieme-powell.

13. Singal, J. (2014). Kajieme Powell died because police have become America's mental-health workers. *The Cut*. Retrieved from https://www.thecut.com/2014/08/police-kajieme-powell-and-mental-illness.html.

14. Schankman, P., & Bernthal, J. (2015). Officers who shot, killed Kajieme Powell will not be charged. *Fox 2 Now: St. Louis*. Retrieved from https://fox2now.com/2015/11/03/officers-who-shot-killed-kajieme-powell-will-not-be-charged/.

15. To view a copy of the official Kajieme Powell lawsuit, which was filed July 19, 2017, *see*: https://www.courthousenews.com/wp-content/uploads/2017/07/Kajieme.pdf.

16. Harris, J. (2017). Mother of police shooting victim Kajieme Powell sues St. Louis. *Courthouse News Service*. Retrieved from https://www.courthousenews.com/mother-police-shooting-victim-kajieme-powell-sues-st-louis/.

17. Ibid.

18. King, S. (2015, April 5). American tragedy: At least 50% of police shooting victims struggled with mental illness. *The Daily Kos*. Retrieved from https://www.dailykos.com/stories/2015/4/5/1375335/-American-tragedy-A-staggering-percentage-of-police-shooting-victims-struggled-with-mental-illness.

19. Beam, R. A., Brownlee, B. J., Weaver, D. H., & Di Cicco, D. T. (2009). Journalism and public service in troubled times. *Journalism Studies, 10*(6), 734–753.

20. Aymer, S. R. (2016). "I can't breathe": A case study—Helping Black men cope with race-related trauma stemming from police killing and brutality. *Journal of Human Behavior in the Social Environment, 26*(3–4), 374.

21. Goldsmith, S. (2016). The brief, poignant life of MarShawn McCarrel. *Columbus Monthly*. Retrieved from https://www.columbusmonthly.com/lifestyle/20161025/brief-poignant-life-of-marshawn-mccarrel.

22. Lowery, W., & Stankiewicz, K. (2016, February 15). "My demons won today": Ohio activist's suicide spotlights depression among Black Lives Matter leaders. *Washington Post*. Retrieved from https://www.washingtonpost.com/news/post-nation/wp/2016/02/15/my-demons-won-today-ohio-activists-suicide-spotlights-depression-among-black-lives-matter-leaders/.

23. Wang, Y. (2016). Ohio officer fired after calling Black Lives Matter activist's suicide "happy ending." *Chicago Tribune*. Retrieved from https://www.chicagotribune.com/news/nationworld/ct-ohio-officer-fired-black-lives-matter-20160308-story.html.

24. Schneider, K. (2013). *The polarized mind: Why it's killing us and what we can do about it*, p. 19. Colorado Springs, CO: University Professors Press.

25. Lowery, W., & Stankiewicz, K. (2016, February 15). 'My Demons Won Today': Ohio Activist's Suicide Spotlights Depression among Black Lives Matter leaders. *The Washington Post*.

26. Ibid.

27. Lowery, W. (2016, September 7). Who killed Ferguson activists Darren Seals? *The Washington Post*.

28. Haddad, V. (2018). Nobody's protest novel: Novelistic strategies of the Black Lives Matter Movement. *The Comparatist, 42*(1), 40–59.

29. Johnson, J. (2017, May 5). Ferguson, Mo., activists are dying and it's time to ask questions. *The Root*. Retrieved from https://www.theroot.com/ferguson-activists-are-dying-and-it-s-time-to-ask-quest-1794955900.

30. Nadal, M. C. (2017, May 5). https://twitter.com/MariaChappelleN/status/860467497589510144.

31. Ibid.

32. McDonell-Parry, A. (2018, November 2). Ferguson activist claims son was "lynched" as police investigate his death as suicide. *Rolling Stone*. Retrieved from https://www.

rollingstone.com/culture/culture-news/ferguson-danye-jones-death-lynching-suicide-melissa-mckinnies-751275/.

33. Packnett, B. (2018, October 31). https://twitter.com/MsPackyetti/status/1057614304181133313.

34. Ibid.

35. Dickson, E. J. (2019, March 18). Mysterious deaths leave Ferguson activists "on pins and needles." *RollingStone.com*. Retrieved from https://www.rollingstone.com/culture/culture-news/ferguson-death-mystery-black-lives-matter-michael-brown-809407/.

36. Associated Press. (2019). Activists unnerved by deaths of men tied to Ferguson protests. *Associated Press*. Retrieved from https://www.apnews.com/436251b8a58c470eb4f69099f43f2231.

37. Lawler, O. G. (2018, November 28). Another Ferguson protester has died. *The Cut*. Retrieved from https://www.thecut.com/2018/11/another-ferguson-protester-bassem-masri-has-died.html.

38. For Brittany Packnett's original Tweet, about the Ferguson protestor deaths, *see*: https://twitter.com/MsPackyetti/status/1067545002631487488.

39. Sanfiorenzo, D. (2018). Bassem Masri is the fourth Ferguson protestor to die since the uprising. *Okayplayer*. Retrieved from https://www.okayplayer.com/news/how-ferguson-protester-bassem-masri-died-details.html.

40. To view the complete Democratic National Convention speech from the Mothers of the Movement, *see*: https://youtu.be/4GaaDiAwa6Y.

41. Toure. (2018, January 8). "This thing" killed her father: Then it killed Erica Garner. *The Daily Beast*. Retrieved from https://www.thedailybeast.com/this-thing-killed-her-father-then-it-killed-erica-garner.

42. Wood, A. (2005). Lynching photography and the visual reproduction of white supremacy. *American Nineteenth Century History, 6*(3), 373–399.

43. Ibid.

44. Apel, D. (2003). Review of on looking: Lynching photographs and legacies of lynching after 9/11. *American Quarterly, 55*(3), 457–478. https://doi.org/10.1353/aq.2003.0020.

45. For the 2016 CNN report featuring Diamond Reynolds' uncut Facebook livestream of Philando Castile's last moments, *see*: https://youtu.be/VeVv9kJLAk4. The network did not blur his face, leaving viewers to observe his dying countenance just as those who were present to view a lynching in the 1900s would have seen the last expressions of the hanged victim. This mediated dehumanization of African American victims of excessive police force may diminish the impact of the black witnesses' work, if this newsroom practice is left unchecked. To function as a tool of change, networks must use these smartphone videos sparingly in ongoing mainstream reports.

46. For an example of how legacy news media have failed to blur the dying faces of victims of police brutality in a CBS news report, *see*: https://youtu.be/pdGXhSQvTKc.

47. For another example, in a *Wall Street Journal* report, of how legacy media fail to shield victims of police brutality from "looped" play online, *see*: https://youtu.be/z6tTfoifB7Q.

48. In this *Los Angeles Times* video, which features Oscar Grant's fatal police encounter, his face is not blurred. *See*: https://youtu.be/Q2LDw5l_yMI.

49. For a virtual tour of the National Memorial for Peace and Justice in Montgomery, Alabama, *see*: https://museumandmemorial.eji.org/memorial.

50. Armstrong, J. B. (2011). *Mary Turner and the memory of lynching*, p. 37. Athens: University of Georgia Press.

51. Ibid., 99.

52. NAACP. (1918). Memorandum for Govenor Dorsey from Walter F. White. Papers of the NAACP, Group I. Series C, Box 353, Washington, DC: Library of Congress.

53. White, W. (1918). The work of a mob. *The Crisis* 16, 221.

54. Raiford, L. (2011). *Imprisoned in a luminous glare: Photography and the African American freedom struggle*, p. 54. Chapel Hill, NC: University of North Carolina Press.

55. Benjamin, W. (1970 [1934]) The author as producer. John Heckman trans. New Left Review, *62*(July/August), 235.

56. Toure, 2018.

57. Fecile, J. (2018, Oct. 1). "Banned in 46 countries"—is *Faces of Death* the most shocking film ever? *The Guardian*. Retrieved from https://www.theguardian.com/film/2018/oct/01/banned-in-46-countries-is-faces-of-death-the-most-shocking-film-ever.

58. I have included the phrase "gore pornography" here in quotes since I did not coin it. I first read of *Faces of Death* as the world's first viral video in an article from *The Independent. See*: https://www.independent.co.uk/arts-entertainment/films/features/faces-of-death-snuff-movie-video-nasty-mundo-underground-horror-mary-whitehouse-jg-ballard-a8428161.html.

59. Reign, A. (2016, July 6). Why I will not share the video of Alton Sterling's death. *Washingtonpost.com*. Retrieved from http://link.galegroup.com.libproxy2.usc.edu/apps/doc/A457218533/AONE?u=usocal_main&sid=AONE&xid=9b31e883.

60. Tufekci, Z. (2013). "Not this one" social movements, the attention economy, and microcelebrity networked activism. *American Behavioral Scientist, 57*(7), 848–870.

61. Kilgo, D., Mourao, R., & Sylvie, G. (2015). Study finds unusual coverage patterns in Ferguson stories. *Gateway Journalism Review, 45*(338), 18–19.

62. McCoy, T. (2015). Freddie Gray's life a study on the effects of lead paint on poor blacks. *The Washington Post, 29*.

63. Belonsky, A. (2018). How the NAACP fought lynching—by using the racists' own pictures against them. *The Guardian*. Retrieved from https://www.theguardian.com/us-news/2018/apr/27/lynching-naacp-photographs-waco-texas-campaign.

64. Muhammad, K. G. (2018). The history of lynching and the present of policing. *The Nation*. Retrieved from https://www.thenation.com/article/archive/the-history-of-lynching-and-the-present-of-policing/.

65. Wood, M. (2013). Valency and abjection in the lynching postcard: A test case in the reclamation of black visual culture. *Slavery and Abolition, 34*(2), 202–221.

66. Apel, D. (2003). On looking: Lynching photographs and legacies of lynching after 9/11. *American Quarterly, 55*(3), 466.

67. Toure, 2018.

68. Raiford, L. (2009). Photography and the practices of critical black memory. *History and Theory, 48*(4), 112–129.

Chapter 9

1. Missouri Senate Bill 628 would have required some of the state's police officers to wear body cams while on duty. The bill died in committee. For the proposed law, *see*: https://www.legiscan.com/MO/text/SB628/2016.

2. For Anthony Scott's original petition in support of police-worn body cameras, *see*: https://www.change.org/p/congress-pass-the-police-camera-act.

3. The *Washington Post* conducted an in-depth report of how many fatal police encounters have resulted in an officer's prosecution. For the complete study, *see*: https://www.washingtonpost.com/sf/investigative/2015/04/11/thousands-dead-few-prosecuted/?utm_term=.c111447a2736.

4. After the Korryn Gaines killing, the Baltimore County PD accelerated the rollout of its body cam program to equip all 1,400 of its uniformed officers with the technology by September 2017. The initial deadline was December 2018, according to a *Washington Post* report.

5. Frumin, A. (2016, July 7). After Baton Rouge shooting, questions swirl around body cam failures. *NBCNews.com*. Retrieved from https://www.nbcnews.com/news/us-news/after-baton-rouge-shooting-questions-swirl-around-body-cam-failures-n605386.

6. Marq Claxton, director of the Black Law Enforcement Alliance, told MSNBC that body cams dislodging from officers during a struggle are not uncommon. Claxton's interview was posted to YouTube a day after Alton Sterling's death. More than 500 of the 800 comments under the video are disapproving, as indicated by a "thumbs down" rating. To read the entire thread that surrounded the missing Alton Sterling body cam footage, *see*: "Body camera video in Alton Sterling shooting may not be available," https://www.youtube.com/watch?v=lpHiNoxOdEI. To view the body cam video that the Baton Rouge PD released eventually, two years after the Sterling killing, *see*: "Body camera shows officer threatened to shoot Alton Sterling within seconds," *CNN.com*. Retrieved from https://www.cnn.com/2018/03/31/us/alton-sterling-police-videos-hearings/index.html.

7. CNN Business. (2015). A year after Michael Brown, the body cam business is booming. Retrieved from https://www.youtube.com/watch?v=eBuXirb2ErA.

8. Fan, M. D. (2019). Police power and the video revolution: Proof, policing, privacy, and audiovisual big data, p. 3. Cambridge University Press.

9. Wasserman, H. M. (2014). Moral panic and body cameras. *Washington University Law Review, 92*(831), 546.

10. While police body cams pose many legal dilemmas surrounding privacy, I am focusing as a media scholar on the ways that body cams complicate the black sousveillant gaze. To read more about the problem of body cams from a legal perspective *see*: Fan, M. D. (2019). *Police power and the video revolution: Proof, policing, privacy, and audiovisual big data*. Cambridge, UK: Cambridge University Press.

11. Williams, D., Martins, N., Consalvo, M., & Ivory, J. D. (2009). The virtual census: Representations of gender, race and age in video games. *New Media & Society*, *11*(5), 815.

12. Ibid., 831.

13. Passmore, C. J., Birk, M. V., & Mandryk, R. L. (2018, April). The privilege of immersion: Racial and ethnic experiences, perceptions, and beliefs in digital gaming. In *Proceedings of the 2018 CHI Conference on Human Factors in Computing Systems*, 383. New York, NY: Association for Computing Machinery.

14. Acosta, M. M., & Denham, A. R. (2018). Simulating oppression: Digital gaming, race and the education of African American children. *The Urban Review*, *50*(3), 345–362.

15. Mastro, D. (2009). Effects of racial and ethnic stereotyping. *Media Effects*, 341–357.

16. Gerbner, G., & Gross, L. (1976). Living with television: The violence profile. *Journal of Communication*, *26*(2), 172–199.

17. Murray, S. (2005). High art/low life: The art of playing grand theft auto. *PAJ: A Journal of Performance and Art*, *27*(2), 91–98.

18. Yang, G. S., Gibson, B., Lueke, A. K., Huesmann, L. R., & Bushman, B. J. (2014). Effects of avatar race in violent video games on racial attitudes and aggression. *Social Psychological and Personality Science*, *5*(6), 698–704.

19. Ibid., 698.

20. Morrison, C. M. (2017). Body camera obscura: The semiotics of police video. *American Criminal Law Review*, *54*(791), 823.

21. Ibid., 824.

22. For a *VICE News* report on HBO as but one example of how the so-called "Operation Varsity Blues" college admissions scandal of 2019 was reported, *see*: https://youtu.be/0v5yHnWCiLE. Rather than feature moments of the 50 alleged white-collar criminals being arrested, legacy media instead rolled footage of the indicted A-list actresses on the red carpet. The remainder of the report focused on how "broken" the college admissions process is, writ large. When legacy media fail to show accused white-collar criminals' encounters with police in the same way they would loop blue-collar run-ins with the law, the former group (which is largely white) is underrepresented in TV news, while the latter group (which is largely black or brown) is overrepresented in TV news.

23. Morrison, C. M. (2017). Body camera obscura: The semiotics of police video. *American Criminal Law Review*, *54*(791), 824.

24. Glanton, D. (2018). Laquan McDonald was shot down by police, and he took the mayor's career down with him. *Chicago Tribune*. Retrieved from https://www.chicagotribune.com/news/columnists/glanton/ct-met-rahm-emanuel-dahleen-glanton-laquan-mcdonald-20180905-story.html.

25. While there are dozens of YouTube videos that feature everyday citizens trying to make meaning of the seemingly missing frames in the Sandra Bland surveillance footage in Waller County Jail, her family first raised the concern to legacy media. *See*: Hennessy-Fiske, M. (2015, July 21). Jail video points to why Sandra Bland's family says her death is a mystery. *The Los Angeles Times*. Retrieved from https://www.

latimes.com/nation/la-na-sandra-bland-jail-video-20150721-story.html. *See* also HBO. (2018). *Say her name: The life and death of Sandra Bland.*

26. Wasserman, H. M. (2008). Orwell's vision: Video and the future of civil rights enforcement. *Maryland Law Review, 68*, 600.

27. Morrison, C. M. (2017). Body camera obscura: The semiotics of police video. *American Criminal Law Review, 54*(791), 824.

28. Pew Research Center. (2016). On views of race and inequality, blacks and whites are worlds apart. Retrieved from http://www.pewsocialtrends.org/2016/06/27/on-views-of-race-and-inequality-blacks-and-whites-are-worlds-apart/.

29. The full agenda of the inaugural Los Angeles County Civilian Oversight Commission conference held October 15, 2018, is available online. I participated on the panel: "Does my camera report the truth, the whole truth, and nothing but the truth?" *See:* https://coc.lacounty.gov/Conference2018.

30. Although many grassroots leaders pushed for the establishment of a Civilian Oversight Commission in Los Angeles, Patrisse Khan Cullors defines her extensive lobbying for it in chapter 10 of her 2018 autobiography, *When They Call You a Terrorist: A Black Lives Matter Memoir.* I recognize her leadership in this space to acknowledge one of the many changes to policing that the movement spurred.

31. Legal scholar Mary Fan coined the term "toutveillance" to describe "the multi-directional pervasiveness of recording." Toutveillance has created overlapping panopticons, she claims. *See:* Fan, M. D. (2019). *Police power and the video revolution: Proof, policing, privacy, and audiovisual big data.* Cambridge: UK: Cambridge University Press.

Epilogue

1. Smith, C. (2019, May 7). https://twitter.com/clintsmithiii/status/112577614921956 1474?s=12.

References

Abad-Santos, A. (2013). My star witness is black: Rachel Jeantel's testimony makes Trayvon a show trial. *The Atlantic*. Retrieved from http://www.thewire.com/national/2013/06/rachel-jeantel-testimony-trayvon-martin-trial/66652/.

Abraham, L., & Appiah, O. (2006). Framing news stories: The role of visual imagery in priming racial stereotypes. *The Howard Journal of Communications, 17*(3), 183–203.

Acosta, M. M., & Denham, A. R. (2018). Simulating oppression: Digital gaming, race and the education of African American children. *The Urban Review, 50*(3), 345–362.

Akom, A. A. (2003). Reexamining resistance as oppositional behavior: The Nation of Islam and the creation of a black achievement ideology. *Sociology of Education, 76*(4), 305–325.

Alexander, E. (1994). "Can you be BLACK and look at this?": Reading the Rodney King video(s). *Public Culture, 7*(1), 77–94.

Allan, S., & Peters, C. (2015). Visual truths of citizen reportage: Four research problematics. *Information, Communication & Society, 18*(11), 1348–1361.

Anon. (2014, December 8). Looks like Chicago PD had a Stingray out at the Eric Garner protest last night. *Privacy SOS*. Retrieved from https://privacysos.org/blog/looks-like-chicago-pd-had-a-stingray-out-at-the-eric-garner-protest-last-night/.

Anon. (2014). Black guy on the phone. *Know your meme*. Retrieved from https://knowyourmeme.com/memes/black-guy-on-the-phone.

Anon. (2018). BBQ Becky. *Know your meme*. Retrieved from https://knowyourmeme.com/memes/bbq-becky.

Anon. (2014). Guy Fawkes and the protest mask: An album. *Getty Images*. Retrieved from https://www.gettyimages.com/album/guy-fawkes-and-the-protest-mask-a-look-at-the--WcPVlZg1o0i-3VXXbxrhtQ#demonstrators-wearing-guy-fawkes-masks-as-they-block-traffic-during-a-picture-id459536504.

Anon. (2014). When did die-ins become a form of protest? *BBC News Magazine Monitor Blog*. Retrieved from https://www.bbc.com/news/blogs-magazine-monitor-30402637.

Anon. (2019). Activists unnerved by deaths of men tied to Ferguson protests. *Associated Press*. Retrieved from https://www.apnews.com/436251b8a58c470eb4f69099f43f2231.

Antony, M. G., & Thomas, R. J. (2010). "This is citizen journalism at its finest": YouTube and the public sphere in the Oscar Grant shooting incident. *New Media & Society, 12*(8), 1280–1296.

Apel, D. (2003). On looking: Lynching photographs and legacies of lynching after 9/11. *American Quarterly, 55*(3), 466.

Arendt, F., Steindl, N., & Vitouch, P. (2015). Effects of right-wing populist political advertising on implicit and explicit stereotypes. *Journal of Media Psychology, 27*, 178–189.

Armstrong, C. L., & Gao, F. (2010). Now tweet this: How news organizations use Twitter. *Electronic News, 4*(4), 218–235.

Armstrong, J. B. (2011). *Mary Turner and the memory of lynching*. Athens, GA: University of Georgia Press.

Aymer, S. R. (2016). "I can't breathe": A case study—Helping Black men cope with race-related trauma stemming from police killing and brutality. *Journal of Human Behavior in the Social Environment, 26*(3–4), 367–376.

Badger, E. (2016, July 13). Why highways have become the center of civil rights protest. *Washington Post.* Retrieved from http://link.galegroup.com.libproxy1.usc.edu/apps/doc/A457904179/AONE?u=usocal_main&sid=AONE&xid=ebc18072.

Baker, H. A. (1994). Critical memory and the black public sphere. *Public Culture, 7*(1), 3–33.

Bal, H. M., & Baruh, L. (2015). Citizen involvement in emergency reporting: A study on witnessing and citizen journalism. *Interactions: Studies in Communication & Culture, 6*(2), 213–231.

Barlow, W. (1999). *Voice over: The making of black radio.* Philadelphia, PA: Temple University Press.

Basu, T. (2015, February 25). The Guantanamo-like torture warehouse of Chicago. *The Atlantic.* Retrieved from https://www.theatlantic.com/national/archive/2015/02/behind-the-disappeared-of-chicagos-homan-square/385964/.

Bates, K. G. (2016). Private equity firm buys *Ebony* and *Jet* magazines. *NPR.* Retrieved from https://www.npr.org/2016/06/16/482279802/private-equity-firm-buys-ebony-and-jet-magazines.

BBC News Staff. (2018). Black Lives Matter "human chain" protest on Heathrow Road. *BBC News.* Retrieved from https://www.bbc.com/news/video_and_audio/headlines/36983828/black-lives-matter-human-chain-protest-on-heathrow-road.

Beam, R. A., Brownlee, B. J., Weaver, D. H., & Di Cicco, D. T. (2009). Journalism and public service in troubled times. *Journalism Studies, 10*(6), 734–753.

Belonsky, A. (2018). How the NAACP fought lynching—by using the racists' own pictures against them. *The Guardian.* Retrieved from https://www.theguardian.com/us-news/2018/apr/27/lynching-naacp-photographs-waco-texas-campaign.

Benjamin, W. (1970). The author as producer. *New Left Review, 1*(62), 1–9.

Benkler, Y. (2011). A free irresponsible press: Wikileaks and the battle over the soul of the networked Fourth Estate. *Harvard Civil Rights-Civil Liberties Law Review, 46*, 311.

Benson, T. W. (1974). Rhetoric and autobiography: The case of Malcolm X. *Quarterly Journal of Speech, 60*(1), 1–13.

Bertens, L. M. (2017). "Okay ladies, now let's get in formation!": Music videos and the construction of cultural memory. *Open Cultural Studies, 1*(1).

Blackmon, D. A. (2009). *Slavery by another name: The re-enslavement of black Americans from the Civil War to World War II.* New York, NY: Anchor.

Blassingame, J. W. (Ed.). (1977). *Slave testimony: Two centuries of letters, speeches, interviews, and autobiographies.* Baton Rouge, LA: Louisiana State University Press.

Bluett, T. (1734). *Some memoirs of the life of Job, the son of Solomon, the high priest of Boonda in Africa; who was a slave about two years in Maryland; and afterwards being brought to England, was set free, and sent to his native land in the year 1734.* London: Richard Ford. Retrieved from http://docsouth.unc.edu/neh/bluett/bluett.html.

Bogado, A. (2015). Clergy stage a die-in at Congressional cafeteria for Black Lives Matter. *Colorlines.* Retrieved from https://www.colorlines.com/articles/clergy-stage-die-congressional-cafeteria-black-lives-matter.

Born in slavery: Slave narratives from the Federal Writers' Project, 1936–1938. Digital Collections. Library of Congress. Retrieved from https://www.loc.gov/collections/

slave-narratives-from-the-federal-writers-project-1936-to-1938/about-this-collection/.

Brock, A. (2012). From the blackhand side: Twitter as a cultural conversation. *Journal of Broadcasting & Electronic Media, 56*(4), 529–49.

Brown Givens, S. M., & Monahan, J. L. (2005). Priming mammies, jezebels, and other controlling images: An examination of the influence of mediated stereotypes on perceptions of an African American woman. *Media Psychology, 7*(1), 87–106.

Brucato, B. (2015). Policing made visible: Mobile technologies and the importance of point of view. *Surveillance & Society, 13*(3/4), 455–473.

Bruns, A., & Stieglitz, S. (2013). Towards more systematic Twitter analysis: Metrics for tweeting activities. *International Journal of Social Research Methodology, 16*(2), 91–108.

Bry, D. (2014). Dear fellow white people: Keep protesting police violence. Just don't throw bottles from the back. *The Guardian*. Retrieved from https://www.theguardian.com/commentisfree/2014/dec/27/white-people-protesting-police-violence-black-lives-matter.

Buchholz, K. (2014). Colorado underreports officer-involved shootings. *CU News Corps*. Retrieved from https://cunewscorps.com/1261/gun-dialog-project/colorado-underreports-officer-involved-shootings/.

Campbell, C. P. (1995). *Race, myth and the news*. Thousand Oaks, CA: SAGE Publications.

Carey, N. (2011, August 23). Special report: In Libya, the cellphone as weapon. *Reuters.com*. https://reut.rs/2L8Kn9N.

Carson, C., & Shepard, K. (2001). *A call to conscience: The landmark speeches of Dr. Martin Luther King, Jr*. New York, NY: Hachette Book Group.

CBS News. (2011). Media, MLK and the Civil Rights Movement. Retrieved from https://youtu.be/pll_5s10ils?t=68.

CBS Staff. (2014, December 6). Activists say Chicago police used "Stingray" technology during protests. *CBS Chicago*. Retrieved from https://chicago.cbslocal.com/2014/12/06/activists-say-chicago-police-used-stingray-eavesdropping-technology-during-protests/.

Chan, J. L. (2016). Colin Kaepernick did not stand during the National Anthem. *Niners Nation*. Retrieved from https://www.ninersnation.com/2016/8/27/12669048/colin-kaepernick-did-not-stand-during-the-national-anthem.

Chavez, N., Grinberg, E., McLaughlin, E. (2018, October 31). Pittsburgh synagogue gunman said he wanted all Jews to die, criminal complaint says. *CNN*. Retrieved from https://www.cnn.com/2018/10/28/us/pittsburgh-synagogue-shooting/index.html.

Cherney, E. (2017, January 13). Chicago lawyer files federal lawsuit over police cellphone tracking system. *Chicago Tribune*. Retrieved from https://www.chicagotribune.com/news/local/breaking/ct-chicago-police-stingray-lawsuit-0113-20170112-story.html.

Chiricos, T., & Eschholz, S. (2002). The racial and ethnic typification of crime and the criminal typification of race and ethnicity in local television news. *Journal of Research in Crime and Delinquency, 39*(4), 400–420.

Ciccariello-Maher, G. (2015, May 4). Riots work: Wolf Blitzer and the *Washington Post* completely missed the real lesson from Baltimore. *Salon*. Retrieved from https://www.salon.com/2015/05/04/riots_work_wolf_blitzer_and_the_washington_post_completely_missed_the_real_lesson_from_baltimore/.

Clabaugh, J. (2018, March 5). 2 DC ZIP codes among nation's "most gentrified." *WTOP*. Retrieved from https://wtop.com/real-estate/2018/03/most-gentrified-zip-codes-dc/.

Clark, M. (2014). *To tweet our own cause: A mixed-methods study of the online phenomenon Black Twitter*. Chapel Hill, NC: The University of North Carolina at Chapel Hill.

Cleary, T. (2018). Jennifer Schulte, "BBQ Becky": 5 fast facts you need to know. *The Heavy*. Retrieved from https://heavy.com/news/2018/05/jennifer-schulte-bbq-becky/.

Clifton, D. (2016, August 9). How protests in Ferguson inspired the occupation of "Freedom Square." *Chicago Reader*. Retrieved from https://www.chicagoreader.com/chicago/freedom-square-homan-square-occupation-ferguson/Content?oid=23089791.

Clifton, D. (2018, January 30). Russian trolls stoked anger over Black Lives Matter more than was previously known. *Mother Jones*. Retrieved from https://www.motherjones.com/politics/2018/01/russian-trolls-hyped-anger-over-black-lives-matter-more-than-previously-known/.

CNN Business. (2015). A year after Michael Brown, the body cam business is booming. Retrieved from https://www.youtube.com/watch?v=eBuXirb2ErA.

CNN Staff. (2008). Close-up: Jesse Jackson crying. *CNN*. https://www.youtube.com/watch?v=CKWKlDznDPE.

CNN Staff. (2014). Cops kill man at Walmart carrying a BB gun. *CNN*. Retrieved from https://youtu.be/BtPt6GrnE6s.

CNN Staff. The Disruptors. *CNN*. Retrieved from http://www.cnn.com/interactive/2015/08/us/disruptors/.

Coates, T. (2012). Florida's self-defense laws and the killing of Trayvon Martin. *The Atlantic*. Retrieved from https://www.theatlantic.com/national/archive/2012/03/floridas-self-defense-laws-and-the-killing-of-trayvon-martin/254396/.

Cobb, J. (2013). Rachel Jeantel on trial. *The New Yorker*. Retrieved from https://www.newyorker.com/news/news-desk/rachel-jeantel-on-trial.

Collective, B. P. S. (Ed.). (1995). *The black public sphere: A public culture book*. Chicago, IL: University of Chicago Press.

Collins, P. H. (2000). Gender, black feminism, and black political economy. *The Annals of the American Academy of Political and Social Science, 568*(1), 41–53.

Collins, P. H. (2009). *Another kind of public education: Race, schools, the media, and democratic possibilities*. Boston, MA: Beacon Press.

Compaine, B. M. (2001). *The digital divide: Facing a crisis or creating a myth?* Cambridge, MA: MIT Press.

Conrad, J., Knowles, O., & Simmons, A. (2018). *Heart of darkness*. Cambridge, UK: Cambridge University Press.

Craven, J. (2015, April 29). Wolf Blitzer fails to goad protester into condemning violence. *The Huffington Post*. Retrieved from https://www.huffingtonpost.com/2015/04/29/wolf-blitzer-baltimore-protests_n_7168964.html.

Crilly, R. (2014, August 16). Dramatic pictures emerge of Michael Brown shooting in Ferguson, Missouri. *The Telegraph*. Retrieved from https://www.telegraph.co.uk/news/worldnews/northamerica/usa/11038527/Dramatic-pictures-emerge-of-Michael-Brown-shooting-in-Ferguson-Missouri.html.

Cullors, P., & Bandele, A. (2018). *When they call you a terrorist. A Black Lives Matter memoir*. New York, NY: St. Martin's Press.

Currier, J. (2018, July 26). Race for St. Louis County prosecutor focuses on experience, criminal justice reform. *St. Louis Post-Dispatch*. Retrieved from https://www.stltoday.com/news/local/crime-and-courts/race-for-st-louis-county-prosecutor-focuses-on-experience-criminal/article_a364b660-6f7a-5be0-83b9-2e78c889a6c0.html.

Curry, T. J. (2012). The fortune of Wells: Ida B. Wells-Barnett's use of T. Thomas Fortune's philosophy of social agitation as a prolegomenon to militant civil rights activism. *Transactions of the Charles S. Peirce Society: A Quarterly Journal in American Philosophy, 48*(4), 456–482.

Curtis, M. V. (1988). Understanding the black aesthetic experience. *Music Educators Journal, 75*(2), 23–26.

Davies, Hannah. (2018). *The Rachel divide* won't make you like Rachel Dolezal, but it might help you understand her. *Refinery 29*. Retrieved from https://www.refinery29.uk/the-rachel-divide.

Davis, A. (1994). Afro images: Politics, fashion, and nostalgia. *Critical Inquiry, 21*(1), 37–45. https://doi.org/10.1086/448739.

Dawkins, W. (1997). *Black journalists: The NABJ story*. Merrillville, IN: August Press.

De Bruijn, M. (2009). *Mobile phones: The new talking drums of everyday Africa*. Oxford, UK: African Books Collective.

Denvir, D. (2016, July 11). Criminalizing the hustle: Policing poor people's survival strategies from Eric Garner to Alton Sterling. *Salon*. Retrieved from https://www.salon.com/2016/07/08/criminalizing_the_hustle_policing_poor_peoples_survival_strategies_from_erin_garner_to_alton_sterling/.

Dickson, E. J. (2019, March 18). Mysterious deaths leave Ferguson activists "on pins and needles." *RollingStone.com*. Retrieved from https://www.rollingstone.com/culture/culture-news/ferguson-death-mystery-black-lives-matter-michael-brown-809407/.

Dingle, D. (2017). 45 Great moments in black business—No. 36: Essence sale continues debate over black ownership. *Black Enterprise*. Retrieved from https://www.blackenterprise.com/great-moments-in-black-business-no-36-essence-sale-continues-debate-over-black-ownership/.

Dixon, T. L., & Linz, D. (2000a). Race and the misrepresentation of victimization on local television news. *Communication Research, 27*(5), 547–573.

Dixon, T. L., & Linz, D. (2000b). Overrepresentation and underrepresentation of African Americans and Latinos as lawbreakers on television news. *Journal of Communication, 50*(2), 131–154.

Djan, O. S., & Cockin, M. S. (1942). Drums and victory: Africa's call to the empire. *Journal of the Royal African Society, 41*(162), 29–41.

Dodge, J. (2014, October 1). After denials, Chicago Police Department admits cell-phone spying devices. *CBS Chicago*. Retrieved from https://chicago.cbslocal.com/2014/10/01/chicago-police-department-admits-purchase-of-cell-phone-spying-devices/.

Doggett, J. A. (2015, April 29). Five code words the media needs to stop using to describe black people. *Essence*. Retrieved from http://www.essence.com/2015/04/29/5-code-words-media-needs-stop-using-describe-black-people.

Domonoske, C. (2016, August 3). During fatal standoff, police asked Facebook to deactivate woman's account. *NPR*. Retrieved from https://www.npr.org/sections/thetwo-way/2016/08/03/488500830/during-fatal-standoff-police-asked-facebook-to-deactivate-womans-account.

Douglass, F. (1960). *Narrative of the life of Frederick Douglass, an American slave*. New York, NY: Oxford University Press.

Du Bois, W. E. B. (1903). *The souls of black folk*. New York, NY: Oxford University Press.

Dunbar, P. L. (1896). We wear the mask. *Poets.org*. Retrieved from https://www.poets.org/poetsorg/poem/we-wear-mask.

Eco, U. (1965). Towards a semiotic inquiry into the television message. *Television: Critical Concepts in Media and Cultural Studies, 2*, 3–19.

Elkouby, Sebastien. (2015, May 1). A quick lesson on Baltimore: What they're not showing you. *JetMag*. Retrieved from https://www.jetmag.com/talk-back-2/quick-lesson-baltimore/.

Entman, R. M. (1992). Blacks in the news: Television, modern racism and cultural change. *Journalism Quarterly, 69*(2), 341–361.

Entman, R. M. (1994). Representation and reality in the portrayal of blacks on network television news. *Journalism & Mass Communication Quarterly, 71*(3), 509–520.

Estes, S. (2006). *I am a man!: Race, manhood, and the Civil Rights Movement*. Chapel Hill, NC: The University of North Carolina Press.

Fanon, F. (1952). *Black skin, white masks*. New York, NY: Grove Press.

Fecile, J. (2018, October 1). "Banned in 46 countries"—is *Faces of death* the most shocking film ever? *The Guardian*. Retrieved from https://www.theguardian.com/film/2018/oct/01/banned-in-46-countries-is-faces-of-death-the-most-shocking-film-ever.

Felman, S., & Laub, D. (1992). *Testimony: Crises of witnessing in literature, psychoanalysis, and history*. New York, NY: Routledge.

Fields, R. (2017, November 15). New York City launches committee to review maternal deaths. *ProPublica*. Retrieved from https://www.propublica.org/article/new-york-city-launches-committee-to-review-maternal-deaths.

Fogel, R. W., & Engerman, S. L. (1995). *Time on the cross: The economics of American Negro slavery*. New York, NY: W.W. Norton & Company.

Folami, A. (2007). From Habermas to "get rich or die tryin'": Hip hop, the Telecommunications Act of 1996, and the black public sphere. *Michigan Journal of Race & Law, 12*, 235.

Fraser, N. (1990). Rethinking the public sphere: A contribution to the critique of actually existing democracy. *Social Text*, (25/26), 56–80. https://doi.org/10.2307/466240.

Frazier, E. F. (1997). The Negro press and wish-fulfillment. In *Black bourgeoisie*, pp. 174–194. New York, NY: Free Press Paperbacks.

Freelon, D., McIlwain, C. D., & Clark, M. (2016). Beyond the hashtags: #Ferguson, #Blacklivesmatter, and the online struggle for offline justice. Center for Media & Social Impact, American University. Retrieved from *http://creativecommons.org/licenses/by-nc-sa/4.0/*.

Frosh, P., & Pinchevski, A. (Eds.). (2008). *Media witnessing: Testimony in the age of mass communication*. New York, NY: Springer.

Frumin, A. (2016, July 7). After Baton Rouge shooting, questions swirl around body cam failures. *NBCNews.com*. Retrieved from https://www.nbcnews.com/news/us-news/after-baton-rouge-shooting-questions-swirl-around-body-cam-failures-n605386.

Fryer, R. G., Jr. (2018). Reconciling results on racial differences in police shootings. *American Economic Review Papers and Proceedings, 108*, 228–233.

Garcia, S. (2018, January 4). With sale, *Essence* is once again a fully black-owned magazine. (National Desk). *The New York Times*.

Garfield, G. (2007). Hurricane Katrina: The making of unworthy disaster victims. *Journal of African American Studies, 10*(4), 55–74.

Garza, A. (2014). A herstory of the #BlackLivesMatter movement. In Hobson, J. (Ed.), *Are all the women still white? Rethinking race, expanding feminisms*, pp. 23–28. Albany, NY: SUNY Press.

Gentzkow, M., Glaeser, E. L., & Goldin, C. (2006). The rise of the Fourth Estate. How newspapers became informative and why it mattered. In Glaeser, E. L., & Goldin, C. (Eds.), *Corruption and reform: Lessons from America's economic history*, pp. 187–230. Chicago, IL: University of Chicago Press.

Gerbner, G., & Gross, L. (1976). Living with television: The violence profile. *Journal of Communication*, 26(2), 172–199.

Gilliam, F. D., Jr., & Iyengar, S. (1998). The superpredator script. *Nieman Reports*, 52(4), 45.

Gilliam, F. D., Jr., Iyengar, S., Simon, A., & Wright, O. (1996). Crime in black and white: The violent, scary world of local news. *The Harvard International Journal of Press/Politics*, 1(3), 6–23.

Gilroy, P. (1982/2008). The myth of black criminality. In Spalek, B. (Ed.), *Ethnicity and crime: A Reader*, pp. 113–127. New York, NY: Open University Press.

Glanton, D. (2018). Laquan McDonald was shot down by police, and he took the mayor's career down with him. *Chicago Tribune*. Retrieved from https://www.chicagotribune. com/news/columnists/glanton/ct-met-rahm-emanuel-dahleen-glanton-laquan-mcdonald-20180905-story.html.

Goldenberg, S. (2016, September 12). Records show increased earnings for officer involved in Garner death. *Politico*. Retrieved from https://www.politico.com/states/new-york/ albany/story/2016/09/officer-in-eric-garner-death-boosts-overtime-pay-105359.

Goldsmith, S. (2016). The brief, poignant life of MarShawn McCarrel. *Columbus Monthly*. Retrieved from https://www.columbusmonthly.com/lifestyle/20161025/ brief-poignant-life-of-marshawn-mccarrel.

Goldstein, M. (2006). The other beating. *Los Angeles Times*. Retrieved from http://articles. latimes.com/2006/feb/19/magazine/tm-holiday8.

Goodman, J. D. (2014). Man who filmed fatal police chokehold is arrested on weapons charges. *The New York Times*. Retrieved from https://www.nytimes.com/2014/08/04/ nyregion/after-recording-eric-garner-chokehold-ramsey-orta-gets-charged-with-gun-possession.html.

Govaki, M. (2016). Mother of Crawford's sons in prison for child endangerment. *Dayton Daily News*. Retrieved from https://www.daytondailynews.com/ news/crime--law/mother-crawford-sons-prison-for-child-endangerment/ q6F0AIs3GsOwQpSu0PosVK/.

Greenwell, A. V. (2012). Twentieth-century ideology meets 21st-century technology: Black news websites and racial uplift. *Fire!!!: The Multimedia Journal of Black Studies*, 1(2), 111–138.

Gregory, S. (1994). Race, identity and political activism: The shifting contours of the African American public sphere. *Public Culture*, 7(1), 147–164.

Gregory, S. (2016). "Human rights in an age of distant witnesses." In *Image operations*. Manchester, UK: Manchester University Press. Retrieved from https://www. manchesterhive.com/view/9781526108647/9781526108647.00023.

Gressman, E. (1952). The unhappy history of civil rights legislation. *Michigan Law Review*, 50(8), 1323–1358.

Guerrero, L. (2016). Can I live?: Contemporary black satire and the state of postmodern double consciousness. (2016). *Studies in American Humor*, 2(2), 266–279.

Gunaratne, S. A. (2006). Public sphere and communicative rationality: Interrogating Habermas's eurocentrism. *Journalism & Communication Monographs*, 8(2), 93–156.

Habermas, J. (1991). *The structural transformation of the public sphere: An inquiry into a category of bourgeois society*. Cambridge, MA: The MIT Press.

Haddad, V. (2018). Nobody's protest novel: Novelistic strategies of the Black Lives Matter Movement. *The Comparatist, 42*(1), 40–59.

Hall, A. V., Hall, E. V., & Perry, J. L. (2016). Black and blue: Exploring racial bias and law enforcement in the killings of unarmed black male civilians. *American Psychologist, 71*(3), 175.

Hall, S. (2001). The spectacle of the other. In Wetherell, M., Taylor, S., & Yates, S. J. (Eds.), *Discourse theory and practice: A reader*. Los Angeles, CA: SAGE Publications.

Halverson, J. R., Ruston, S. W., & Trethewey, A. (2013). Mediated martyrs of the Arab Spring: New media, civil religion, and narrative in Tunisia and Egypt. *Journal of Communication, 63*(2), 312–332.

Harlow, S., & Johnson, T. J. (2011). Overthrowing the protest paradigm? How the I, global voices and Twitter covered the Egyptian revolution. *International Journal of Communication, 5*, 16.

Harris, A. (2015). Has Kendrick Lamar recorded the new black national anthem? *Slate*. Retrieved from http://www.slate.com/articles/arts/culturebox/2015/08/black_lives_matter_protesters_chant_kendrick_lamar_s_alright_what_makes.html.

Harris, J. (2017). Mother of police shooting victim Kajieme Powell sues St. Louis. *Courthouse News Service*. Retrieved from https://www.courthousenews.com/mother-police-shooting-victim-kajieme-powell-sues-st-louis/.

Harris-Lacewell, M. (2004). *Barbershops, bibles, and BET: Everyday talk and black political thought*. Princeton, NJ: Princeton University Press.

Hayes, K. (2016). Black organizers in Chicago get in "Formation" for Black Lives and public education. *TruthOut*. Retrieved from https://truthout.org/articles/inspired-by-beyonce-black-organizers-get-in-formation-to-disrupt-nfl-draft/.

Haygood, C. (2017). The influence of Zora Neale Hurston's films on Beyonce's *Lemonade*. *Kenyon Review*. Retrieved from https://www.kenyonreview.org/2017/12/influence-zora-neale-hurstons-films-beyonces-lemonade/.

Healy, J., & Turkewitz, J. (2015, July 16). Guilty verdict for James Holmes in Aurora attack. *The New York Times*. Retrieved from https://www.nytimes.com/2015/07/17/us/james-holmes-guilty-in-aurora-movie-theater-shooting.html.

Heitzeg, N. A. (2015). "Whiteness," criminality, and the double standards of deviance/social control. *Contemporary Justice Review, 18*(2), 198.

Heusel, J. (2015). Postracial justice and the trope of the "race riot." In Gibson, S., & Lando, A. L. (Eds.), *Impact of communication and the media on ethnic conflict*, pp. 195–213. Hershey, PA: Information Science Reference.

Hirschfield, P. J., & Simon, D. (2010). Legitimating police violence: Newspaper narratives of deadly force. *Theoretical Criminology, 14*(2), 155–182.

Holson, L. M. (2018). Hundreds in Oakland turn out to BBQ while black. *The New York Times*. Retrieved from https://www.nytimes.com/2018/05/21/us/oakland-bbq-while-black.html.

Honey, M. K. (2011). *Going down Jericho Road: The Memphis Strike, Martin Luther King's last campaign*. New York, NY: W. W. Norton & Company, Inc.

hooks, b. (2014). *Black looks: Race and representation*. Boston, MA: South End Press.

Howard, P. N., Duffy, A., Freelon, D., Hussain, M. M., Mari, W., & Maziad, M. (2011). *Opening closed regimes: What was the role of social media during the Arab Spring?* Retrieved from https://ssrn.com/abstract=2595096; http://dx.doi.org/10.2139/ssrn.2595096.

Huie, W. B. (1956). The shocking story of approved killing in Mississippi. *Look, 20*(2), 46–50. Retrieved from https://www.pbs.org/wgbh/americanexperience/features/till-killers-confession/.

Hurston, Z. N. (1995). The Eatonville anthology. In *Folklore, memoirs, & other writings,* 813–826. New York: NY: Library of America.

Isaksen, J. L. (2012). Resistive radio: African Americans' evolving portrayal and participation from broadcasting to narrowcasting. *Journal of Popular Culture, 45*(4), 749–68.

Iyengar, S., & Hahn, K. S. (2009). Red media, blue media: Evidence of ideological selectivity in media use. *Journal of Communication, 59*(1), 19–39.

Jackson, J. L., & Alvite, D. (2012). Unlikely hero: Rapping with Petey Greene. *Journal on African Philosophy, 6.* Retrieved from https://www.africaknowledgeproject.org/index.php/jap/article/view/1511.

Jackson, R. (2016). If they gunned me down and criming while white: An examination of Twitter campaigns through the lens of citizens' media. *Cultural Studies? Critical Methodologies, 16*(3), 313–319.

Java, A., Song, X., Finin, T., & Tseng, B. (2007). Why we twitter: Understanding micro-blogging usage and communities. In *Proceedings of the 9th WebKDD and 1st SNA-KDD 2007 workshop on Web mining and social network analysis,* 56–65. San Jose, California.

Johnson, J. (2017, May 5). Ferguson, Mo., activists are dying and it's time to ask questions. *The Root.* Retrieved from https://www.theroot.com/ferguson-activists-are-dying-and-it-s-time-to-ask-quest-1794955900.

Johnson, J. H., & Bennett, L. (1989). *Succeeding against the odds: The inspiring autobiography of one of America's wealthiest entrepreneurs.* New York, NY: Warner Books.

Johnson, R. E. (1991, March 14) Backstage. *Jet.* Retrieved from https://tinyurl.com/y2ex6a6r.

Joseph, G. (2015, July 24). Exclusive: Feds regularly monitored Black Lives Matter since Ferguson. *The Intercept.* Retrieved from https://theintercept.com/2015/07/24/documents-show-department-homeland-security-monitoring-black-lives-matter-since-ferguson/.

Kast, S. (2010, June 23). Morgan State finds its MOJO. *Maryland Morning: NPR.* Retrieved from https://mdmorn.wordpress.com/2010/06/22/623102-morgan-state-finds-its-mojo/.

Khan-Cullors, P. (2018). *When they call you a terrorist.* New York, NY: St. Martin's Press.

Khazan, O. (2018, May 08). In one year, 57,375 years of life were lost to police violence. *The Atlantic.* Retrieved from https://www.theatlantic.com/health/archive/2018/05/the-57375-years-of-life-lost-to-police-violence/559835/.

Khondker, H. H. (2011). Role of the new media in the Arab Spring. *Globalizations, 8*(5), 675–679.

Kilgo, D., Mourao, R., & Sylvie, G. (2015). Study finds unusual coverage patterns in Ferguson stories. *Gateway Journalism Review, 45*(338), 18–19.

King, S. (2015, April 5). American tragedy: At least 50% of police shooting victims struggled with mental illness. *The Daily Kos.* Retrieved from https://www.dailykos.com/stories/2015/4/5/1375335/-American-tragedy-A-staggering-percentage-of-police-shooting-victims-struggled-with-mental-illness.

Klein, E. (2014). Did the St. Louis police have to shoot Kajieme Powell?" *Vox.* Retrieved from https://www.vox.com/2014/8/20/6051431/did-the-st-louis-police-have-to-shoot-kajieme-powell.

Kohns, O. (2013). Guy Fawkes in the 21st century. A contribution to the political iconography of revolt. *Image & Narrative, 14*(1), 89–104.

La Ganga, M. L., & Dolan, M. (2009, January 15). Oakland shooting protest ends in violence: Some of those protesting the death of Oscar J. Grant III damage businesses and cars, a former transit police officer is charged in the case. *Los Angeles Times*, p. 1.

Lartey, J. (2018, January 28). We've ignited a new generation: Patrisse Khan-Cullors on the resurgence of black activism. *The Guardian*. https://www.theguardian.com/us-news/2018/jan/28/patrisse-khan-cullors-black-lives-matter-interview.

Laughland, O., and Swaine, J. (2015, August 17). "I dream about it every night": What happens to Americans who film police violence? *The Guardian*. Retrieved from https://www.theguardian.com/us-news/2015/aug/15/filming-police-violence-walter-scott-michael-brown-shooting.

Laurent, O. (2015, April 30). Go behind *TIME's* Baltimore cover with aspiring photographer Devin Allen. *TIME Lightbox Photo Blog*. Retrieved from http://time.com/3841077/baltimore-protests-riot-freddie-gray-devin-allen//.

Lawler, O. G. (2018, November 28). Another Ferguson protester has died. *The Cut*. Retrieved from https://www.thecut.com/2018/11/another-ferguson-protester-bassem-masri-has-died.html.

LeDuff, K. M. (2012). National news coverage of race in the era of Obama. In Campbell, C. P., LeDuff, K. M., Jenkins, C. D., & Brown, R. A. (Eds.), *Race and news: Critical perspectives*, pp. 43–63. New York, NY: Routledge.

LeMelle, T. J. (2002). The HBCU: Yesterday, today and tomorrow. *Education, 123*(1), 190.

Leonard, J. (2010, June 24). Court releases dramatic video of BART Shooting. Retrieved from https://youtu.be/Q2LDw5l_yMI.

Leopold, J. (2015, June 24). Fearing a "catastrophic incident," 400 federal officers descended on the Baltimore protests. *VICE News*. Retrieved from https://news.vice.com/en_us/article/8x393b/fearing-a-catastrophic-incident-400-federal-officers-descended-on-the-baltimore-protests.

Levenson, E. (2017, December 31). Activist Erica Garner, 27, dies after heart attack. *CNN*. Retrieved from https://www.cnn.com/2017/12/30/us/erica-garner-eric-death/index.html.

Lichtblau, E., & Flegenheimer, M. (2017). Jeff Sessions confirmed as Attorney General, capping bitter battle. *The New York Times*. Retrieved from https://www.nytimes.com/2017/02/08/us/politics/jeff-sessions-attorney-general-confirmation.html.

Liebelson, D., & Reilly, R. J. (2015, October 9). Inside Hillary Clinton's meeting with Black Lives Matter. *The Huffington Post*. Retrieved from https://www.huffingtonpost.com/entry/black-lives-matter-hillary-clinton_us_56180c44e4b0e66ad4c7d9fa.

Liebelson, D., & Reilly, R. J. (2015, September 16). Black Lives Matter activists meet with Bernie Sanders to make sure he is on board. *The Huffington Post*. Retrieved from https://www.huffingtonpost.com/entry/bernie-sanders-black-lives-matter_us_55f9ca9ce4b00310edf57b02.

Lind, D. (2015, December 17). There are huge racial disparities in how US police use force. *Vox*. Retrieved from *https://www.vox.com/cards/police-brutality-shootings-us/us-police-racism*.

Linke, U. (1999). Formations of white public space: Racial aesthetics, body politics and the nation. *Transforming Anthropology, 8*(1–2), 129–161.

Lopez, C. E. (2018, November 11). Here's why Jeff Sessions' parting shot is worse than you thought. *The Marshall Project*. Retrieved from https://www.themarshallproject.org/2018/11/19/here-s-why-jeff-sessions-parting-shot-is-worse-than-you-thought.

Lotan, G., Graeff, E., Ananny, M., Gaffney, D., & Pearce, I. (2011). The Arab Spring| The revolutions were tweeted: Information flows during the 2011 Tunisian and Egyptian revolutions. *International Journal of Communication*, *5*, 31.

Lowery, W. (2016, September 7). Who killed Ferguson activists Darren Seals? *The Washington Post*.

Lowery, W., & Stankiewicz, K. (2016, February 15). "My demons won today": Ohio activist's suicide spotlights depression among Black Lives Matter leaders. *WashingtonPost.com*.

Lubbers, M., Scheepers, P., & Vergeer, M. (2000). Exposure to newspapers and attitudes toward ethnic minorities: A longitudinal analysis. *Howard Journal of Communication*, *11*(2), 127–143.

Luckie, M. (2015, September 18). What it's really like being black in Silicon Valley. *USA Today*. Retrieved from https://www.usatoday.com/story/tech/columnist/2015/09/18/silicon-valley-diversity-being-black-in-tech-companies-mark-luckie/72399254/.

Luckie, Mark S. (2018, November 27). Facebook is failing its black employees and its black users. *Facebook*. Retrieved from https://www.facebook.com/notes/mark-s-luckie/facebook-is-failing-its-black-employees-and-its-black-users/1931075116975013/.

Lund, J. (2015, April 29). CNN and Baltimore: A crossfire with 100 percent casualties. *RollingStone.com*. Retrieved from https://www.rollingstone.com/tv/tv-news/cnn-and-baltimore-a-crossfire-with-100-percent-casualties-72812/.

Manjoo, F. (2010, August 10). How black people use Twitter. *Slate.com*. Retrieved from https://slate.com/technology/2010/08/how-black-people-use-twitter.html.

Mann, S., & Ferenbok, J. (2013). New media and the power politics of sousveillance in a surveillance-dominated world. *Surveillance & Society*, *11*(1/2), 18.

Mastro, D. (2009). Effects of racial and ethnic stereotyping. In Bryant, J., & Oliver, M. B. (Eds.), *Media Effects*, 341–357.

McBride, D. A. (2001). *Impossible witnesses: Truth, abolitionism, and slave testimony.* New York, NY: NYU Press.

McCorvey, J. J. (2016, August 3). Before the police killed Korryn Gaines, Facebook deactivated her account. *Fast Company*. Retrieved from https://www.fastcompany.com/4015851/before-the-police-killed-korryn-gaines-facebook-deactivated-her-account.

McCoy, T. (2015, April 29). Freddie Gray's life a study on the effects of lead paint on poor blacks. *The Washington Post*. Retrieved from https://www.washingtonpost.com/local/freddie-grays-life-a-study-in-the-sad-effects-of-lead-paint-on-poor-blacks/2015/04/29/0be898e6-eea8-11e4-8abc-d6aa3bad79dd_story.html.

McDonell-Parry, A. (2018, November 2). Ferguson activist claims son was "lynched" as police investigate his death as suicide. *Rolling Stone*. Retrieved from https://www.rollingstone.com/culture/culture-news/ferguson-danye-jones-death-lynching-suicide-melissa-mckinnies-751275/.

McKinley, J. (2009, January 8). In California, protests after man dies at hands of transit police. (National Desk)(Oscar Grant III). *The New York Times*, p. A10.

McLeod, J. D., Jr. (2017). If God got us: Kendrick Lamar, Paul Tillich, and the advent of existentialist hip hop. *Toronto Journal of Theology*, *33*(1), 123–135.

Mills, Q. T. (2013). *Cutting along the color line: Black barbers and barber shops in America.* Philadelphia, PA: University of Pennsylvania Press.

Miranda, C. (2016). "It hasn't left me": How Black Lives Matter used performance to create unforgettable 2016 moments. *Los Angeles Times*. Retrieved from http://www.latimes.com/entertainment/arts/miranda/la-ca-cm-year-end-black-lives-matter-artists-20161218-story.html.

Moreno, J. (2015). People are making badass art of the woman who removed the Confederate flag. *Buzzfeed*. Retrieved from https://www.buzzfeed.com/javiermoreno/bree-newsome-confederate-flag-art?utm_term=.hamz8kjK5D#.acMYwgZkq5.

Morrison, C. M. (2017). Body camera obscura: The semiotics of police video. *American Criminal Law Review, 54*, 791.

Mortensen, M. (2011). When citizen photojournalism sets the news agenda: Neda Agha Soltan as a Web 2.0 icon of post-election unrest in Iran. *Global Media and Communication, 7*(1), 4–16.

Muhammad, K. G. (2018). The history of lynching and the present of policing. *The Nation*. Retrieved from https://www.thenation.com/article/archive/the-history-of-lynching-and-the-present-of-policing/.

Murray, S. (2005). High art/low life: The art of playing grand theft auto. *PAJ: A Journal of Performance and Art, 27*(2), 91–98.

NAACP. (1918). Memorandum For Governor Dorsey from Walter F. White. Papers of the NAACP, Group I. Series C, Box 353, Washington, DC: Library of Congress.

NAACP. (2019). *History of lynchings*. Retrieved from https://www.naacp.org/history-of-lynchings/.

NBC Staff. (2015). #Selma50: What the media and Hollywood got wrong about Bloody Sunday. *NBC News*. https://www.nbcnews.com/news/nbcblk/media-studies-selma-n319436.

Neville, H. A., Coleman, M. N., Falconer, J. W., & Holmes, D. (2005). Color-blind racial ideology and psychological false consciousness among African Americans. *Journal of Black Psychology, 31*(1), 27–45.

NewsOne Staff. (2014). Angela Williams: Woman's death following Walmart shooting ruled homicide. *NewsOne*. Retrieved from https://newsone.com/3056226/angela-williams-womans-death-following-walmart-shooting-ruled-homicide/.

Noble, S. U. (2018). *Algorithms of oppression*. New York, NY: NYU Press.

Norris, P. (2001). *Digital divide: Civic engagement, information poverty, and the Internet worldwide*. Cambridge, UK: Cambridge University Press.

Ogletree, C. (2012). *The presumption of guilt: The arrest of Henry Louis Gates Jr. and race, class and crime in America*. New York, NY: St. Martin's Press.

Olumhense, E. (2019). 20 years after the NYPD killing of Amadou Diallo, his mother and community ask: What's changed? *Intelligencer*. Retrieved from http://nymag.com/intelligencer/2019/02/after-the-nypd-killing-of-amadou-diallo-whats-changed.html.

Omi, M., & Winant, H. (2014). *Racial formation in the United States*. New York, NY: Routledge.

Parks, G. (1966/2010). *A choice of weapons*. St. Paul, MN: Minnesota Historical Society Press.

Paschalidis, G. (2015). Mini cameras and maxi minds: Citizen photojournalism and the public sphere. *Digital Journalism, 3*(4), 634–652.

Passmore, C. J., Birk, M. V., & Mandryk, R. L. (2018). The privilege of immersion: Racial and ethnic experiences, perceptions, and beliefs in digital gaming. In *Proceedings of the 2018 CHI Conference on Human Factors in Computing Systems*, p. 383. ACM.

Penrice, R. R. (2014, February 14). Why Malcolm X rifle image still strikes a chord. *The Grio*. Retrieved from https://thegrio.com/2014/02/14/why-malcolm-x-rifle-image-still-strikes-a-chord/.

Pesca, M. (2005, September 5). Are Katrina's victims "refugees" or "evacuees"? *NPR*. https://www.npr.org/templates/story/story.php?storyId=4833613.

Peters, J. (2001). Witnessing. *Media, Culture & Society, 23*(6), 707–723.

Peters, J. (2015, April 28). Where are the police? When cities spasm with violence for complicated reasons, that's the only question CNN wants to ask. *Slate.* Retrieved from https://slate.com/news-and-politics/2015/04/baltimore-freddie-gray-riots-why-cnn-is-incapable-of-understanding-why-violence-erupts-in-cities.html.

Pew Research Center. (2016). On views of race and inequality, blacks and whites are worlds apart. Retrieved from http://www.pewsocialtrends.org/2016/06/27/on-views-of-race-and-inequality-blacks-and-whites-are-worlds-apart/.

Pew Research Center. (2018, February 5). *Mobile Fact Sheet.* Retrieved from http://www.pewinternet.org/fact-sheet/mobile/.

Phillips, J. (2016). Caliver, Ambrose: 1894–1962. *Black Past.* Retrieved from http://www.blackpast.org/aah/caliver-ambrose-1894-1962.

Plevin, R. (2016). Black Lives Matter rally blocks 405 freeway in Inglewood. *KPCC.* Retrieved from https://www.scpr.org/news/2016/07/11/62495/black-lives-matter-rally-blocks-405-freeway-in-ing/.

Poindexter, P. M., Smith, L., & Heider, D. (2003). Race and ethnicity in local television news: Framing, story assignments, and source selections. *Journal of Broadcasting & Electronic Media, 47*(4), 533.

Pough, G. D. (2015). *Check it while I wreck it: Black womanhood, hip-hop culture, and the public sphere.* Boston, MA: Northeastern University Press.

Powell, E. (1968, April 20). Rivers of blood. *Speech at Birmingham.* Retrieved from http://www.toqonline.com/archives/v1n1/TOQv1n1Powell.pdf.

Price, W. (2014, August 11). Ferguson protest: "I am a man." Retrieved from http://www.stlamerican.com/gallery/wiley_price_photojournalism/ferguson-protest-i-am-a-man/image_056c85f8-2181-11e4-842b-001a4bcf887a.html.

Pullen, K. (2011). If ya liked it, then you shoulda made a video: Beyoncé Knowles, YouTube and the public sphere of images. *Performance Research 16*(2), 145–146. https://doi.org/10.1080/13528165.2011.578846.

Raiford, L. (2007). "Come let us build a new world together": SNCC and photography of the Civil Rights Movement. *American Quarterly, 59*(4), 1129.

Raiford, L. (2009). Photography and the practices of critical black memory. *History and Theory, 48*(4), 112–129.

Raiford, L. (2011). *Imprisoned in a luminous glare: Photography and the African American freedom struggle.* Chapel Hill, NC: UNC Press Books.

Ramsey, F. (2015). She left the flagpole in handcuffs. Now artists reimagine her as a superhero. *Upworthy.* Retrieved from https://www.upworthy.com/she-left-the-flagpole-in-handcuffs-now-artists-reimagine-her-as-a-superhero.

Ransby, B. (2015). The class politics of Black Lives Matter. *Dissent, 62*(4), 31–34.

Reid, E. (2017). Why Colin Kaepernick and I decided to take a knee. *The New York Times.* Retrieved from https://www.nytimes.com/2017/09/25/opinion/colin-kaepernick-football-protests.html.

Reign, A. (2016, July 6). Why I will not share the video of Alton Sterling's death. *The Washington Post.* Retrieved from http://link.galegroup.com.libproxy2.usc.edu/apps/doc/A457218533/AONE?u=usocal_main&sid=AONE&xid=9b31e883.

Rhodan, M. (2017). This photo of MLK kneeling has power amid the NFL protests. Here's the story behind it. *TIME.* Retrieved from http://time.com/4955717/trump-protests-mlk-martin-luther-king-kneeling/.

Richardson, A. (2016). The platform: How Pullman porters used railways to engage in networked journalism. *Journalism Studies, 17*(4), 398–414.

Roberts, G., & Klibanoff, H. (2007). *Race Beat: The press, the civil rights struggle, and the awakening of a nation.* New York, NY: Vintage Books.

Rogers, A. (2015). What is Anonymous doing in Ferguson? *TIME.* Retrieved from http://time.com/3148925/ferguson-michael-brown-anonymous/.

Ross, L. C. (2001). *The Divine Nine: The history of African American fraternities and sororities.* New York, NY: Kensington Books.

RT News. (2014, August 21). GRAPHIC: St. Louis police officer shoots Kajieme Powell. *YouTube.* Retrieved from https://www.youtube.com/watch?v=sEuZiTcbGCg&t=41s.

Samara, R. (2013). What white people don't understand about Rachel Jeantel. *GlobalGrind.* Retrieved from https://bit.ly/2NDRMuT.

Samsung Staff. "From Zero to Infinity": The Five-year Journey of the Samsung Galaxy. Retrieved from https://news.samsung.com/global/from-zero-to-infinity-the-five-year-journey-of-the-samsung-galaxy-s.

Sanders, J. (2015). *How racism and sexism killed traditional media: Why the future of journalism depends on women and people of color.* Santa Barbara, CA: ABC-CLIO.

Sandritter, M. (2017). A timeline of Colin Kaepernick's national anthem protest and the athletes who joined him. *SBNation.* Retrieved from https://www.sbnation.com/2016/9/11/12869726/colin-kaepernick-national-anthem-protest-seahawks-brandon-marshall-nfl.

Sanfiorenzo, D. (2018). Bassem Masri is the fourth Ferguson protestor to die since the uprising. *Okayplayer.* Retrieved from https://www.okayplayer.com/news/how-ferguson-protester-bassem-masri-died-details.html.

Schankman, P., & Bernthal, J. (2015). Officers who shot, killed Kajieme Powell will not be charged. *Fox 2 Now: St. Louis.* Retrieved from https://fox2now.com/2015/11/03/officers-who-shot-killed-kajieme-powell-will-not-be-charged/.

Schiappa, J. (2015). # IfTheyGunnedMeDown: The Necessity of "Black Twitter" and Hashtags in the Age of Ferguson. *ProudFlesh: New Afrikan Journal of Culture, Politics and Consciousness, 10.*

Schildkraut, J. V. (2014). *Mass murder and the mass media: An examination of the media discourse on US rampage shootings, 2000–2012.* San Marcos, TX: Texas State University.

Schneider, K. (2013). *The polarized mind: Why it's killing us and what we can do about it.* Colorado Springs, CO: University Professors Press.

Schoetz, D. (2008). Cops cleared in groom's 50-shot slaying. *ABC News.* Retrieved from https://abcnews.go.com/US/story?id=4725206&page=1.

Schudson, M. (2001). The objectivity norm in American journalism. *Journalism, 2*(2), 149–170.

Schwartz, I. (2014, November 17). Eric Holder likens Michael Brown to Emmett Till: "The struggle goes on." *Real Clear Politics.* Retrieved from https://www.realclearpolitics.com/video/2014/11/17/eric_holder_likens_michael_brown_to_emmett_till_the_struggle_goes_on.html.

Selle, J., & Dolan, M. (2015). Black like me? Civil rights activist's ethnicity questioned. *Coeur d'Alene/Post Falls Press.* Retrieved from http://www.cdapress.com/archive/article-385adfeb-76f3-5050-98b4-d4bf021c423f.html.

Sessions. J. (2018). Memorandum: Principles and procedures for civil consent decrees and settlement agreements with state and local governmental entities. *Office of the Attorney General.* Retrieved from https://www.justice.gov/opa/press-release/file/1109621/download.

Shade, C. (2016). Police violence and the American caste system. *Literary Hub.* Retrieved from https://lithub.com/police-violence-and-the-american-caste-system/.

Sharma, S. (2013). Black Twitter? Racial hashtags, networks and contagion. *New Formations, 78*(78), 46–64.

Sharpe, J. A. (2005). *Remember, remember: A cultural history of Guy Fawkes Day.* Cambridge, MA: Harvard University Press.

Sicha, C. (2009). What were black people talking about on Twitter last night? *The Awl.* https://medium.com/the-awl/what-were-black-people-talking-about-on-twitter-last-night-4408ca0ba3d6.

Singal, J. (2014). Kajieme Powell died because police have become America's mental-health workers. *The Cut.* Retrieved from https://www.thecut.com/2014/08/police-kajieme-powell-and-mental-illness.html.

Smith, B., Gottinger, P., and Klippenstein, K. (2014, December 7). Anonymous: Chicago police surveilled activists, including politician's daughter. *Reader Supported News.* Retrieved from https://readersupportednews.org/news-section2/318-66/27362-focus-anonymous-chicago-police-surveilled-activists-including-politicians-daughter.

Smith, C. (2006). Moneta Sleet Jr. as active participant: The Selma march and the Black Arts Movement. In Collins, L. G., & Crawford, M. N. (Eds.), *New Thoughts on the Black Arts Movement,* 210–226. New Brunswick, NJ: Rutgers University Press.

Snider, M. D. (2018). White woman called out for racially targeting black men having BBQ in Oakland. *YouTube.* Retrieved from https://youtu.be/Fh9D_PUe7QI.

Squires, C. R. (2002). Rethinking the black public sphere: An alternative vocabulary for multiple public spheres. *Communication Theory, 12*(4), 446.

Squires, C. R. (2009). *African Americans and the media.* Cambridge, UK: Polity Press.

Stange, M., & Vogel, T. (2001). Photographs taken in everyday life: Ebony's photojournalistic discourse. In Marcus, J., & Levine, R. S. (Eds.), *The black press: New literary and historical essays,* pp. 188–206. New Brunswick, NJ: Rutgers University Press.

Stovall, C., & Phillips, E. (2016). Today in Black Twitter: An actual black person who worked at Twitter speaks his mind. *BET.com.* Retrieved from https://www.bet.com/news/lifestyle/2016/15/today-in-black-twitter--an-actual-black-person-who-worked-at-twi.html.

Stratton, J. (2014). Ob-la-di ob-la-da: Paul McCartney, diaspora and the politics of identity. *Journal for Cultural Research, 18*(1), 5.

Sumlin, T. (2015, June 24). Charleston shooting suspect's Burger King meal gets national attention. *The Charlotte Observer.* Retrieved from https://www.charlotteobserver.com/news/local/article25394389.html.

Swaine, J. (2014). Ferguson police officer was "doing his job," say supporters. *The Guardian.* Retrieved from https://www.theguardian.com/world/2014/aug/18/ferguson-supporters-police-killed-teenager-protest.

Swaine, J. (2014). Ohio Walmart video reveals moments before officer killed John Crawford. *The Guardian.* Retrieved from https://www.theguardian.com/world/2014/sep/24/surveillance-video-walmart-shooting-john-crawford-police.

Swaine, J. (2014). Video shows John Crawford's girlfriend aggressively questioned after Ohio police shot him dead in Walmart. *The Guardian.* Retrieved from https://www.theguardian.com/us-news/2014/dec/14/john-crawford-girlfriend-questioned-walmart-police-shot-dead.

Swaine, J. (2015). Girlfriend of John Crawford, man killed by police in Walmart, dies in car crash. *The Guardian.* Retrieved from https://www.theguardian.com/us-news/2015/jan/02/girlfriend-john-crawford-dies-car-crash-tasha-thomas.Swaine, J., & Ryan, M. (2014). Police officer who shot black man in Walmart lied, victim's mother says. *The Guardian.* Retrieved from https://www.theguardian.com/world/2014/sep/30/police-officer-shot-john-crawford-walmart-lied-victims-mother-says/.

Tait, D. (2009). Reading the "Negro Bible": online access to *Jet* and *Ebony*. *Resources for American Studies, 62*.

Teague, M., & Laughland, O. (2016, July 7). Alton Sterling shooting: New footage appears to show police taking gun from body. Retrieved from https://www.theguardian.com/us-news/2016/jul/06/alton-sterling-gun-baton-rouge-new-video.

Testimony before the credentials committee by Fannie Lou Hamer. *Say It Plain*. American Public Radio. Retrieved from http://americanradioworks.publicradio.org/features/sayitplain/flhamer.html.

The Tribe CLT. (2015). #KeepitDown Confederate flag takedown. Retrieved from https://www.youtube.com/watch?v=gr-mt1P94cQ.

Toch, H. (2012). *Cop watch: Spectators, social media, and police reform*. Psychology, crime, and justice series. Washington, DC: American Psychological Association. http://dx.doi.org/10.1037/13618-000.

Touré. (2018, January 8). "This thing" killed her father: Then it killed Erica Garner. *The Daily Beast*. Retrieved from https://www.thedailybeast.com/this-thing-killed-her-father-then-it-killed-erica-garner.

Tuchman, G. (1972). Objectivity as strategic ritual: An examination of newsmen's notions of objectivity. *American Journal of Sociology, 77*(4), 660–679.

Tufekci, Z. (2013). "Not this one": Social movements, the attention economy, and microcelebrity networked activism. *American Behavioral Scientist, 57*(7), 848–870.

Tufekci, Z., & Wilson, C. (2012). Social media and the decision to participate in political protest: Observations from Tahrir Square. *Journal of Communication, 62*(2), 363–379.

Tyson, T. B. (2017). *The blood of Emmett Till*. New York, NY: Simon & Schuster.

Vassell, O., & Burroughs, T. S. (2014). "No other but a Negro can represent the Negro": How black newspapers "founded" Black America and Black Britain. *Journal of Pan African Studies, 7*(4), 256–268.

Victor, D. (2018). When white people call the police on black people. *The New York Times*. Retrieved from https://www.nytimes.com/2018/05/21/us/oakland-bbq-while-black.html/.

Victor, D., & McPhate, M. (2016). Critics of police welcome Facebook Live and other tools to stream video. *The New York Times*. Retrieved from https://www.nytimes.com/2016/07/08/us/critics-of-police-welcome-facebook-live-and-other-tools-to-stream-video.html.

Vincent, R. (2013). *Party music: The inside story of the Black Panthers' band and how Black Power transformed soul music*. Chicago, IL: Lawrence Hill Books.

Wallace, A. (2017). A critical view of Beyoncé's "Formation." *Black Camera, 9*(1), 189–196.

Wang, Y. (2016). Ohio officer fired after calling Black Lives Matter activist's suicide "happy ending." *Chicago Tribune*. Retrieved from https://www.chicagotribune.com/news/nationworld/ct-ohio-officer-fired-black-lives-matter-20160308-story.html.

Washburn, P. S. (2006). *The African American newspaper: Voice of Freedom*. Evanston: IL: Northwestern University Press.

Wasserman, H. M. (2008). Orwell's vision: Video and the future of civil rights enforcement. *Maryland Law Review, 68*, 600.

Wasserman, H. M. (2014). Moral panic and body cameras. *Washington University Law Review, 92*(831), 546.

Watts, J. (2011). BlackPlanet's founder talks MySpace, why he was skeptical of Twitter, and if Facebook may have peaked. *Complex*. Retrieved from https://www.complex.com/pop-culture/2011/03/interview-blackplanet-founder-talks-myspace-twitter-facebook.

Weinstein, A. (2013, July 12). This, courtesy of MSNBC, is Trayvon Martin's dead body. Get angry. *Gawker.* Retrieved from https://gawker.com/this-courtesy-of-msnbc-is-trayvon-martins-dead-body-753370712/.

Wells-Barnett, I. B., & Douglass, F. (1894). *A red record: Tabulated statistics and alleged causes of lynchings in the United States, 1892–1893–1894. Respectfully submitted to the nineteenth century civilization in "the land of the free and the home of the brave."* Chicago, IL: Donohue & Henneberry.

Wells, I. B. (1892/2014). *Southern horrors: Lynch law in all its phases.* The Floating Press. Retrieved from http://readingsinjournalism.pbworks.com/f/Ida%20B.%20Wells,%20Southern%20Horrors%20%20SHORT%20PAMPHLET--%20READ%20THIS.pdf.

Wells, I. B. (2014). *The light of truth: Writings of an anti-lynching crusader.* New York, NY: Penguin.

White, W. (1918). The work of a mob. *The Crisis 16,* 221.

Wiggins, D. K. (1992). "The year of awakening": Black athletes, racial unrest and the Civil Rights Movement of 1968. *The International Journal of the History of Sport, 9*(2), 188–208.

Williams, D., Martins, N., Consalvo, M., & Ivory, J. D. (2009). The virtual census: Representations of gender, race and age in video games. *New Media & Society, 11*(5), 815.

Wilson, C. C., & Gutierrez, F. (1985). *Minorities and the media.* Thousand Oaks, CA: SAGE Publications.

Winfrey, O. (2013). Why Michael B. Jordan says black males are America's pitbulls. *Oprah's Next Chapter.* Retrieved from http://www.oprah.com/own-oprahs-next-chapter/why-michael-b-jordan-says-black-males-are-americas-pit-bulls-video.

Wood, A. (2005). Lynching photography and the visual reproduction of white supremacy. *American Nineteenth Century History, 6*(3), 373–399.

Wood, M. (2013). Valency and abjection in the lynching postcard: A test case in the reclamation of black visual culture. *Slavery and Abolition, 34*(2), 202–221.

Word. (2014). Martin Baker gets blasted for being the lone black guy at a pro-Darren Wilson rally. *Uproxx.* Retrieved from https://web.archive.org/web/20140918021916/http://uproxx.com/smokingsection/2014/08/martin-baker-memes/.

Wyche, S. (2016). Colin Kaepernick explains why he sat during the national anthem. *NFL.* Retrieved from http://www.nfl.com/news/story/0ap3000000691077/article/colin-kaepernick-explains-why-he-sat-during-national-anthem.

Yang, G. S., Gibson, B., Lueke, A. K., Huesmann, L. R., & Bushman, B. J. (2014). Effects of avatar race in violent video games on racial attitudes and aggression. *Social Psychological and Personality Science, 5*(6), 698–704.

Yesko. P. (2018). Acquitting Emmett Till's killers. *American Public Radio.* Retrieved from https://www.apmreports.org/story/2018/06/05/all-white-jury-acquitting-emmett-till-killers.

Young, R. (2017). The viral video that set a city on fire. *CNN.* Retrieved from https://cnn.it/2LbM72h.

Zelizer, B. (2010). *About to die: How news images move the public.* New York, NY: Oxford University Press.

Index

Barlow, William, 34–35
Barnett, Ferdinand, 29
Basie, Count, 34
Baton Rouge Police Department,
     Louisiana, 191–92
BBQ Becky (meme), 147–48, 150–51
bearing witness while black, introduction,
     xii–xvii. *See also* African American
     media history
   memorialization function of, xii–xiii
   as protest journalism, xii–xiii
   research questions and methods,
     xv–xvii, 120
   summary conclusion, 191–96
Beautiful Ghetto, A (Allen), 194
Beavercreek Police Department,
     Ohio, 153–54
Becker, Ernest, 160
Becton, Dajerria, 170–71
#BeforeYouWatch, activist reports from
     the field, 113–33
   advantages of smartphones, 114–16
   authentication, 127
   carving out the counterpublic, 127–30
   disadvantages of smartphones, 116–20
   editorial workflow, 124–30
   establishing digital enclaves, 125–27
   estimating audience
     engagement, 123–24
   estimating engagement with
     favorites, 124
   new protest #journalism, 130–33
   original content vs. pass-along
     content, 122–23
   quantifying commitment, 120–22
   trends from timelines/
     frontlines, 120–24
Beitler, Lawrence, 176
Bell, Sean, 37–39
Bell, Wesley, 85
Benjamin, Walter, 173
Bennett, Naftali, 8–9
Bertens, Laura, 147
Between the World and Me (Coates), 3–4
Beyoncé. *See* Knowles-Carter, Beyoncé
Black Arts Movement, 107
black barbershops, 20
Blackbird, 119–20

black blogs. *See* African American media
     history; *specific blogs*
black bourgeoisie (Frazier), 32
Black Caucus of the American Library
     Association, 194
black criminality myth, 60–65, 70, 71,
     168–69, 183
blackening (Collins), 13
Black Enterprise (magazine), 33
Black Futures Lab, 192–93
"Black Guy on the Phone" (meme), 147–48
black inferiority myth, 21
black journalistic activism. *See* African
     American media history
Black Lives, Black Lungs (documentary),
     50–51, 109–10
#BlackLivesMatter
   creation of hashtag, x, 15, 48
   number of tweets using, x
Black Lives Matter Chicago, 108, 117, 129
Black Lives Matter Movement, 197. *See
     also* Movement for Black Lives; new
     protest #journalism; *specific leaders
     and participants*
   bias in news coverage of, 68
   as black counterpublic, 20
   chapter-based network, xiv
   distinguished from MAU, 108
   diverse Atlanta rally, 59–60
   Facebook censorship of, 80
   Freedom Square Occupation,
     Chicago, 89–90
   international news coverage, 95
   international organization of, xiv
   M. Brown and, ix–x
   number of protests through May
     2015, 144–45
   petition to declare as terrorist
     organization, 113–14
   public health and, 50–51
   Russian web infiltration of, 127
   Trayvon's death as tipping point, 43
Black Looks: Race and Representation
     (hooks), 82
black magazines and newspapers. *See*
     African American media history;
     specific magazines and newspapers
black marginality news myth, 65–67